Content Management Systems in Libraries

Case Studies

Edited by
Bradford Lee Eden

THE SCARECROW PRESS, INC.
Lanham, Maryland • Toronto • Plymouth, UK
2008

SCARECROW PRESS, INC.

Published in the United States of America
by Scarecrow Press, Inc.
A wholly owned subsidiary of
The Rowman & Littlefield Publishing Group, Inc.
4501 Forbes Boulevard, Suite 200, Lanham, Maryland 20706
www.scarecrowpress.com

Estover Road
Plymouth PL6 7PY
United Kingdom

British Library Cataloguing in Publication Information Available

Library of Congress Cataloging-in-Publication Data

Content management systems in libraries : case studies / edited by Bradford Lee Eden.
p. cm.
Includes bibliographical references and index.
ISBN-13: 978-0-8108-5692-9 (alk. paper)
ISBN-10: 0-8108-5692-1 (alk. paper)
1. Library Web sites—Management—Case studies. 2. Web site development—Case studies. 3. Digital media—Management—Case studies. I. Eden, Bradford Lee.
Z674.75.W67C66 2008
025.04—dc22 2008001105

∞™ The paper used in this publication meets the minimum requirements of American National Standard for Information Sciences—Permanence of Paper for Printed Library Materials, ANSI/NISO Z39.48-1992.
Manufactured in the United States of America.

Contents

Introduction

Content management systems (CMSs) within libraries are becoming more and more important as mechanisms for content and services to be provided in the digital environment. They allow for consistency in branding, look and feel, and the delivery of information; they also help to centralize input and maintenance of content and services by allowing multiple authors and creators to manage and edit their content without an intermediary, i.e., another staff person. In addition, CMSs have the capability to produce test environments that assist libraries in exploring new tools, services, and presentation of content, without having to recreate these environments manually multiple times.

This book documents case studies related to two types of CMS implementations: those that manage content on library websites, and those that manage digital content. These chapters first appeared as articles in a special issue in *Library Hi Tech* (v. 24, no. 1–2, 2005). I would like to thank Emerald for this opportunity to provide a broader venue of dispersion and publication for these valuable and interesting implementations related to CMSs, and *Library Hi Tech* editor Michael Seadle.

Matt Benzing's chapter examines how an XML-based application named Luwak was implemented at the Rensselaer Polytechnic Institute. Paul F. Bramscher and John T. Butler's contribution describes how the University of Minnesota developed an open-source CMS for web pages. Ioannis Papadakis and Christos Douligeris examine the benefits of using a CMS to manage e-journals. Library staff at Georgia State University discuss their experience with implementing a CMS, as does Texas A&M staff in their chapter. A small college CMS case study is provided by Terry Huttenlock et al., at Wheaton College, and a homegrown CMS solution at Kent State is provided by Rick Wiggins et al. Migrating content to a CMS is detailed by Tom Kmetz and Ray Bailey at Morehead State University, and a collection-specific CMS solution is detailed by Regina Beach and Miqueas Diál for their library. Yan Han examines how an RDF-based digital library CMS might work. Evolving in-house systems for CMS solutions is detailed by Marilyn Lutz and Curtis Meadow in their chapter, Edward Iglesias discusses consensus building when implementing a CMS, and Yu Su demonstrates how a CMS has been implemented to manage a university photographic museum. Finally, library staff at the University of Oklahoma provide assessment research based on the internal use of their library's intranet.

It is hoped that these case studies will assist libraries currently in the process of researching and implementing CMSs.

1

Luwak: A Content Management Solution

Matt Benzing

HTML was originally designed to be a content description language. Appearance and layout were secondary concerns, especially in the early days when text-based browsers like Lynx were the only way to access the web. With the development of graphical browsers, however, HTML became increasingly cluttered with page layout and descriptive tags that did nothing to describe content.

XML was developed as a solution to this problem. The idea was to once again sever form from content so that content could easily be adapted or transformed into new formats. In XML systems, content is kept within XML tags and form and design is applied through XSLT, a style sheet language. This means that information can be transmitted through a variety of handheld devices, browsers, printers, and other output mechanisms without the time-consuming process of adapting information for each medium. A separate style sheet is invoked for each use, which then transforms the content into an acceptable form. It also means that persons inputting information do not necessarily have to know anything about layout and design and can simply follow a template or use a series of forms to deposit their information into an XML database.

Rensselaer Research Libraries are a part of Rensselaer Polytechnic Institute, a technologically oriented university in Troy, New York. Like many institutions, Rensselaer Research Libraries were dealing with the difficulties caused by users accessing their website with multiple browser types, with the need to adapt web pages with sizable headers and navigation systems into usable handouts, and with the need for a variety of librarians of various skill levels to create and update web pages that were in synch with the site as a whole. The closest that the libraries had come to a content management system was the staffwide adoption of Macromedia Dreamweaver as a site management and design tool.

Dreamweaver helped with some of the issues of design consistency through the use of templates, but it did nothing to fill the need for quick and easy transformation of pages for different needs. Also, even with the template and check in/check out feature, it was still susceptible to the occasional misstep by a librarian new to HTML: It was far too easy to accidentally erase or alter large numbers of pages or to overwrite or distort design features.

The solution for a content management system that corrected these problems was found in an XML-based application developed by the Communication & Collaborative Technologies division of Rensselaer Polytechnic Institute named Luwak. Luwak was originally devised as a solution to the problem of how to adapt web pages for users of PDAs and other handheld devices without having to maintain multiple copies of the same information. It was first implemented as an application for maintaining the campus newsletter. As such it had features that were suited to short articles and time-sensitive information. The application itself was written in Java and built on the Jakarta Struts MVC framework. The content is maintained in a MySQL database. All of the software used in the implementation of Luwak is open source and free.

Luwak is named after the ferretlike Asian mammal (also known as the Palm Civet) and the coffee that bears its name and benefits from its biological functions. For those uninformed about the secrets of the gourmet coffee world, Kopi Luwak coffee is one of the most expensive brews on the planet. This rare delicacy is created when the Luwak consumes ripe red coffee beans. After passing through its unique digestive system, the beans are harvested by coffee pickers from the fresh scat of the beast.

While this may not sound especially appetizing to the average coffee drinker, it does provide a metaphor for what the system does. As value is added to the java beans that pass through the luwak's bowels, so the content that passes through the java-fueled innards of the Luwak application gains value through the processing that it receives.

While Luwak had been deployed successfully for the KIOSK newsletter, the RPInfo campuswide information system, and the school of engineering newsletter, the libraries presented a greater challenge than any of these. The libraries' site was both broader and deeper and featured many more authors as well as a complex interaction among items on different servers, including the website itself, the libraries, catalog, and the class reserves system.

A number of specific features of Luwak interested the library staff. The system had a number of "roles" built into it. Users could be assigned as "writers," "editors," or "administrators." This meant that an individual librarian, classified as writer, could create or edit content within the system but that this librarian could not add material to or alter the live website without the content or changes being approved by one of the librarians assigned as editor. Changes to the format of the website, including changing the basic structure or style sheets or the creating or destroying of new directories could only be performed by administrators.

Some of this functionality was already available to the libraries by the use of the AFS file permissions system. The drawback to this system was that there was no fine-tuning of access available. Librarians had access to a file or directory or they did not; there was no way to restrict them to merely the content section on an individual HTML file. Luwak would allow librarians who simply wanted to add a few lines to a pathfinder or change a URL in a list of resources to do just that without worrying about creating any other unintended changes to pages.

Another desirable feature was the ability to create different style sheets for different devices that would be applied on the fly. The libraries had begun thinking about the need to supply information to users of handheld devices. Since that was one of the original catalysts for the creation of Luwak, it served that need well. This same feature also solved the problem of handouts. Previously, librarians had spent time stripping headers and footers and navigational systems from pages in order to make them printer-friendly. A few attempts had been made to do this with JavaScript, but they proved unwieldy. Luwak promised to do these chores effortlessly.

Luwak's database-driven design also solved a number of other problems with library web pages. Because each of the pages within the site would become a database element rather than an independent file, and because links between pages and the content of the pages themselves would be generated with each page request, Luwak promised to alleviate the plague of orphaned pages and dead links that seemed to creep up year after year. A start and end date assigned to each piece of content upon its introduction to the system meant that time-sensitive announcements could be written in advance and held within the bowels of Luwak until the proper time came for them to emerge, or that outdated information could quietly fade away, without librarians being concerned about making these changes in real time. Announcements could even expire in the middle of the night if necessary, without anyone having to groggily log in from home at 1 a.m. Also, the separation between content and form created by the system's use of XML made it possible on the one hand for a librarian to change content without worrying about damaging the page layout and on the other hand for a web designer to implement design changes that would instantly be effective across the site. In addition, the application offered to allow librarians to submit their content either in XHTML or as plain text. All input was done through a form that resembled the type of form used in forum postings. After entering content into the form, the users had the option to view it as it would appear in a live page, to save it to work on later, or to send it to the "editor" to be published. All content would be processed through the JTidy validator and if invalid, information would be given to the librarian on how to correct errors. Of course, as a homegrown application based on open source technology, the price was right, and having the developers of the product a short walk away in the computer center made for convenient customer support.

After a demo by the creators of the application, the library management team approved its implementation. Since the Luwak application would reside on a different server, the original library website could be maintained while the Luwak site was being built. All of the pages that existed in the original site had to be moved over to the Luwak site. This mostly involved cutting and pasting, although there was a substantial amount of line-by-line editing necessary, since many of the pages in the original site were not valid XHTML. Common problems were tables that lacked summary tags, unclosed paragraphs, format tags such as FONT and COLOR, and missing ALT tags for images. While tedious, this did provide a valuable motivation for bringing the library site into conformance with the Americans with Disabilities Act and with proper coding practice. Images also provided a special problem: They could not be submitted into the Luwak database; instead, they had to be maintained on a separate server and referenced from the web pages through an absolute URL. This was not a huge obstacle, but it did require some getting used to for librarians who were used to the ease with which they were able to create in-line images with Dreamweaver. Pages that resided within other systems on other servers, such as the libraries' catalog, the interlibrary loan and class reserves system, and the electronic journals database all needed to be carefully edited so that they matched the new format and so that links from these systems to various parts of the old site would be valid.

While it might have been expected that librarians would have resented the loss of control that a system like Luwak threatened, the opposite was the case. Librarians not directly involved in web design welcomed the break from having to be concerned with accidentally deleting or altering a design and with having to be concerned with whether the code they were writing or that Dreamweaver supplied them with was valid. Most wanted to concentrate on the content of the pages that they were responsible for and wanted as little as possible to do with layout and design. Although the system of "editors" and "writers" initially seemed attractive, the librarians decided to start with having all content providers able to publish their own content in order to avoid possible bottlenecks that could arise from an editor being out of the office or overwhelmed with too many updates to approve. Since the librarians had been writing directly to the live site for years with only the occasional serious mishap, it seemed like a reasonably prudent choice. Only the Reference Coordinator and the Information Technology Librarian, however, would have administrative rights over the system.

The Information Technology Librarian worked closely with the CC&T staff at implementing a default style sheet for the site as well as a style sheet for printing that simplified the header and footer, removed most images, and added URLs within parentheses to linked text so that users could find out what links were active within the page as it appeared live on the web. Style sheets for handheld devices were put off until a later day, and style sheets for different browsers were declared unnecessary after testing the site design on then current versions of Internet Explorer, Netscape, Opera, and Mozilla.

IMPLEMENTATION

The switch over to the new site went smoothly. A redirect was employed to send users from the old library site to the new. As a content management tool, Luwak was largely transparent to the users, so user feedback was largely unnecessary (although feedback about the simultaneous design change was valuable). Feedback from librarians was positive, for the most part. Although the system itself was fairly simple, like any piece of homegrown software, it had quirks that arose on occasion. Going from a traditional static website to a dynamic database-driven one required different modes of thinking. Some of the features librarians had grown used to in Dreamweaver, like a WYSIWYG interface and spell checking, were missing (although it was discovered that spell checking could be provided by plugins if the librarians were using Mozilla Firefox as their browser). The JTidy validation process brought occasional headaches. Common errors like leaving the closing bracket off a tag were difficult to pinpoint in long, complex pages. Some of the validation error messages were helpful and very specific, while others were vague and called for line-by-line combing for irregularities. Although the validator caught most errors, it was possible for a submission with certain types of code errors to crash a directory. Fortunately, the development team was a short walk away, so that most difficulties were quickly resolved.

CONCLUSION

Over the past year the library staff has adapted to thinking and editing in the Luwak environment. Further work needs to be done on providing a useful on-the-fly style sheet for handheld devices and in exploiting some of the design and functionality capabilities of the system, such as providing collapsible hierarchies of links, multiple page skins, and the importation of library news bulletins into an RSS feed. The website as it now stands is more flexible, efficient, and consistent than it has ever been.

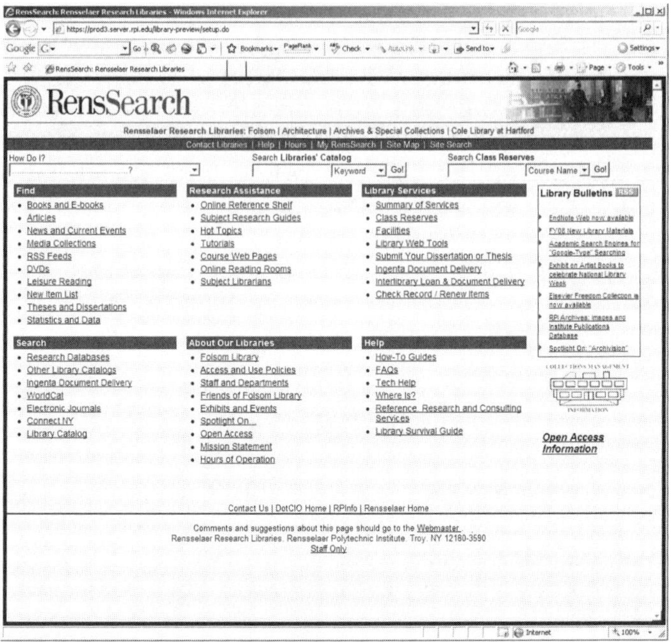

Figure 1.1. RensSearch, the Rensselaer Libraries' website, as it appears to the user.

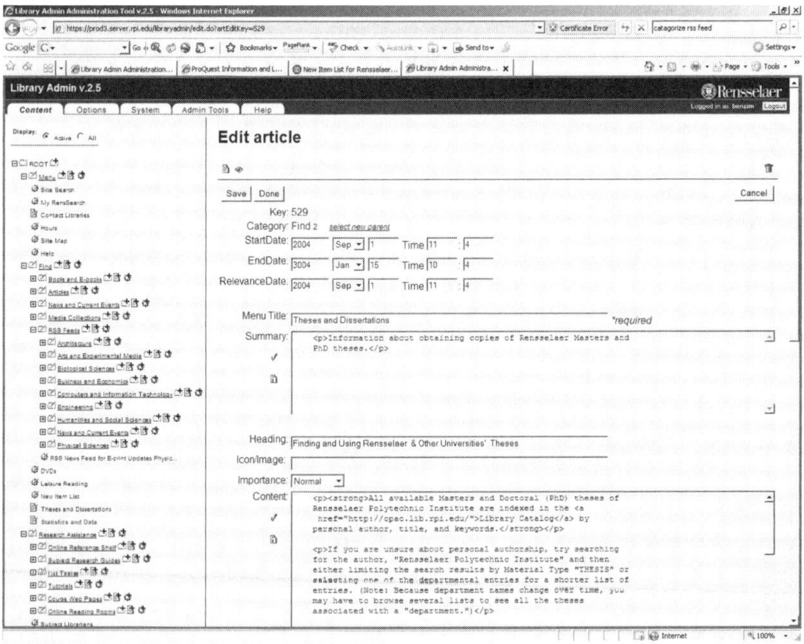

Figure 1.2. View of a typical page in the Luwak system.

REFERENCES

Bishop, K., A. Johnson, and D. Wentorf. 2002. From dated to dynamic: A campus newsletter unfolds as a web service. Proceedings of the 30th Annual ACM SIGUCCS Conference on User Services, Providence, Rhode Island.

World Wide Web Consortium. *Extensible markup language (XML) 1.0 (third edition).* Available at www.w3.org/TR/REC-xml/

2

LibData to LibCMS: One Library's Evolutionary Pathway to a Content Management System

Paul F. Bramscher and John T. Butler

As a first step on its path toward a content management system (CMS), the University of Minnesota Libraries developed LibData, a data repository built with open source technologies (Bramscher 2003). Consisting of approximately 40 relational tables, LibData contains resources, subjects, information types, staff, libraries, library services, and numerous other entities and enables extensive and rich relationships between them.

Moving beyond simple data-entry forms, LibData provides multiple authoring mechanisms allowing these entities to be pulled together in various ways to meet identified information delivery needs. This approach may be roughly analogized to arranging DNA nucleotides in chains to produce an "information molecule." Three authoring environments have been developed progressively, in the sequence presented below, in response to an expanding range of page-publishing needs:

- Research QuickStart (RQS)—an authoring mechanism currently serving up over 200 subject-oriented web pages. This mechanism offers a standardized graphical layout and an information structure from subject to subject. Resources are arranged alphabetically under information types that also are presented in alphabetical order. This mechanism produces high homogeneity and user predictability at the cost of the author's creative license. The overall appearance is controlled centrally by a webmaster. When first implemented, Research QuickStart demonstrated the notion of replacing static HTML subjects guides on a library's website with those that are created dynamically from a database. This method has now become widely implemented (Dupuis 2004; Sennema 2004).

- CourseLib and PageScribe (CLPS)—a common mechanism currently delivering over 1,100 course-supporting and general-purpose library pages. At present, CLPS provides approximately 20 styles (themes or "skins") to authors, each containing a header/footer/CSS wrapper around page content available for various libraries and special types of pages. Pages are assembled from elements in tree or outline fashion: with parents, siblings, children, etc., and their relationships. The elements may be resources, libraries, library services, staff, RQS pages, or any free text optionally wrapped in a URL or in-line CSS/HTML. Authors may place and rearrange elements in any desired order and select from among a limited number of webmaster-defined font definitions available for each style. Elements are bulleted automatically to the level of their generation or indention.
- LibCMS—at the time of this writing, over 100 pages representing the core of the University of Minnesota Libraries website are delivered through this new mechanism. LibCMS, deliberately, contains no hard-coded formatting limitations, although there is capacity to introduce them. It creates containers for authors to deposit any sort of page source (HTML, server-side scripts, XML, RSS, etc.) into a site hierarchy. The hierarchy is tree-driven, but rather than driving elements on individual pages, it applies to how pages themselves relate to one another across site architecture.

The complete LibData source code has been released under the GPL license and is available for free download on SourceForge (at libdata.sourceforge.net). Since its release in late 2003, LibData has been installed by six of the largest public and private college and university libraries in Minnesota, and by others nationally. As a new extension to LibData, LibCMS is not, at the time of this writing, part of the release, although it will likely be included in late 2005 or in 2006. The code for LibData/LibCMS is generally written in the PHP server-side scripting language for the MySQL database, providing a workable foundation for further customization or improvement. LibData/LibCMS is a modest project receiving no special funding, but it is designed specifically with library needs and open source technologies in mind.

This chapter highlights perspectives on and design decisions made on implementing a CMS in a large academic library environment, using the multiyear experience of developing LibData/LibCMS as context. It will emphasize Minnesota's pathway to a CMS: a logical evolution from granular and relational database elements to increasingly complex authoring tools and forward to the edge of the CMS paradigm. Presented are overall observations about CMSs and their implementation as well as the requirements and design outcomes of LibCMS. The rationale for developing LibCMS locally, as a means to ensure that design followed the requirements of an academic library environment and service/business model, is also provided. It is hoped that these insights may assist other libraries in the process of prospecting or actively developing a CMS.

THOUGHTS ABOUT CONTENT MANAGEMENT SYSTEMS: LOOK BEFORE YOU LEAP

Brendan Quinn of Clueful Consulting in Australia maintains an active listing of over 300 CMSs and, as the site says, "the list is growing every week" (Quinn). At the same time, there are indications that the failure rate of CMS implementations is high. A highly cited 2003 industry analyst report placed the rate at about 60 percent (Jupitermedia Corporation 2003). The "Failed CMS Projects" thread on the CMS-forum discussion list (cms-forum.org/) includes anecdotal reasons cited by many of its subscribers: cost overruns, complexity, and misapplying the technology. One might read some other reasons between the lines: perhaps the nature of an immature technology, failure or inability to commit long term on the part of the organization, a bad match with the organization's business model, too dynamic or chaotic a business model, or an attempt to do too many things using a "Swiss Army knife" approach.

These reports suggest that organizations might consider stepping back from unrealistic expectations of the CMS as a slam dunk transformative technology. Instead, organizations might carefully consider a simple, but key, question: What should a CMS reasonably strive to accomplish in the context of an organization's needs, aspirations, and established business processes? (Jenkins 2004; Arnold 2003) Martin White states that, ultimately, "[t]he adroit implementation of a CMS should enable the organization to provide a high degree of customization for users so that key user communities feel that the site has been designed expressly for them" (White 2005). In fact, a CMS should ideally enable greater levels of customization, when necessary, and uniformity, also as necessary. The ease of pushing out digital material or objects (Content) by nontechnical staff, facilitating decisions regarding site architecture and distribution of authorship and editorial roles (Management), and providing the mechanisms to carry this out (System) are all roles critical to the success of a CMS as a technology that enables an organization to meet the needs of its users. This view of CMSs as not primarily a technology but rather as a process framework has been applied specifically to the library environment and its content management realm (Browning 2001).

The content (information), management (organization), and system (technology) roles in a generic CMS implementation are illustrated in Figure 2.1.

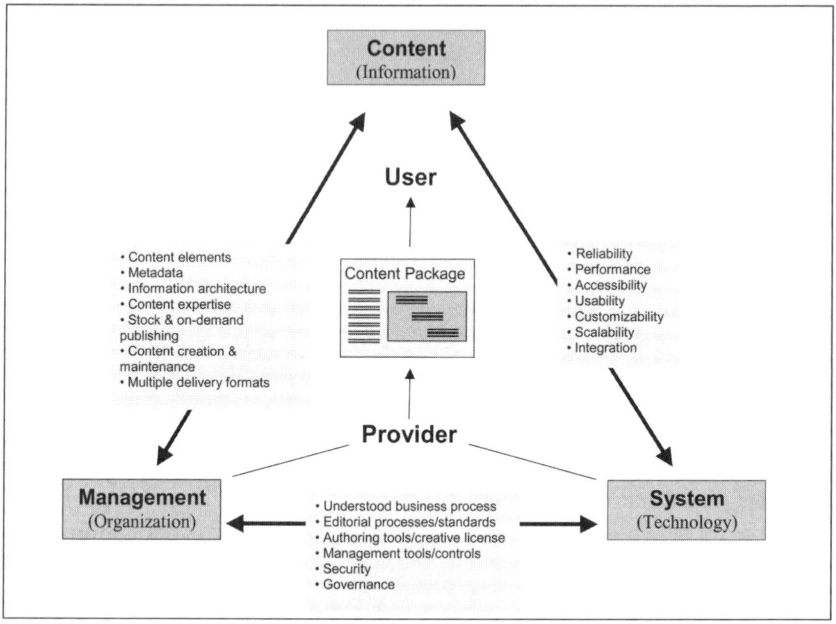

Figure 2.1. Roles in a content management system implementation. Adapted from White, Martin. 2005. *Content management handbook*. Abingdon: Facet Publishing. 11.

An inherent push-pull tension between these roles, set in triangular formation, is implied. The tensions here are structural and necessary. They are only unhealthy if the ultimate balance between roles does not optimally serve the requirements and reflect business processes and the cultural characteristics of the implementing organization. Tilting the balance of control among these three roles may lead to a dysfunctional CMS implementation, with impeding rather than enabling effects on the organization's ability to deliver content effectively. The CMS ought to be viewed as a set of coordinated technologies and processes (Borbone 2003).

Engineering Tensions and Trade-offs

Programmers and database developers find themselves constantly confronting these tensions and making design compromises to maintain optimal balance. For instance, slightly denormalizing a table away from so-called Third Normal Form (or higher) in some use cases will result in substantial SELECT performance increases, but it must incur costs elsewhere in the design. Most any sort of engineering encounters fundamental tugs of advantage and disadvantage: More strength may mean more weight; greater reusability may entail tighter coupling and overhead to handle additional dependencies. Fundamental and insurmountable limits may eventually be reached: No four-sided triangles or three-sided squares are allowed.

These trade-offs are conspicuously present in choosing a path for a CMS. "Content" and "system" liabilities may include loss of freedom for technical staff. For instance, nearly any CMS under consideration will likely impact decisions or require compromises around the operating system and version upgrade cycle of the server on which it resides. It may not interface well with local databases and scripting languages, or it may not fit well into an organization's security or authentication requirements. It may introduce a whole host of new migration and URL persistency issues. Or, it may ultimately be more of a document management system, powerful in what it does but not well suited for managing dynamic content or complex algorithmic scripting.

Greater ability to "manage" site content and architecture appears to confer no particular disadvantages in itself, though it may impinge on existing departmental autonomy or professional creative license if used heavy-handedly to enforce homogeneity. The sort of management a CMS offers must play in tune to the organization's business arrangement. It should neither impose its own rules nor fail to capture existing rules to a degree that is highly incompatible with how the library functions. It is important that even before exploring CMS options, a library ought to carefully flowchart its own business functions and the sort of content it creates—as it genuinely operates, not as it would ideally operate.

Management Roles

There is often subtle role differentiation along functional lines in an organization that must be understood in advance of making technical decisions. For example, department heads occupy a managerial, titled, or vested position in various library operations, and yet their role in the CMS—functionally speaking—may differ in practice. If much of the editing/proofing and daily work falls into the hands of a subordinate, then that subordinate is the functional manager role in the CMS.

The LibData project encountered these issues and was compelled to create some rather complex access rules. For instance, authors may create and manage their own content, or content for which other authors (or higher) identify them as a co-maintainer. Managers can do the same and, in addition, may edit the content of any author in their departmental units and modify special systemwide setup tables. DBAs have no restrictions at all. The manager level proved to be the most difficult to implement in practice since actual departmental managers were generally not involved in day-to-day web maintenance. Anthropologically speaking, a role-based mechanism should most closely mirror the realized functional or behavioral aspects of the organization, not necessarily its political or hierarchical entitled roles.

To make this point about those with experience, but not official or entitled authority, we borrow the *Wife of Bath's Prologue* (Chaucer, 1387–1400), with license:

> Experience, though no authority
> Were in this world, were good enough for me,
> To speak of woe that is in all content management systems;
> For, masters, over passing technologies and tech-isms,
> Thanks be to the computer which forever chugs along fine,
> Of CMSs have I had nine;
> For CMSs so many times have CMS'd for me;
> And all were worthy in their degree.

TOWARD A SOLUTION: TO BUILD OR BUY

Before embarking on LibData (the system that was first developed and from which LibCMS was extended), considerations whether to build or buy were weighed. There were no easy answers here, as many of the variables were beyond the project's control. The following arguments framed the case to build:

- Complete technical control of the source code, API, and development process. Technological autonomy and self-determination.
- Designed specifically with the institution's needs in mind, ability to interface with existing applications, enterprise authentication schemas, the University of Minnesota portal, etc.
- Important learning and teamwork opportunity for the librarians and technology staff involved. A rich professional-development and collaborative journey.
- No licensing or proprietary issues. Chance to release work as open source (GPL) to a broader community for study, collaboration, improvement, etc.
- Applications that serve a central role in the library and information sciences discipline might ideally be developed and owned by that community. Disciplinary risks may be entailed from excessive proxying or subcontracting to outside entities, of what may arguably be professional disciplinary turf in the Internet age.
- Arguably cheaper Total Cost of Ownership (TCO) over the long run. If the system is built to the desired level of maturity and baseline functional requirements, no license fees are ever encumbered into perpetuity.

Conversely, these arguments were considered in the case to buy or outsource:

- Buying seems most prudent in situations presented by perennial or ubiquitous business problems (e.g., word processing) and little is gained for the profession of library and information science by building one's own.
- Something exists on the market, which ideally suits the library's needs; perhaps it is a highly affordable vended application or an existing open source project that may require little or no customization.
- May be cheaper in the short run and require less in-house permanent staffing.

As a large research institution with its own engrained, traditional, and perhaps stubborn ways of doing business (which may generally be the norm), Minnesota found a path of least resistance in the "case to build" LibData in the early 2000s.

Extending the LibData Architecture to LibCMS

At the time of considering CMS options, LibData had been in place at Minnesota for about two years with high levels of adoption, expanded capability, and notable increases in web publishing output and impact. This clearly biased the decision to extend LibData to provide more CMS-like features with LibCMS. Project developers, as well as the organization itself, were well poised to take it to the next level, rather than to embark on an unrelated project and make necessary customizations to enable clean convergence. The pathway to a CMS, as sketched earlier, moved along these lines: database/repository =>data-entry interfaces =>multiple authoring mechanisms to assemble dynamic pages =>a management system to organize relationships of pages. To extend the analogy given earlier, granular data evolved into "information organisms" in want of some sort of taxonomic management tool.

For others, it may be a document management impetus, or a top-down need to impose homogeneity and sensibility across a site that will plow the pathway to a CMS. The decision and rationale each library makes ought to harmonize with its own needs, requirements, and organizational circumstances.

Requirements Analysis

The LibCMS project started by identifying core functionality, and we arrived at a list of minimal requirements. This was an important soul-searching opportunity as well. Rather than evaluating existing applications and asking how they might be engineered to work in Minnesota's environment, or how to take advantage of feature XYZ, which is offered but for which there is no current use, the project returned to basic software engineering methodologies to identify core needs first. While LibData eventually culminated in a specifications document of over 300 items, LibCMS's core functionality specs were much leaner, and they are reasonably condensed into the following:

- Versioning mechanism; storing potentially an infinite number of versions.
- A nonpublic "draft" area that would allow various pre-published alternatives to be viewable by design committees for consideration.
- However, it should not entail a cumbersome or Byzantine publishing arrangement. A simple role-based authorization schema with public and draft capacity would be adequate. Multiple checkoffs and a more elaborate editorial process would be desirable theoretically, but it would not match the reality of the organization's business practices and staffing arrangement.
- It must be capable of storing HTML/CSS/XML/JavaScript and any server-side scripting language (Perl, PHP, etc.) for execution.
- Dynamic breadcrumb navigation and a site map.
- A self-indexing mechanism.
- Authoring side must be delivered entirely over an SSL connection to mesh with our enterprise authentication and security requirements.
- It must be trivial to build connections and APIs to the LibData database.

Table 2.1 provides another view of prioritized LibCMS functionality using a value scale against commonly offered CMS functionality. It is not expected that the priorities expressed here, those of a large research library, would entirely mirror that of an organization with a contrasting mission, culture, and business processes.

Weaknesses Analysis

Probably as important as identifying minimal requirements is making a list of known weaknesses in a particular model. What does the model *not* support initially? Can some features be added at a later date? If X is enacted, is Y therefore not possible?

For instance, the LibCMS project did not want, or have the resources, to build a desktop-quality WYSIWYG HTML editor. Several plug-in editors were investigated, some of which were judged to be excessively JavaScript intensive. In the end it was decided to settle on a very minimalist JavaScript editor, with built-in capability for authors to write content with their desktop editor of choice and upload the resulting source into the CMS.

Table 2.1. Value That LibCMS Design Placed on Common CMS Functionality

CMS Functionality	*Value**	*Notes*
Authoring/Publishing		
• Web-based, server-side	High	Enabling authors and site managers with time/place independent means to create and maintain web pages, rapidly and efficiently, with minimal technical barriers, proved critical to wide adoption of the system. Database-driven content, a range of optional page templates, customizable skins, page cloning, and author-controlled collaborative authorizations were key to customization at scale.
• Basic WYSIWYG	High	
• Optional interface templates	High	
• Dynamic publishing	High	
• Collaborative authoring	Medium	
• Ability to accommodate executable programming code	High	
• Ability to upload page source	High	
• Page cloning	High	
• Schedulable publishing/unpublishing	Medium	
Workflow/Review Management		
• Commenting	Low	Workflow controls were of lower importance in supporting business processes and cultural norms (i.e., distributed authority for content creation).
• Change approval	Low	
• Approval & sign-off	Low	
Version Control		
• Published/draft modes	Medium	Versioning needs stemmed from occasional page recovery needs, not audit or compliance purposes.
• Roll back/forward	Medium	
Repository/Metadata Management		
• Web-based record entry/editing	High	Library websites tend to be data- and link-intensive, highlighting the criticality of a robust and easy-to-manage content repository. Support for multiple levels of descriptive metadata enabled repository to become a powerful means to support resource discovery and selection in page authoring functions.
• Discovery tools for content selection	High	
• URL management	High	
• High-level classification scheme	High	
• Granular resources tagging	High	
• Search, drilldowns, global editing	High	
Conversion/Repurposing		
• Word/RTF-to-web conversion	Low	The need for publishing symmetrical versions of web and formal print products (e.g., PDF) deemed of diminishing importance. Of ascending value are XML-based outputs, used to interoperate with and present data in other environments.
• Web-to-Word/RTF/PDF conversion	Medium	
• Printer-friendly output	High	
• XML/RSS outputs	High	

(continued)

Table 2.1. *(continued)*

CMS Functionality	*Value**	*Notes*
Management Tools/Controls		
• User management • Role-based authorizations • Use statistics • Site structure and management • Security (SSL login to admin)	High High High High High	Robust management capabilities are essential for supporting a high-performing content repository, authoring, and publishing system. Typically, research libraries have highly distributed authoring and site coordinators, making user and content management tools critical to operations.
Enterprise Interoperability		
• Central authentication hub • Campus portal • Integrated library system • Course management system	High High High High	Enterprise interoperability is of growing importance for effective distributed content management at the institutional level. Leveraging data in other systems creates opportunities for customized feeds and presentations.

* Indicates the relative value (and importance) of basic CMS functionalities in requirements for LibCMS at the University of Minnesota Libraries.

LibCMS currently offers no capability to upload multimedia files, partially the upshot of security concerns from system administration, architectural challenges, and limited technology staffing. LibCMS presently requires that a user have the ability to securely transfer (SFTP) multimedia files into a separate library or reference off-site images for content.

Here, the earlier discussion on basic engineering tugs is again relevant. A central media library could possibly result in highly reusable components, for example, various branding graphical logos. On the other hand, the more reusable the component becomes, the less it should be readily modifiable by staff at large (i.e., changes would be far-reaching across the site and mistakes potentially disastrous). Given these inherent tensions, it is reasonable to consider that managing a multimedia file library may be basically a human function. While leveraging technology to make certain aspects easier, ultimately, the greatest management challenge of multimedia in an enterprise environment may no longer be technical.

Content

In the broader context of CMSs, content includes any sort of web-delivered data or object, including:

- Flat documents; these may be persisting documents (hopefully, with persistent links) or digital ephemera deliberately designed for a short life cycle
- News, events, calendars
- Database-driven content
- Multimedia objects (images, sound, video, anything that requires a special plug-in, etc.)

Typically, library websites have some special types of content, not necessarily exclusive to the domain, but heavily leaned on nonetheless. These include:

- Records in databases, singly or in sets. These produce point-of-query algorithmic or computed content. They may be instantiated in the form of search results based on permuted user selections. They don't exist as assembled content until an end user creates a set of conditions such that they congeal.
- A search interface or list of databases itself is potential content.
- Subject headings and other controlled field names. Controlled vocabulary within various fields, requiring additional management.

Content in the LibData system echoes typical library web content types (above), noting that the content created and managed consists of granular and reusable database records in a relatively complex relational schema.

Separation of Content from Presentation

LibData's public interfaces settled on two sorts of separation of content and presentation as briefly described in the introduction of this chapter. Research QuickStart's interface was designed to achieve homogeneity from subject to subject, despite heterogeneity of subject emphases and subject specialists authoring them. This required enforcing of a common server-side includes header, footer, and overall page cascading style sheet (CSS). The gain in homogeneity and predictability from a user perspective came at a cost of creative license from the authors. The resources under each subject are divided into information types, and these are alphabetized across all subjects. Some authors would like to adjust various categories up or down based on their importance to the subject at hand, but doing so would entail a design consideration based on knowledge hidden to the uninitiated user. The librarian possesses a greater knowledge set regarding which information type is most important for the subject at hand. The end user, however, is not guaranteed to be privy to it beforehand and might be confused as he or she scans the information types across subjects presented in differing orders.

And yet, building an entire site under constraints like this would not, ultimately, be politically possible or ultimately semantically useful. For example, readers of books generally expect an index to be found at the end of a book, and that it be alphabetized. The reader, however, expects chapter headings to be arranged in whatever order the author sees fit. These functions of the book serve important, but differing and complementary, purposes.

In acknowledging the need to support these differing purposes, the authoring engine of CourseLib and PageScribe (CLPS), in contrast to the precast nature of the Research QuickStart presentation, grants authors the capability to order page elements in any desired fashion and to group them hierarchically. Furthermore, LibData provides "styles" that wrap pages with a header, footer, and overall CSS created by a web designer, at least one schema for each department. An entire page could be fitted with a "style" (more commonly referred to as a "skin" or "theme" in today's usage) or flipped to another one as desired without modifying page content. This did not achieve 100 percent separation of content and presentation, but it seems to be a highly feasible approach.

In the "tug" between an author's creative license and central control, the compromise provided by the CLPS mechanism was still somewhat tipping in favor of control. Ultimately, this motivated a design push to make LibCMS impose less, rather than more, structure in certain ways. Note that these authoring mechanisms—RQS, CLPS, and LibCMS—are not meant to deprecate but rather to complement one another. They intend to offer varying balances of power in authoring and site management.

LIBCMS: THE SYSTEM DELIVERED AND LESSONS LEARNED

In fall 2005, the first production instance of LibCMS was successfully implemented in support of a completely redesigned website at the University of Minnesota Libraries (www.lib.umn.edu). Through implementation and to date, the development of LibCMS has achieved the set of initial and deliberately modest goals. Following is a description of the significant architectural choices made with regard to the implemented design. This list is by no means complete, but it offers a sampling of the interesting trade-offs and decisions one might make by building a CMS in-house or by adopting and modifying an existing open source project.

A Forest and Its Trees

In designing LibCMS, the lead developer conceptualized a website as a tree of pages, and an enterprise site as a forest of trees. In computer science terminology, tree structures generally have only a single root or node. In wanting the LibCMS mechanism to potentially scale out to additional units or libraries on campus, each with its own index page, the root node in this tree was subjugated into a virtual, unused, node in the tree. The effect of this simple move is to secure the potential for unlimited numbers of other virtual document roots. What would have been secondary pages below a single root page (a single website) are now treated as multiple root pages, each enjoying its own descendants (an enterprise library site). LibCMS's initial rollout is limited to the "core" pages of Minnesota's main library site, but it can be extended architecturally for root or index pages of other libraries in our enterprise.

Tree structures are accompanied by typical operations: add, delete, move, or edit a node. The design of LibCMS has added a few others: delete and promote the children, delete a sub-tree recursively, reorder siblings, etc. All relevant operations may be made at the site level, and all changes affect the dynamically generated breadcrumb navigation (see next section), denoting primary-secondary-tertiary-quaternary page relationships. The underlying functions to support this are standard algorithmic fare in computer science, simple recursion, and crafty SQL in some places.

The one caveat deliberately built into the system to achieve URL continuity, despite the ability to change the page's position on the fly in the hierarchy, is that all pages must first have a unique page name, and second must all be located in the same directory (with the exception of the root page). This presents another engineering trade-off. The page relationships are encoded back-end in the system database, and they are evident to users via the dynamically built menus and navigational breadcrumbs. They are not tied, however, to the physical or logical location in the file system, nor are they evident in the URL. This transparency achieves much toward URL persistence but requires divorcing the URL from its (potentially volatile) architectural placement in the overall site.

The goal of separation of content and presentation remains critical in chaotic and changing presentation environments. Also desirable should be the goal of separation of page relationships from hard-coded markers such as directory structure and its URL—in a realm in which page relationships are also somewhat unsettled. For example, if a website is built to roughly mirror library service offerings, or departments, and due to organizational or other reasons some are merged, dropped, or added, then a system that has encoded such relationships in hard format will cause a 404 error, redirect, or some other issue for people who've bookmarked the now obsolete and exposed architecture. The LibCMS response to this is certainly not perfect, but it renders some of the underlying messiness transparent to the end user.

Dynamic Breadcrumbs

Breadcrumbs and the user's browser history (capable of being manipulated by JavaScript, often with mixed results) serve very different functions.

Browser history represents an artifact of the user's behavior: successes and failures alike. Large, complex library sites such as Minnesota's offer many ways to link from page to page—not merely the simple tree structure discussed above. And yet, they are also not quite a "fully connected graph" (one in which any two destinations are accessible by a single edge or path). In LibCMS, breadcrumbs are conceived as offering the minimal or preferred route between any page and the site index or root page. In a sense, they are reminiscent of problems known in graph theory or the Traveling Salesman Problem well known in computer science literature. The parallel problem in a CMS breadcrumb schema should be to develop a means for the user to traverse from any page to the root page in the most direct route possible from an information delivery and architecture perspective.

"Widgets"

Systems such as wikis offer special markups to shorthand aspects of display formatting, obviating the need to be an HTML expert. LibCMS offers a series of tools, tentatively called "widgets," which might be seen as a dynamic tag.

The currently published version of a LibCMS page is written to a file on the server. This file may be completely flat (HTML, XML, etc.) or it may contain server-side scripting code. Widgets offer another sort of dynamism. When a page is invoked by an end user, an output buffer is initiated by a call from PHP to the Apache server. Any server-side scripts involved in generating that page are resolved. The resulting page source—no longer dynamic, but still not quite ready to ship to the end user—is then parsed for regular expressions against widgets (see syntax below). These widgets are in turn resolved dynamically against the database, replaced with their retrieved results, and the output buffer is then released to the end user. Widgets essentially offer a second chance at content/database dynamism. They can be placed anywhere on a page and are typically wrapped in CSS or HTML formatting rules to improve their appearance. LibCMS's current set of widgets is as follows:

- ##nav Generate a dynamic breadcrumb navigation to the root/index page.
- ##parent Display a linkable title to the parent page.
- ##siblings Display a linkable menu of siblings (if any).
- ##children Display a linkable menu of child pages (if any).
- ##res=N Display a linkable resource present in the LibData database by ID.
- ##resdec=N Display that resource's description by ID.

- ##binfo=N Generate a list of resources matching a particular "base information type," a field that LibData uses to group resources together.
- ##cms=N Link to another CMS page by ID.

Handling Foreign Characters

Foreign character sets, quotes, double-quotes, etc., typically pose issues for data storage. LibCMS gets around this by converting all page source code to base64 (and hexadecimal in a special case). This limits the character set to a universally implemented subset, effectively negating all special character issues from a database perspective.

Publishing Methodology

LibCMS does not necessarily publish flat pages; rather, it publishes pages that may be flat, but may also be fully scripted, or perhaps lightweight-dynamic (as discussed in the widget section). Essentially, an author may achieve or operate at his or her own desired level of dynamism. The publishing mechanism is engineered to interact with two locations on the web server: a publicly visible site content directory and a draft directory. The system allows for unlimited versioning of CMS pages, only one of which may be published "live" at any point. Multiple drafts may be published for viewing in the draft area. All versions are stored in the database, with content encoded in base64 format transparently to the end user. If desired, pages may exist *only* in the database awaiting additional work. That is, their source need neither be published nor drafted.

When a page is published or drafted, a number of things occur:

- LibCMS verifies that the current user has sufficient access rights.
- The system reserves file names and establishes control with unique IDs stored in the supporting database. It's possible for a new version to replace an existing published version of the same page, but no cross-page operations are possible (i.e., the version of one page may not accidentally overwrite a completely unrelated page). This serves both as a check against accidental operations as well as a form of authority control.
- The page is written to the live site or draft area, depending on the operation selected.
- LibCMS opens a socket in the background, as if it were a client visiting the site itself, and pulls down the fully rendered page source. HTML and JavaScript are stripped from the source code, and the page text is inserted into a contents field for indexing (refer to upcoming discussion of self-indexing).

Self-Indexing

A mechanism was built to self-index pages in the following way: Once the author published a page, a process would open an HTTP socket to the page as it appears to an end user. The process strips out all HTML tagging and client-side script, compresses trailing and leading spaces, and inserts the results into a text-type database field. This field can be indexed by MySQL and serviced by a simple interface for searching page content. All levels of page dynamism, including the widgets discussed earlier, are indexed in their final, resolved format.

External URLs

LibCMS allows the author the ability to create stubs in the navigational schema of resources that lie outside its bounds. For example, a link to a library catalog, operating in a separate environment, might be added as a page in the schema. A user could link to it as a child page and leave the LibCMS portion of the site. And yet, that external page may be designated as a parent page for other sites in the managed system.

Content Creation

LibCMS provides (deliberately) no authoring capability beyond simple bold/italics/anchoring and other basic HTML, a link to a spell-checker, and the ability to upload a file.

LibCMS pages, however, have potentially three main blocks or cells for source code (in addition to a number of metadata tags). The first block offers an opportunity to perform a server-side include—perhaps to include a standard header look and feel, etc. The second or middle block contains main page content. The third block provides an opportunity to include a page footer. The system enforces nothing: It is possible to write a completely blank page, a valid XML or RSS document, a dynamic data-driven site in PHP, etc. In this sense, it accomplished a high degree of freedom by not requiring anything—but offering some architectural management tools and hooks to the LibData database.

Security Arrangement

All authoring interfaces of both LibData and the LibCMS extension are delivered through SSL. A secure cookie containing a session ID is checked with the server for validity for every administrative task.

It is desirable for large academic libraries to have the ability to interface with a campus authentication mechanism or, at the very least, there exists a strong likelihood that library systems ought to adhere to formalized enterprise security standards. The University of Minnesota Libraries have developed a number of objects and scripts that allow enterprise security interoperability for both in-house applications and as wrappers around vended products.

In an increasingly security-conscious environment, a CMS system that cannot interface with enterprise security and authentication, or one that offers administrative functions over unencrypted sockets, could potentially be a showstopper. Libraries must interact frequently with vended databases, in-house databases, and proxy systems—some of which may require sensitive connection parameters or passwords. If a CMS system is involved in the storing and crafting of this sort of sensitive content, it must do so completely through SSL.

CONCLUSION

Any CMS ought to accomplish simple tasks simply and complex tasks as simply as possible. An effective CMS ought to manage site architecture, manage relationships between pages, provide role-based authorizations, and offer reasonable authoring, editorial, and publishing processes that fit the library's business model. If in an adopted system there are features that an organization will never use, they may actually become a liability (i.e., a larger application footprint, possible security issues, upgrading/patching issues, etc.).

Minnesota's main approach to a CMS system was not to replicate or supplant bona fide content creation environments and multimedia tools (for example, Dreamweaver, Adobe Photoshop, or a programming IDE). Rather, the emphasis was to approach CMS design more as a Source or Version Control System for web pages, with easy data hookups and useful architectural/navigational tools. The rationale for local development was to extend LibData's capabilities to site-level management concerns and to fully control the API and source. This would provide an avenue for integration with campus authentication and other enterprise applications (e.g., integrated library system, campus portal, course management system, etc.). On this point, the LibData/LibCMS system has already demonstrated capabilities for interoperating with academic and administrative systems to dynamically deliver content to environments beyond the library.

The local development of LibCMS allowed the design to be driven, from the ground up, by the requirements of a library environment and its service/business model. In general, the larger and more gradual path taken to develop both LibData/LibCMS became itself a method of ensuring that the system was right-sized and well tuned for the organization.

Through the experience of developing and implementing LibCMS, several design challenges were confronted. These included the need to balance page dynamism with static content, loose-data coupling with desires for high-data reusability, and creative license in authoring with standardization requirements of the organization. Additional challenges included making a CMS of dynamic pages searchable for page content; incorporating external pages (URLs outside the CMS system) in the overall site tree structure; creating environments in which page authors can upload binary objects while supporting a common area in which objects may be reused on multiple pages and managed for their integrity and persistence; and implementing the system across multiple virtual domains where needed in the organization. These challenges have been addressed to various degrees and provide a path for ongoing (and continued evolutionary) development.

REFERENCES

Arnold, S. E. 2003. Content management's new realities. *Online* 27(1): 36–40.

Borbone, M. 2003. Common sense content management: What organizations need to know. *Managing Information* 10(10): 36–38.

Bramscher, P., S. Nackerud, and J. Butler. 2003. LibData: A library web management system. Digital Library Federation Fall Forum. Albuquerque: New Mexico. 17–19 November 2003. Available at www.diglib.org/forums/fall2003/fallforum03.htm#p19

Browning, P., and M. Lowndes. 2001. Content management systems: Who needs them? *Ariadne* issue 30. Available at www.ariadne.ac.uk/issue30/techwatch/intro.html

Chaucer, G. (ca. 1387–1400). Wife of Bath's prologue (The prologe of the wyves tale of bathe). *The Canterbury tales*. Available through the Internet Medieval Sourcebook at www.fordham.edu/halsall/source/CT-prolog-bathpara.html

Dupuis, J., P. Ryan, and M. Steeves. 2004. Creating dynamic subject guides. *New Review of Information Networking* 10(2): 271–7.

Jenkins, T. 2004. What is content management: When should a content management system be considered? *Information Management & Technology* 37(2): 70–71.

Jupitermedia Corporation. 2003. *Web content management: Matching needs and solutions*. Darien, Connecticut: Jupitermedia Corporation.

Quinn, B. Clueful Consulting's content management systems directory. Available at www.clueful.com.au/cmsdirectory/

Sennema, G. 2004. Creating an internal content management system. *Computers in Libraries* 24(1): 8–13.

White, M. 2005. *Content management handbook*. Abingdon: Facet Publishing.

3

Issues and Opportunities in E-journal CMSs

Ioannis Papadakis and Christos Douligeris

Electronic publishing (e-publishing) has emerged in the last few years as a viable alternative to the traditional print-based scholarly publishing process. The most significant reason for this trend is the fact that an ever-increasing number of people and certainly the majority of scientists and researchers (at least in certain disciplines like computer science and physics) depend on the web to perform and deliver their work. The immediate availability of a variety of sophisticated tools and technologies that support e-publishing has contributed to the wide acceptance of this new way of publishing.

Content management systems (CMSs), one of the latest trends on the web, are devoted to the efficient management of web content by taking into consideration the special nature of such information. More specifically, a CMS allows average users to rapidly publish content on their desktop and/or the web without requiring them to have any knowledge regarding computer-specific technologies and/or standards (e.g., HTML) (Robertson 2003).

A special case of a web-based CMS is with electronic journals (e-journals). E-journals were first conceived 20 years ago as paperless journals consisting of "*computer output microform*" (Sondak and Schwartz 1973). Since then, e-journals have evolved to cover a significant part of the overall scholarly publishing process (Weller 2000). Even though information inside an e-journal is logically organized according to the printed journal paradigm and at first it was only intended to map the traditional life cycle of a printed journal to the emerging, much promising web environment, it was not long before it was realized that the web had a whole lot more to offer to the scholarly publishing process than was initially estimated. The obvious capability of the web to promote collaboration together with the inherent ease of use of the new digital medium inspired many researchers and vendors to provide models and services that have literally transformed the way all the stakeholders of the scholarly publishing community operate.

The goal of this chapter is to present the e-journal as a special case of a web-based CMS and to provide guidelines for the design of such systems based on ongoing efforts in the web community. Current technological trends on the web are identified and an assessment is made about the appropriateness of such technologies in the e-journal paradigm. It is argued that interoperability should be a fundamental requirement of such web-based infrastructures. In order to accomplish interoperability, modern e-journal CMSs should rely on well-defined standards. In this direction, the backbone of a web-based e-journal CMS capable of keeping up with current and future web developments should be the XML standard (www.w3.org/XML).

The rest of this chapter is structured as follows: the next section compares the traditional scholarly publishing process with the emerging e-publishing process as applied to the e-journal paradigm. Such a comparison intends to inform the reader how the traditional steps of the scholarly publishing process find their way into the new, challenging web environment. The following section aims at revealing the true power of e-journals through the presentation of various innovative, value-added services that can only be realized in the digital environment. Section 4 refers to various issues that have arisen since the emergence of the first e-journal infrastructures on the web. Section 5 presents basic guidelines for building robust, efficient, and long-living web-based, e-journal CMSs. Special attention is given to the fact that modern e-journal CMSs should rely on widely available common standards like XML. Finally, the last section concludes the chapter with a critical as well as visionary view of the role of e-journal CMSs and their widest possible user acceptance.

1. SHIFTING FROM TRADITIONAL TO E-JOURNAL PUBLISHING

The traditional publishing process relies on the printed medium for the delivery of its services to the academic community. It would be unfair to ignore the benefits from printed materials over the years. Rawlins (1998) discusses the great benefits of printing and how it has made information available to everyone over the last 500 years. "Printing led to pagination, indices, and bibliographies since they were now possible and they made searching easier." The rewards of using print as a medium to exchange knowledge have been cultivated in multiple forms. Rawlins notes that "print has democratized knowledge, increased accuracy, made fiction possible, made propaganda possible, created public libraries, and created the idea of authorship."

Scholars and researchers publish their findings according to the traditional printing model in order to promote science and disseminate knowledge. The advent of the web, however, has brought to the surface several weaknesses of such a model. Collaboration between researchers is discouraged due to unacceptable waiting times between submission and publication in most well-known scientific, scholarly journals. Moreover, the paper medium restricts authors in several ways. Space limitations, cost limitations, and the two-dimensional format limit are only the most obvious restrictions imposed by the traditional printed journal model (Resh 1998).

In order to overcome such deficiencies and at the same time take advantage of the inherent opportunities provided by the web, the electronic publishing model and particularly e-journals have emerged. The primary goal of e-journals is to handle and disseminate scholarly information on the web. The employment of CMS technology resulted in the emergence of several e-journal CMSs, capable of providing numerous advantages as compared to their printed equivalents. Thus, from the authors' point of view, such systems allow papers to be interactive by providing the capability not only to link different parts of a paper but also to connect different papers of similar content. The considerably faster production and publication times in the e-journal sector (Menon and Raymond 2002) have contributed to their acceptance by research communities that suffered considerably long publication queues. With conventional journals, once a paper has been approved for publication, there can be a considerable delay while the issue is being printed and distributed. In contrast, electronic papers can be converted into a form suitable for immediate electronic publishing instantaneously. Moreover, accessibility is considerably better because online papers can be readily available for downloading.

From a publisher's point of view, updating printed issues can be very costly, and thus it is rarely done in scholarly journals. For the purpose of avoiding the re-publication of an issue, procedures are usually implemented for identifying corrections, amendments, or errata to the readers. Such procedures tend to be time-consuming and prone to errors, and they often fail to reach the intended audience on time. With e-journal CMSs, republishing a complete issue and keeping track of different versions of a paper is a relatively fast and inexpensive procedure. Additionally, e-journal CMSs allow authors to be more directly involved within the publishing process than printed ones (Kling and Callahan 2002).

The above comparison clearly indicates that publishing scholarly journals on the web through adequate CMSs is considerably more efficient than following the traditional way of printed publishing. Furthermore, the scholarly publishing process is greatly enhanced by taking advantage of certain inherent features of the web as an information highway. The next section summarizes these features and examines their applicability to the scholarly publishing sector. As will be discussed later in the chapter, however, certain concepts and procedures that were taken for granted in the printed publishing process should be reexamined when applied to the new digital environment.

2. EXTENDING THE TRADITIONAL PUBLISHING PROCESS

The transition from the printed to the electronic medium opens new horizons with potentially great benefits to the stakeholders of the publishing process (i.e., researchers, librarians, publishers). Towards this direction, the next section outlines a number of features and services that are currently found in the e-publishing sector. Such features and services should be incorporated in future e-journal CMSs in order to provide scalable, modern, user-oriented functionality to the scholarly publishing community.

2.1. Citation Analysis

One of the most important features of an e-journal is the acquisition of knowledge through linking, and in particular, the linking that takes the reader from the document she or he is currently reading to another of similar content. Traditionally, documents that come from the scholarly publishing community always contain references to ones of similar content. In this direction, the field of citation analysis (Garfield 1955) emerged. Citation analysis refers to the development of tools capable of handling references that have been automatically extracted from documents in various ways. The domination of the web as a standard way of disseminating knowledge has boosted the development of citation analysis. Thus, it is now possible to access distributed repositories containing numerous documents across disciplines very efficiently and cost-effectively. Web-based citation services take advantage of this opportunity and provide the research community with very interesting tools (Hitchcock et al. 2002). It is also encouraging to observe that the members of the scholarly publishing community have concluded that citation-based tools can be most useful when they work across publications and across publishers.

CrossRef (Brand 2001), for example, was incorporated as a collaborative venture among 12 of the world's top scientific and scholarly publishers, both commercial and nonprofit, to enable cross-publisher reference linking throughout the journal literature. Furthermore, one of the first approaches aimed at exploiting citations within scientific papers was the Science Citation Index (SCI) (Garfield 1964). The SCI has kept citations of papers in virtually all scientific journals since 1982, using a semiautomated procedure. NEC's ResearchIndex (Lawrence et al. 1999) maintains an index that automatically catalogs documents' citations by linking them with the cited works. Thus, users are able to rank papers according to the citations they have.

Similarly, the Stanford Linear Accelerator Center (SLAC) maintains the SPIRES-HEP Literature Database (SPIRES-HEP) (www.slac.stanford.edu/spires/hep/), which is an automatically updated database of references and a search system that enables the counting and ordering of the most cited papers. This web-based application builds on top of the ArXiv.org E-print Archives project (Pack and Pemberton 2001). Another application based upon the E-print Archives project is Citebase (Cameron 1997), which can be described as a web-based citation and impact-ranked search service. The difference between the two systems is that the SPIRES-HEP approach is not fully automated in terms of data collection and checking, as opposed to the software approach of Citebase.

CERN's Document Server (Claivaz et al. 2001) also exploits citations of documents that are available on the web through e-journals. In contrast to SPIRES-HEP, not all of the document's text is kept and indexed, but only the pointers to cited documents. Another difference between the CERN and SPIRES-HEP citation treatments is that, while SPIRES-HEP is pointing the references to its own database, CERN links references directly to the corresponding e-journal site.

2.2. E-publisher-specific Functionality

The above approaches constitute an abstraction layer on top of the typical e-journal infrastructure since they manipulate fully structured information (i.e., references) from various documents within e-journals belonging to different publishers. Moreover, functionality is provided by dedicated servers belonging to independent institutions that act as service providers to the overall academic community. These systems usually do not keep the full text of the contained papers.

Various e-journals, though, provide extended functionality based on autonomously implemented features and services. The vast majority of such approaches take advantage of the capabilities provided by sophisticated database systems that are appropriately designed to host document-based repositories.

The Perspectives in e-Publishing (PeP) e-journal produced by Hitchcock and Hall (2001) builds upon the idea of bringing together open-access papers of similar content through an innovative link service. Specifically, users are able to add links to any word within the paper, pointing either directly to other papers or indirectly to similar categories and/or keywords stored in an appropriate database. Papers may not be stored locally at the PeP infrastructure. The user-added links of each paper are "glued" on the original paper through an appropriate module, without adding any modifications to the original paper. PeP can be seen as complementary to other e-journals since it enriches remotely hosted papers by adding its own original content and perspectives.

Another way of interacting with e-journals is through discussion forums. Sociological Research Online (SocRes) (www.socresonline.org.uk/) and McLuhan Studies (www.chass.utoronto.ca/mcluhan-studies/) are two e-journals that allow their users to post messages on a message board about the quality of the included papers. Similarly, the MRS Internet Journal of Nitride Semiconductor Research (MIJ-NSR) (nsr.mij.mrs.org/) e-journal utilizes a message board that classifies the incoming messages on a "per article" basis.

2.3. From the Authors' Point of View

From the authors' point of view, many e-journals like Cochrane (www.update-software.com/Cochrane/default.HTM) and Signal Transduction Knowledge Environment (STKE) (www.sciencemag.org/) provide the opportunity to dynamically review the content of the included papers. Such systems tend to come closer to the CMS paradigm, although they do not address themselves as typical CMSs. Specifically, authors are able to review and possibly update the content of their submitted papers after they have been published online.

The Interactive Multimedia Electronic Journal of Computer-Enhanced Learning (IMEJ) e-journal (imej.wfu.edu/) provides a high level of multimedia and interactivity to its users through an appropriate infrastructure, which is capable of including multimedia content throughout the full-text of the published papers. In this context, Conservation Ecology (ConsEcol) (www.consecol/Journal), Internet Journal of Chemistry (IJC) (www.ijc.com), and Internet Archaeology (IntArch) (intarch.ac.uk/) are three peer-reviewed e-journals that rely on systems capable of allowing the inclusion of various "add-ons" (i.e., executable applications, three-dimensional models in Virtual Reality Markup Language—VRML, maps, etc.) to the body of their papers. Such extensions can either be viewed online by the readers or, given the option, downloaded locally for future inspection.

2.4. From the Readers' Point of View

Looking at functionalities from the readers' point of view, various e-journals are able to alert their subscribed members about forthcoming e-journal issues. Moreover, members may bookmark an interesting paper online and examine it at a later time (e.g., Institute of Physics—IOP e-journal [www.iop.org]). There is also the opportunity to download a selected paper in more than one format (i.e., pdf, doc, ps), according to the preferences of each visitor; for example, the IOP e-journal, Biomedicine e-journal (BMJ) (http://www.bmj.com/), and Journal Watch Online (JWO) e-journal (www.jwatch.org/).

2.5. Personalized Content

In the context of providing extended functionality to the research community, various e-publishers attempt to personalize the view of an e-journal, thus providing an intelligent, personalized interface. Such functionality can be implemented through adaptive personalization techniques (Correia and Boavida 2002). The Astrophysical Journal (ApJ) CMS (www.journals.uchicago.edu/ApJ/journal/) employs the SOM classification system (Kohonen 1995) in order to provide customized layout. In the same direction, according to the Journal of Artificial Intelligence Research (JAIR) (http://www.jair.org/) e-journal, readers are prompted to use a specific Application Program Interface (API) in order to visualize a published paper. Moreover, readers are able to classify the contents of an e-journal according to their individual preferences. Another functionality that is derived from the ability to employ adaptive personalization techniques to e-journals is the notion of the virtual journal. This can be compiled from various papers across a number of e-journals, according to the specific needs of each reader.

3. THE OTHER SIDE OF THE COIN

The appearance of numerous e-journals on the web, some of which have been digitized from printed revisions, clearly indicates that "going digital" is not just an additional feature that should be embedded in the traditional, printed scholarly publishing process. As it can be concluded from the previous section, the advantages of e-journals are undoubtedly overwhelming. Moreover, the advent of web-based CMSs capable of efficiently and at the same time intuitively managing the web content suggests an ongoing progress in the area of e-journals.

There are still some major issues in the overall e-publishing sector, however, that need to be addressed. Thus, archiving and preserving digital information has so far proved to be a difficult task with many implications. The most important problem of long-term preservation of digital artifacts such as e-journals is the lack of longevity of the corresponding storage medium. As compared to paper, digital storage media (i.e., CD-ROMs, DVDs, etc.) have major drawbacks. Digital storage media have not been tested through time since they appeared relatively recently in the market. Even if the storage conditions are ideal, such materials remain fragile and have a limited life cycle. So far, it has been very difficult to foresee whether digital storage media will remain operable after a certain period of time (Cervone 2004).

Moreover, new devices, procedures and applications replace products and methods for the creation, storage, and retrieval of digital material every two to five years (Andre et al. 1996). Consequently, valuable information stored in digital format within e-journal CMSs is at risk of becoming inaccessible over time due to the obsolescence of the hardware and software that is employed to store and disseminate such information. Thus, technological obsolescence is an even greater danger than the presumably short life cycle of digital storage media, as access to information kept in digital storage devices is likely to be denied long before these become unavailable (Lyman and Besser 1998).

One way to solve this problem is to periodically transfer digital information to new and more up-to-date storage media. It should be noted, though, that in order to have a successful transition, digital information should be independent of the storage media. Moreover, the new storage media should be compatible with software capable of manipulating the information it contains. Given the current growth rate of information technology in general, such requirements are rather difficult to satisfy. Backwards compatibility is often neglected when new versions of software products are developed. To make things worse, interoperability between different products is regretfully rare (Lorie 2001).

In order to overcome such difficulties, there is always the option of migrating digital artifacts from one hardware/software configuration to another. The migration process is definitely a much more complex, time-consuming, and expensive procedure, which in many cases is difficult to accomplish. Given the above observations, it is of primary importance that a modern, e-journal CMS should to a large extent address the problem of preserving its valuable content in the long term.

Another issue that remains to be solved in the e-journal sector relates to the intellectual properties of the electronically published digital information. The owners of copyrighted material remain skeptical about the fact that digital information can be unlawfully copied and transferred to anybody without permission. It is also beyond any doubt that the pricing policy of the traditional journals cannot be applied as-is to the digital ones (Beagrie and Jones 2001). New formulas should be introduced for the establishment of an efficient pricing policy not only for e-publishers but also for all the remaining stakeholders of the publishing process as well.

Last but not least, the acceptability of e-journals in the academic community remains at a rather low level (Gomes and Meadows 1998). Since the emergence of electronic journals about 20 years ago, electronic publication was viewed as a way to communicate research findings rather than to advance careers. According to various surveys (Galvin 2004), many scholars were unaware that the peer review process was used in scholarly e-journals. Consequently, contributors themselves felt that the electronic publication carried less weight than the print publication. By the mid-1990s the situation slowly began to change, however, as evidenced by several statements by academics and by the involvement of major research universities in scholarly e-journal projects (Galvin 2004). Maybe the most important factor towards the wider acceptability of e-journals is the predominance of a peer-reviewing model capable of maintaining the integrity of science and scholarly communication in the changing electronic environment that is as effective as the traditional, peer-review model of the printed journals (Weller 2000).

4. GUIDELINES FOR BUILDING A WEB-BASED CMS FOR E-JOURNALS

4.1. Interoperability—Relying on Standards

In order to come up with solutions of general acceptance, the above issues should be approached from an organizational rather than a technical point of view. In this context, interoperability between software and/or hardware components emerges as a key requirement for the development of robust, efficient, and long-living e-journal CMSs.

CMSs that are built upon interoperable components provide significant benefits to their users. Moreover, it is common knowledge that a major feature of traditional libraries containing journals is their role as a unique point of access to a variety of resources. Therefore, the transition from physical to digital resources should not compromise this feature. It should be equally easy for a researcher to shift from one scientific area to another from their workstation, as is the case in a physical library. After all, technology is employed to simplify rather than to complicate the quest for knowledge. Various interoperability procedures facilitate the development of diverse e-journal CMSs, which are nevertheless capable of working together in order to provide valuable cross-publisher features.

In the context of interoperable e-journal CMSs, the employment of standards is more than necessary. The adoption of standards in the e-journal sector will allow potentially competitive organizations (i.e., different publishers, libraries, etc.) to agree upon issues that will facilitate better services to the wider user community. In this direction, the Digital Object Identifier (DOI) (Arms 1997) has emerged as an effort to redefine the ISBN equivalent in the digital world. Moreover, as it is argued in the following sections, the ability of the XML standard to encapsulate metadata and thus publish the actual content of the corresponding resource to third-party systems renders this technology ideal for the development of highly interoperable e-journal CMSs.

4.2. XML: The Building Block

One could argue that the fact that the eXtensible Markup Language (XML) as a descendant of Standard Generalized Markup Language (SGML) predetermines a short and unsuccessful future for this technology on the web. Although SGML has been around for more than 15 years, it has never managed to dominate this environment. This was primarily due to the complexity of the language and the overhead that derives from using it. Having this in mind, XML did away with much of the complexity of its ancestor and kept only the parts needed for use on the web (Pardi 1999). Consequently, it is safe to predict that XML-based systems are very likely to dominate the web in the imminent future.

Another argument in favor of employing XML technology for the development of an e-journal CMS is that XML allows the existence of different views of the same data (Liechti et al. 1998) since content is separated from presentation. Such a feature is very useful to the e-journal community where, most frequently, various user profiles require different views of the same data. Also, user interfaces can be maintained easier without having to access the actual data.

From a technical point of view, XML provides a structural representation of data that can be broadly implemented and deployed. Client-server architectures on the web, like e-journal CMSs, greatly benefit from this fact. By taking advantage of the inherent XML support that is provided by current web browsers on the market, XML-based documents may be manipulated, edited, and presented in multiple views without unnecessary return trips to the web server. Servers can therefore become more scalable due to lower computational and bandwidth loads. Also, data exchanged in XML format can be easily merged from different sources, ultimately providing the ability to manipulate diverse data from different organizations.

Moreover, interoperability across different e-publishers can be easily established through the employment of XML and related standards. By defining a common format for data structures that are both human readable and computer understandable, complexity of computer-to-computer interaction is significantly reduced (Aloisio et al. 1999).

In the context of an e-journal CMS, XML could be employed in various ways. According to Robertson (2003), many tenders specify "CMS must be built on top of XML." More specifically, there are a number of key areas in a CMS where XML has a role to play, including authoring, communication, interoperability, storage, and publishing.

As far as authoring is concerned, nearly all major word-processing vendors (including Microsoft's Office 12 edition) rely on XML-based file formats (e.g., OpenDocument format [ODF], Microsoft Office Open XML format) for saving and exchanging editable office documents such as text documents. Thus, an e-journal CMS building on top of such formats would remain interoperable with a wide range of vendors and systems.

In order to promote communication between different CMS vendors, a number of widely used "syndication" formats are readily available. These include Rich Site Summary (RSS) (Milic-Frayling et al. 2003) and NewsML (Allday 2001), which are also based on XML. Consequently, there is a need to customize e-journal CMS solutions to handle these syndication formats.

The evolution of wireless communications urged many manufacturers to develop handheld devices capable of accessing the web through specially designed, low capability browsers. In the context of an e-journal CMS capable of providing "single source publishing" (Fraley 2003), XML has the potential to offer real benefits. By separating presentation from content and employing XSL (http://www.w3.org/) technology, the same piece of information may be rendered differently depending on how it will be used (e.g., on-screen, PDA, printer, etc.).

As far as storage is concerned, keeping data in native XML database management systems would greatly enhance not only functionality within the e-journal CMS but also interoperability between different CMS vendors. Unfortunately, at present, there are no widely accepted solutions in this field.

Of course, greater functionality will become available with the emergence of Semantic Web technologies, aiming at making computers understand the semantics of the information they handle. Although there is considerable activity in this research area, it is still too soon to expect Semantic Web services capable of extending and/or replacing current services on the web. It is estimated that, together with many other trends on the web, e-journal CMSs will significantly benefit from the evolution of the current web to the Semantic Web, according to the vision of Tim Berners Lee, the founder of this new environment (Lee et al. 2001).

Having the above thoughts in mind, it is fair to claim that XML technology can provide a simple and straightforward way of developing and managing robust and functional e-journal CMSs.

4.3. Making a Web-based E-journal CMS Part of the Semantic Web

As intuitively stated in Decker et al. (2000), the web is entering its third generation, passing through the first generation (static web consisting of handwritten HTML pages) followed by the second generation web (consisting of machine-generated and often active HTML pages). Nowadays, the web is evolving to the Semantic Web, aiming at the understanding and sharing of knowledge between humans and computers in a bidirectional way.

In order to keep up with this evolution, an e-journal CMS should be compatible with the infrastructural components consisting of the Semantic

Web. In this context, the notion of the ontology needs to be employed, which is defined as an "explicit specification of a conceptualization" (Gruber 1993), or as a "common vocabulary of terms, some specification of the meaning of the terms and a shared understanding for people and machines" (Goble and De Roure 2002).

Each scientific area has its own set of vocabulary terms with specific meanings among the members of the community defined by this scientific area. The most common gathering points for the members of such communities are the scholarly journals. Therefore, an e-journal CMS should be able to provide the infrastructure to the stakeholders of the corresponding e-journals to author and utilize ontologies. Such ontologies may be used to actually enrich the metadata associated with a document by including implicit entities, which are closely related to the explicitly mentioned entities in the given context (Fisher and Sheth 2003). Moreover, ontologies provide the infrastructure for sophisticated annotation systems that could be employed by e-journal CMSs, in this way enhancing collaboration between the members of scientific communities.

Unfortunately, so far, there are neither well-established standard methodologies for building ontologies nor a field of Ontological Engineering equivalent to Knowledge or Software Engineering. Despite these difficulties, significant initiatives towards this direction, like RDF (www.w3.org/RDF) and OWL (Oberle et al. 2004), as well as ontology-oriented tools like OilEd (Bechhofer et al. 2001) and Protege 2000 (Noy et al. 2001) have been widely accepted.

4.4. Looking at the Wider Picture: Blogs and Wikis

The web is known as a place where technological innovations occur quite often. The democratic nature of this environment ensures that, in the long term, useful innovations get the attention they deserve. Similarly, proposals that do not manage to get enough attention are probably not really noteworthy. It is very important, therefore, to be able to make correct assumptions about certain innovations as early as possible.

In the context of an e-journal CMS, blogs and wikis certainly deserve a closer look. Blogs and wikis are websites that any visitor can add to and edit. The blog resembles someone's personal web diary, while the wiki is the underlying engine implementing the blog. As collaborative technologies for the scholarly publishing sector, blogs and wikis offer a forum for broader and more timely discussion to complement the existing system of peer-reviewed journals. This could enhance science communication, both before publication when generating ideas and after publication when discussing results. Moreover, blogs and wikis offer a unique opportunity to keep up with the latest developments in several scientific fields (Butler 2005).

A community of conservative researchers, however, has a different opinion about the necessity of these new technologies to the scholarly publishing sector. As stated in Butler (2005), some people think "blogs and wikis remain unattractive distractions from real work. Many consider them an online version of coffee-room chatter, background noise that goes against the very ethos of heavily filtered scholarly communication." Another argument against blogging is the fear of being scooped by rivals. It seems like the new generation of scientists and even more of readers believe that the benefits of brainstorming research ideas on blogs far outweigh the corresponding risks (Butler 2005).

It may be the case that blogs should not be treated as a replacement for formal journals. A paper published in a journal is a fixed, archivable work ready to be referenced by future researchers. On the other hand, blogs provide rapid dissemination of ideas to a very wide population of researchers. "Blogs associated with traditional printed and/or e-journals may help bridge the gap between the literature and blogs," says Glenn McGee, editor-in-chief of the American Journal of Bioethics (AJB) (www.bioethics.net/), the leading journal in its field that was the first to create a companion blog, namely Blog.Bioethics.Net. The bioethics blog allows the journal to respond faster and in different ways to public controversies. The blog has a high impact, especially in influencing reporting on ethical issues by the mainstream media.

Maybe it is too early to decide whether blogs and wikis could be integrated and to what extent in a web-based e-journal CMS. Further discussion is required on the way blogs and wikis should be handled by such CMSs. The very nature of the web as an information highway capable of rapidly disseminating new technologies and innovative ideas, however, dictates that the e-publishing sector should be at all times aware of current trends on the web in order to remain competitive and useful to its users.

5. CONCLUSION

The rather short history of e-journals makes it difficult to assess the impact of e-journals in the scholarly publishing community. As compared to the traditional publishing process which has a solid past of several hundred years, e-publishing and specifically e-journals with a life of no more than a couple of decades simply cannot change immediately the way things operate in this sector.

On the other hand, the opportunity to bring scholarly publishing to another, more promising level through the employment of the latest trends on the web should not be neglected. A web-based CMS, adapted to the special needs of scholarly e-publishing, provides the infrastructure for the development of e-journals and accompanying services that go beyond the formal conception of a scholarly journal. Collaboration is greatly enhanced and accessibility is much more efficient, resulting in the widest possible dissemination of knowledge. It seems that all the stakeholders of the publishing process (i.e., researchers, librarians, publishers) will benefit from such progress.

In order to avoid certain pitfalls that lurk in a constantly changing and evolving environment such as the web, an e-journal CMS should follow certain guidelines. Interoperability is the primary feature required by such systems. Without interoperability a killer CMS of today is at risk of becoming obsolete tomorrow. The most consistent vehicle of interoperability is to rely on well-accepted standards. In this context, XML should be the basis of every effort towards a successful, long-living e-journal CMS.

Finally, innovations that occur almost every day on the web should be carefully evaluated in order to assess their appropriateness to the e-journal paradigm. It is crucial to attain the ability to distinguish useful innovations from false alarms. Being on the cutting edge of technology is certainly not an easy task. It seems, however, that this is the only way towards the development of robust e-journal CMSs capable of fulfilling the constantly increasing needs of the scholarly publishing community.

REFERENCES

Allday, T. 2001. NewsML—enabling a standards-led revolution in news publishing? *EBU Technical Review.*

Aloisio, G., G. Millilo, and R. D. Williams. 1999. An XML architecture for high performance web-based analysis of remote-sensing archives. *Future Generation Computer Systems* vol. 16: 91–100.

Andre, P. Q. C., et al. 1996. *Report of the task force on archiving of digital information.* Available at ftp://ftp.rlg.org/pub/archtf/final-report.pdf.

Arms, W. 1997. Digital object identifiers (DOIs) and Clifford Lynch's five questions on identifiers. *ARL: A bimonthly newsletter of research library issues and actions, Association of Research Libraries.* Available at www.arl.org/newsltr/194/arms.html.

Beagrie, N., and M. Jones. 2001. *Preservation management of digital materials: A handbook.* London: The British Library.

Bechhofer, S., I. Horrocks, C. A. Goble, and R. Stevens. 2001. Oiled: A reason-able ontology editor for the Semantic Web. KI '01. Proceedings of the Joint German/Austrian Conference on AI, Springer-Verlag, 396–408.

Brand, A. 2001. CrossRef turns one. *D-Lib Magazine* vol. 7, no. 5. Available at www.dlib.org/dlib/may01/brand/05brand.html.

Butler, D. 2005. Science in the web age: Joint efforts. *Nature* vol. 438: 548–549.

Cameron, R. D. 1997. A universal citation database as a catalyst for reform in scholarly communication. *First Monday* vol. 2, no. 4.

Cervone, F. H. 2004. The repository adventure. *Library Journal.* Available at www.libraryjournal.com/article/CA421033.

Claivaz, J-B, J-Y Le Meur, and N. Robinson. 2001. From full text documents to structured citations: CERN's automated solution. *HEP Libraries Webzine* Issue 5. Available at www.library.cern.ch/HEPLW/5/papers/2/.

Correia, N., and M. Boavida. 2002. Towards an integrated personalization framework: A taxonomy and work proposals. *AH 2002. Proceedings of the workshop on personalization techniques in electronic publishing on the web: Trends and perspectives*, Spain, 9–18.

Decker, S., F. Harmelen, J. Broekstra, M. Erdmann, D. Fensel, I. Horrocks, M. Klein, and S. Melnik. 2000. The semantic web—on the respective roles of XML and RDF. *IEEE Internet Computing* vol. 4, no. 5.

Fisher, M., and A. Sheth. 2003. Semantic enterprise content management. *Practical Handbook of Internet Computing*. CRC Press.

Fraley, L. 2003. Beyond theory: Making single sourcing actually work. *Proceedings of the ACM SIGDOC '03*, San Francisco.

Galvin, J. 2004. The next step in scholarly communication: Is the traditional journal dead? *Electronic Journal of Academic and Special Librarianship* vol. 5, no. 1: Spring 2004. Available at collection.nlc-bnc.ca/100/201/300/ejasl/2004/v05n01/galvin_j01.htm.

Garfield, E. 1955. Citation indexes for science: A new dimension in documentation through association of ideas. *Science* vol. 122, no. 3159: 108–111.

Garfield, E. 1964. Science citation index—a new dimension in indexing. *Science* no. 144: 3619–3649.

Goble, C., and D. De Roure. 2002. The grid: An application of the semantic web. *Technical Report* 4.

Gomes, S., and J. Meadows. 1998. Perceptions of electronic journals in British universities. *Journal of Scholarly Publishing* vol. 29, no. 3: 174–181.

Gruber, T. 1993. A translation approach to portable ontologies. *Knowledge Acquisition* vol. 5, no. 2: 119–220.

Hitchcock, S., D. Bergmark, T. Brody, C. Gutteridge, L. Carr, W. Hall, C. Lagoze, and S. Harnad. 2002. Open citation linking: The way forward. *D-Lib Magazine* vol. 8, no. 10. Available at www.dlib.org/dlib/october02/hitchcock/10hitchcock.html.

Hitchcock, S., and W. Hall. 2001. How dynamic e journals can interconnect open access archives. *ELPUB 2001*, proceedings of the ICCC/IFIP 5th Conference on Electronic Publishing. Italy: IOS Press. 183–193.

Kling, R., and E. Callahan. 2002. Electronic journals, the Internet, and scholarly communication. *Annual Review of Information Science and Technology* vol. 37: 127–177.

Kohonen, T. 1995. *Self-organization maps.* Berlin and Heidelberg: Springer-Verlag.

Lawrence, S., C. Lee Giles, and K. Bollacker. 1999. Digital libraries and autonomous citation indexing. *IEEE Computer* vol. 32, no. 6: 67–71.

Lee, T. B., J. Hendler, and O. Lassila. 2001. The semantic web. *Scientific American* vol. 284, no. 5: 34–43.

Liechti, O., M. Sifer, and T. Ichikawa. 1998. Structured graph format: XML metadata for describing web site structure. *Computer Networks and ISDN Systems* vol. 30: 11–21.

Lorie, R. A. 2001. Long term preservation of digital information. Proceedings of the 1st Joint Conference on Digital Libraries (JCDL) 2001: 346–352.

Lyman, P., and H. Besser. 1998. Defining the problem of our vanishing memory: Background, current status, models for resolution. Margaret MacLean and Ben H. Davis, eds. *Time & Bits: Managing Digital Continuity*. Los Angeles: J. Paul Getty Trust. 11–20.

Menon, G., and F. B. Raymond. 2002. Electronic publishing: An avenue for the dissemination of knowledge. *Electronic Journal of Social Work* vol. 1, no. 1.

Milic-Frayling, N., R. Sommerer, and G. Smyth. 2003. MIDAS: Towards rich site structure and content metadata. Poster. On-line Proceedings of the 12th World Wide Web Conference. Budapest.

Noy, N. F., M. Sintek, S. Decker, M. Crubzy, R. W. Fergerson, and M. A. Musen. 2001. Creating semantic web contents with Protégé 2000. *IEEE Intelligent Systems* vol. 16, no. 2: 60–71.

Oberle, D., R. Volz, B. Motik, and S. Staab (eds.). 2004. *An extensible open software environment*. Springer. 311–313.

Pack, T., and J. Pemberton. 2001. A harbinger of change: The cutting edge library at the Los Alamos National Laboratory. *Online Magazine* vol. 23, no. 2: 34–42. Available at www.onlineinc.com/articles/onlinemag/pack993.html.

Pardi, W. J. 1999. *XML in action*. Microsoft Press.

Rawlins, G. 1998. The new publishing—technology's impact on the publishing industry over the next decade. *Public-Access Computer Systems Review,* vol. 3, no. 8: 5–63. Available at www.roxie.org/papers/publishing/pub.html.

Resh, V. H. 1998. Science and communication: An author/editor/user's perspective on the transition from paper to electronic publishing. *Issues in Science and Technology Librarianship*: 1–7.

Robertson, J. 2003. XML and content management systems. Step two designs. *KM Column*. Available at www.steptwo.com.au.

Sondak, N. E., and R. J. Schwartz. 1973. The paperless journal. *Chemical Engineering Progress* vol. 69, no. 1: 82–83.

Weller, A. C. 2000. Editorial peer review for electronic journals: Current issues and emerging models. *Journal of the American Society for Information Science* vol. 51, Issue 14. Hoboken, NJ: John Wiley & Sons. 1328–1333.

4

Beyond HTML: Developing and Reimagining Library Web Guides in a Content Management System

Doug Goans, Guy Leach, and Teri M. Vogel

BACKGROUND

In 2000 the Georgia State University (GSU) Library had a FrontPage-based website with minimal login security, site architecture planning, and administrative and editorial processes in place. A single librarian served in the role of network coordinator, server administrator, and website manager. At the same time about fifteen liaison librarians, including the government documents librarian, were fulfilling their charge to develop web guides for their assigned subject areas. There were no policies or guidelines in place to assist the liaisons in meeting this responsibility, nor was any formal FrontPage training available. Administrative, technical, and personnel support were minimal, and no editorial control was in place. Liaisons were given complete control of their guides as well as direct, barrier-free access to manage their pages on the web server. The content on the resulting guides and how that content was displayed was extremely inconsistent, which contributed to a lack of organizational voice and credibility.

The web guides were extremely diverse on a visual level. Each librarian, as well as the student assistants and support staff who also worked on the pages, used different fonts, colors, and layout designs. Navigation was hampered by the lack of agreed-upon guidelines for content arrangement and labeling. While some librarians utilized their previous experience with FrontPage or other web-editing programs, others had never created a single web page. The lack of any training system to address these differing web-page and site-building skills among the librarians was also a factor affecting the quality and consistency of the guides.

Since there was no clearly defined or communicated mission for the library guides, the liaisons had different ideas about their purpose. There was no agreement or even discussion about how many guides a librarian should create or even what kinds of content should be included. For some departments or disciplines there was a single guide for all users. For others, multiple guides were developed to support general research, specialized subject areas, and individual classes, each guide a mix of new content and material copied over from other guides. Some guides were extremely content-rich, while others had nothing more than a librarian's contact information. Time, existing workloads, and even enthusiasm also had an impact on the quantity and quality of guides created by each librarian.

Serious technical and administrative problems with the liaisons' guides that went beyond their visual and content variability also existed. The minimal security implemented with the FrontPage system, intended to allow many librarians to publish content quickly and easily to the live website, eventually backfired when the liaisons' sub-web was accidentally deleted. Most of the liaison guides were restored through backups and browser caches. This disruptive event revealed serious weaknesses of the system, while leaving some liaisons reluctant to put additional time and effort into these activities beyond what was minimally required.

In response to the growing nature of library web content and the issues surrounding the FrontPage working environment, the library's first web development librarian was hired in 2000. Implementing website security for FrontPage authors and exploring website infrastructure development were among the first steps he undertook to improve the library's web presence. He also built MySQL applications to manage the lists of databases and electronic journals as well as several major photograph collections for the special collections department.

While the web development librarian was making these significant and sorely needed improvements to the library's web infrastructure, the liaisons' share of the website continued to grow. The liaisons, including those hired to fill new positions, continued creating guides as before, without standards, management, or oversight. By 2003, there were more than 100 guides on the site, with thousands of files in the liaison directory on the web server. Uncontrolled growth had been an ongoing though unresolved concern among the liaisons and web development librarian, but other priorities like library sitewide improvements and liaison department reorganization and reallocation had taken precedence. In 2003 the web development librarian, with help from a liaison staff assistant who was taking on more web-related responsibilities, began working with a small team of liaison librarians to help introduce site standards and better workflow.

To implement those standards, the team surveyed the library's research, subject, and course guides for content and identified four common elements: books, databases, journals, and websites. While surveying guides with similarly arranged content on other library websites, the task force noticed that a few of these sites were database-driven. This observation reinforced the web development librarian's suggestion that database technology could be applied to the GSU guides. This approach would support a scalable and flexible system by shifting the liaisons away from a static HTML content delivery system to one that was more dynamic and automated. A database-driven system could also create a more efficient web publishing workflow for the liaisons as well as the entire library site. The files-and-folders infrastructure could not support the library website indefinitely, and the liaison's component of the site brought the situation to a critical mass.

LIBRARY CONTENT MANAGEMENT SYSTEMS DEFINED

Content management (CM) can be defined as the process of collecting, managing, and publishing content (Boiko 2001; Thamaraiselvi 2002). Calling a content management system a "database" or "repository" is an oversimplification. Databases and other web technologies indeed form the technical foundation of a CMS, but the authors' vision of what a CMS can and should offer a library has evolved from conceptual foundations shaped by the experience at GSU.

Content

In a CMS, the content is disconnected from the layout and design elements of the page. Librarians create their guides in a forms-based environment, which levels the playing field for possessing HTML skills. Anyone, regardless of previous experience creating web pages, can create a basic guide in the system. Instead of devoting time with HTML or FrontPage to create the structural or presentational display where the content resides, the librarians can focus instead on identifying, creating, annotating, and selecting the content itself. The importance of empowering site contributors with the ability to contribute content without having to know markup languages like HTML (Ingersoll 2005) or website architecture issues cannot be overlooked.

In a CMS the scope of what is identified as "content" can be as broadly defined as the organization chooses. For the liaison guides at GSU, this includes:

- Resource links for databases, journals, books, and websites. Some of these links are pulled from existing sources such as the library's lists of databases and electronic journals, while other links are added by the liaisons.
- Web pages built within the CMS using a simplified HTML editor.
- Images files that can be uploaded.
- Files in other formats that can be uploaded and linked from pages in the CMS, including PDFs, PowerPoint presentations, and Word documents.

Another value of the CMS is reusability, that content can be repurposed or repackaged (Fichter 2005). Every resource that has been added, every file or image that has been uploaded, every custom page that has been created is an object in a database. Once that object is in the database, it can be used again and again. Mescan (2004) and Thamaraiselvi (2002) cite the reuse concept, which improves efficiency of the editorial process, as one advantage of moving to a CMS. There should also be levels of access. Some objects can be reused by any of the librarians for their own guides, while other objects can only be accessed and used by the librarian who added or created them. This model of object-oriented site development does not typically exist in a files-and-folders web system, and it is a foundational concept that librarians need to understand when working within a CMS.

Control

Some libraries adopt CMS technology because they want to reduce the "gatekeeper" effect by eliminating barriers that limit library staff from contributing to the website (Ingersoll 2005). The GSU Library had the opposite problem, and it was the lack of technological or managerial barriers that helped to create the existing situation. A CMS can allow more content creators to have direct editorial access to their assigned areas or components of the website, while still functioning as a limited gatekeeper to provide visual and navigational standards for all guides without restricting access to content developers.

ASP-generated templates using cascading style sheets (CSS) are used for the GSU guides to control how content is delivered and presented to the users, from fonts to text placement to branding. By controlling how content is presented, arranged, and structured, the templates create a common style as well as navigational consistency across the guides. Users know what to expect in each guide and how to navigate them, and it is hoped that these standards will improve usability. While the templates control the automated layout of the guides, they can be modified. Over time changes will be made to the guides in order to adapt to changing technologies as well as user needs and preferences. The web development librarian will then be able to make global modifications to the templates to change the structure and presentation of the content without affecting the content itself.

Customization and Context

Customizing (or tagging) content is a crucial feature of the CMS because it 1) allows librarians to work in the same system and create guides for users in different subject disciplines, and 2) allows them to take the reusable content and repackage it in ways that are most meaningful to the users. Librarians have the freedom to group resources into categories of their own choosing, to place them in any particular order (Bills, Cheng, and Nathanson 2003), and to identify key resources within groupings. Each time a resource is selected from an existing database table, the librarian has the opportunity to create a unique description. These features give the system a level of customization that can help alleviate the perceived loss of creativity or professional expression or individual writing style in the move from a free-HTML publishing workflow to the structured template environment of a CMS (Ingersoll 2005; Mosley 2003; Bills, Cheng, and Nathanson 2003).

The ability to customize the metadata for CMS objects within individual guides gives these objects meaning for the user. Librarians can contextualize the content that goes into each guide, whether being a broad or more specialized subject or course guide. They are working within the more structured framework of this system to develop sites that are targeted and customized for specific audiences but are still within an environment that allows librarians to deliver a better product to their users.

Complexity

The CMS can make these concepts a reality in a way that a files-and-folder system cannot even come close to. It offers the scalability necessary to accommodate the growing body of work being developed by library personnel without hindering editing and publishing workflows. The web development staff has more control over assigning access rights for librarians and support staff working on sites. System security and backups are in place to keep the content from being deleted or otherwise damaged accidentally, while allowing content creators to update their sites quickly and easily and remotely, if desired. The CMS should also identify the author or contributor of each resource in the system and protect the content, so that one librarian cannot delete a resource that someone else is using elsewhere on the site.

Part of the complexity of a CMS when compared to simpler database-driven applications is the need for it to be flexible. In an increasingly IT-based learning environment, both on and off campus, the CMS must and should respond accordingly to meet the needs and expectations of library users. Use of the CMS should also not be limited to a single department or group of content creators within a library. It should be able to support the publishing activities of not just other library departments with public pages, such as Special Collections and Access Services, but also groups that use the library's intranet, such as committees, Technical Services units, and departments like Human Resources.

FIRST STEPS TOWARD A CMS ENVIRONMENT

Realizing the limitations and less-than-optimal practices that had emerged out of the FrontPage environment, the web development librarian and liaison team began an informal and largely unstructured exploration of alternative solutions. This exploration was influenced by several factors.

The Commercial Option

Some early discussions about potential commercial software solutions took place informally between the web development librarian, the systems librarian, and within the library administration. Dreamweaver was considered and its feature set weighed against the university-wide FrontPage license that was in effect "free" and that the library was using at the time. While Dreamweaver had some compelling features in contrast to FrontPage, the web development librarian and the systems librarian had concerns about the costs for licenses, recurring upgrades, and training and additional software. Those concerns were not present in FrontPage (aside from training, an issue regardless of the software package) due to the university-wide license that made copies of FrontPage and any ongoing updates available for "free." It was also unknown at the time if Dreamweaver would alleviate the scalability issues that were surfacing over time with FrontPage.

Some libraries have selected commercial CMS solutions, such as Vignette, or taken advantage of outsourcing to create their system (Mosley 2003; Bills, Cheng, and Nathanson 2003). The web development librarian did not believe that either option was feasible mainly due to the even higher costs involved with "shrink-wrap" software solutions. The issues being raised were still new, and a formal review process was not in place to submit an official proposal to persuade the library to move to a new infrastructure with associated licensing and product costs.

With high competition for the limited technology funding available, spending could not be justified for a new website commercial service, software, and future upgrades or maintenance plans when the free FrontPage package was already available. Critical technological needs that could easily be explained and justified in a formal proposal were usually and rightly given the priority for funding. Since the exploration for alternative solutions was only beginning, any further research into a commercial solution and formal proposals was foregone while other alternatives were considered.

The Open Source Option

As an alternative to fee-based licensing for website publishing software and services, open source solutions were a tantalizing option. Open source website systems at the time were often not developed to encompass the range of online services for an entire library web presence in one solution. Some open source solutions would address various library-centric services like the Scout Portal Toolkit to work with lists of resources or general content management systems that could manage HTML-based web page content such as Zope or Midgard. Open source options were viable, but it appeared that most would require "Frankensteining" several products together to facilitate the automation of all website content including research guides, regular web pages, blogs, an intranet, and single authentication to the system.

Additionally, many of these open source solutions tend to be supported or optimized for the Linux/Unix platforms. The library's existing Windows Server platform environment greatly influenced many of the library's technology choices, including this one. Any open source solution not designed for Windows IIS would carry with it the potential requirement of code tweaking and reconfiguration to run in the library's existing web server environment.

The In-House Option

GSU Library had established a precedent with successful in-house web development projects between 2001 and 2003, most notably the blogging system www.library.gsu.edu/news/. Since the databases and code had already been developed for the blogging system as well as online resources and a private intranet login system, the web librarian drafted a prototype using all of the existing technology to illustrate the feasibility of an automated system for the research guides. This prototype was then presented to the liaison team to evaluate suitability as a replacement for FrontPage.

Two liaisons (and article co-authors), the music librarian, and the biology/chemistry librarian offered to test the web guide prototype in the summer of 2003. The newly hired astronomy/physics librarian was invited to join the beta group because she could start fresh with creating guides in the new system instead of working on migrating HTML/FrontPage web guides. They were joined by the liaison assistant, who had been working with the web development librarian and liaison team to improve the guides. The group tested the system and gave extensive feedback to the web development librarian and newly hired web programmer, who programmed the system to accommodate baseline CMS functionality. By August, the librarians were satisfied enough with the improved system to go "live" and replace their FrontPage web guides with ones built in this new system, now dubbed a Content Management System.

An introductory training manual and workshop were tested and refined with the beta group. The library-wide Technology Steering Committee was kept informed of these activities and concluded that the developing CMS would be sufficient as the next-generation tool for the liaison web guides. The web development librarian then set up a schedule with the other liaisons to migrate their existing FrontPage/HTML content into the CMS. Typically, a group of four liaisons would attend a workshop provided by the web development librarian about the CMS and migration process. The session was a nuts-and-bolts workshop on the features and functions of the CMS. He would then meet with each liaison individually to review their existing web content and assist with acclimating them to the new system. The liaison was then given time to review their guides in the CMS, while their FrontPage guides were still active. The web development librarian and liaison then scheduled a "switch-over" date to replace the FrontPage guides with the CMS guides on the live server. The process from initial workshop to switching over generally took four to six weeks but remained flexible to allow for semester schedules and to work around other duties and projects.

At this time, the primary focus was on the top-level research guides (art, mathematics, etc.). Unlike the numerous subject and course guides that splintered off this group, the number of research guides was set at around a more manageable 30. These were also the first guides the users come across on the library website, and the need to "fix" these first was paramount.

While this migration process was moving forward, the Liaison Web Task Force was formed to formalize the various ad hoc liaison web groups. The task force met regularly with the web development librarian and programmer to review the CMS and offer feedback and suggestions on enhancing its features and functionality to support liaison-based web publishing, including the design of the template to control the look and layout of the research guides. The web development librarian and programmer continued to improve the system and develop the rich functionality desired in the CMS for the web guides.

Between August 2003 and June 2004, the liaison web guides were moved into the CMS. Some librarians rebuilt their guides in the new system. Other librarians, either due to having too many guides or too little time to rebuild them during the transition, had their FrontPage guides copied and pasted into the CMS. The web librarian, web programmer, and another liaison assistant managed the copy-and-paste activities, which helped the librarians meet the goal of completing the liaison website transition quickly. The team had met the goal to switch over the entire liaison website to the CMS by the end of June 2004. In November 2004 the FrontPage liaison website was disabled and archived.

THE GSU LIBRARY CMS TECHNOLOGY

Database Design

At the heart of the GSU Library CMS is a MySQL database on a Windows web server. The database is made up of resource tables, metadata tables, and personnel metadata tables. Resource tables store the content objects while metadata tables assign content to templates such as Research Guides. Figure 4.1 shows the entity diagram of the subscription databases in the CMS. The personnel tables shown in Figure 4.2 house data for logging in to the system, assignments for website authoring, and also contact information for display on web pages.

The tables for personnel and subscription resources were already running on the website during the time the team began to explore solutions to replace FrontPage. As part of the early prototype, a new series of tables were designed around a core set of resources, one being the subscription databases that would connect with the personnel tables. By joining these two tables through an administrative interface, librarians can contribute and work with database content as individuals, but also collectively. After the aforementioned meetings with the liaison team to round out the feature requirements of the system and further work with database design, a final design emerged. Figure 4.3 illustrates the tables used in the CMS for the research guides in 2003.

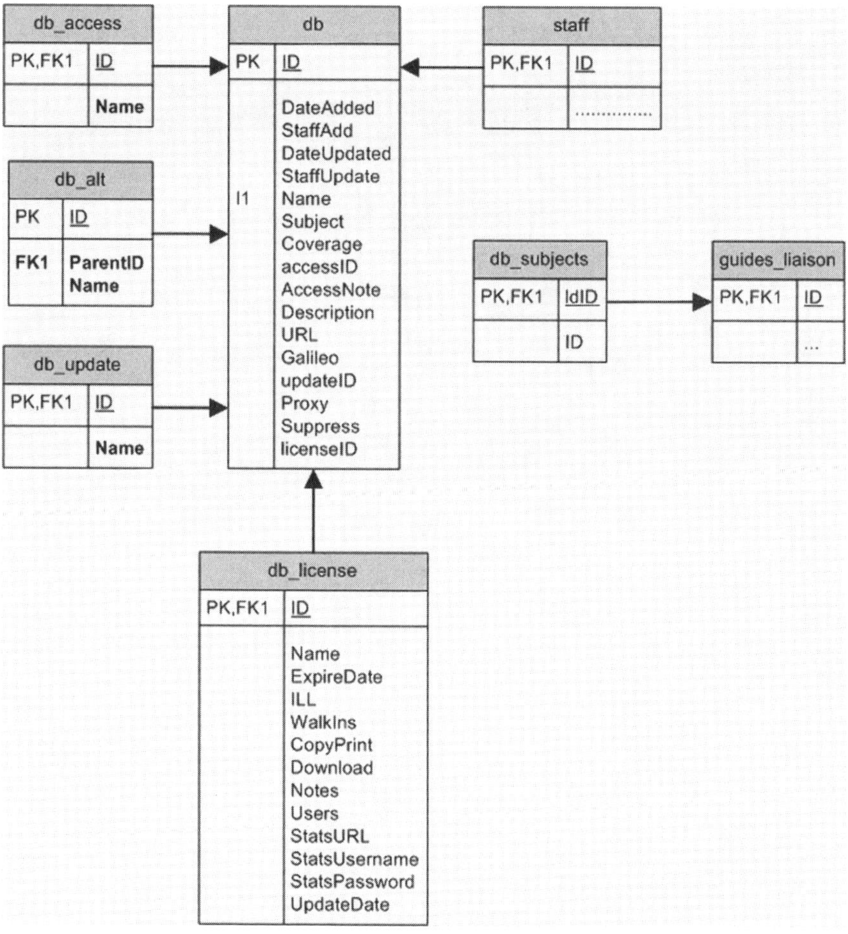

Figure 4.1. Entity tables for subscription databases used for the library's list of databases and connected to research guides.

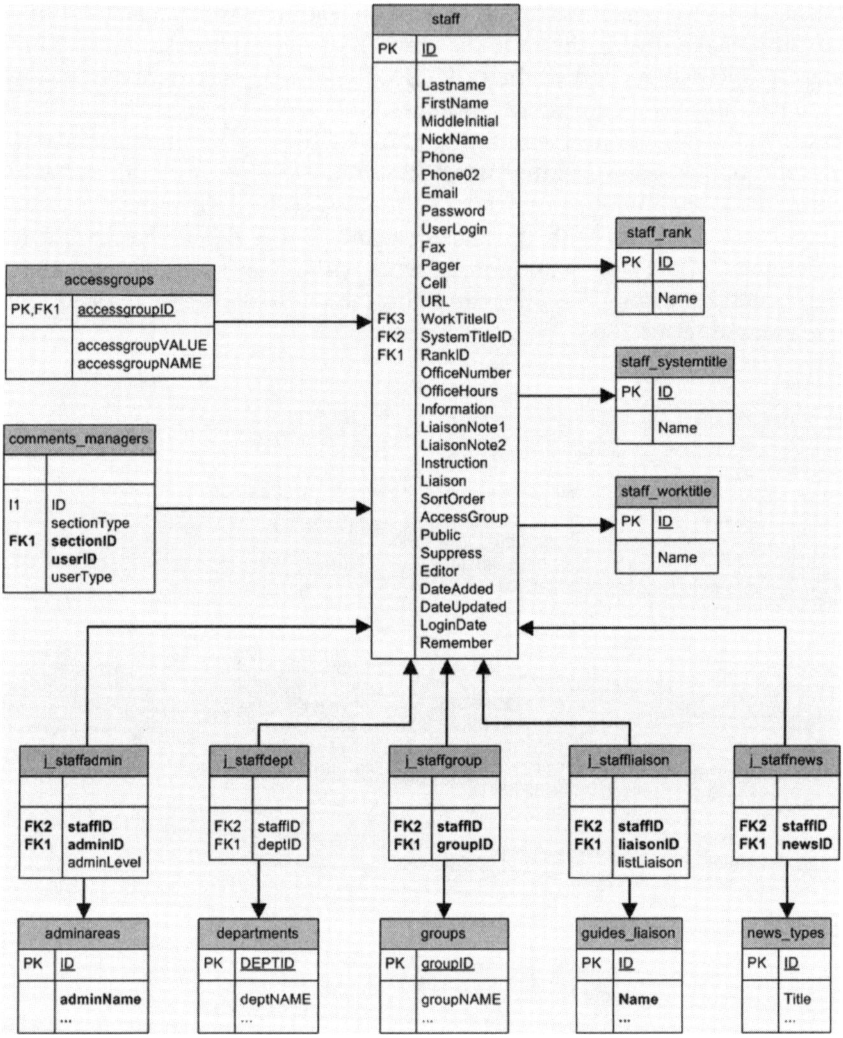

Figure 4.2. Entity tables for staff database (employee database). It sets up liaison status and is used in guide assignment and system login.

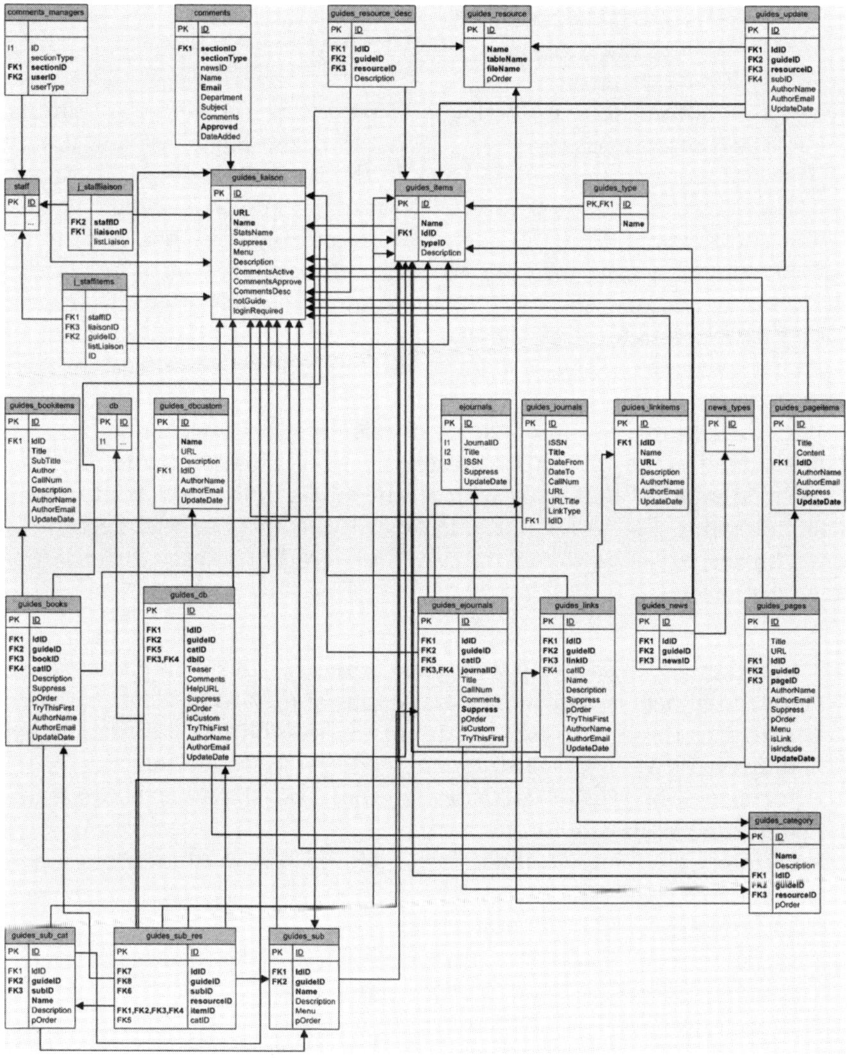

Figure 4.3. Entity tables for liaison research guides. Tables used for the administration and presentation of research guides.

ADMINISTRATION OF THE CMS WITH ACTIVE SERVER PAGE FILES

Web-based administrative interfaces, using online forms, radio buttons, and checkboxes, are password protected and enable librarians and library staff to add content to various tables in the MySQL database. These administrative forms and their various fields map to the associated database tables and fields to allow for the addition and maintenance of content. Various interfaces exist for CMS administrators to work with the personnel tables to add new employees and assign individuals or groups of people to have access to other tables. A series of interfaces also exist for librarians working in the system to add or update resources in their websites.

Files for administration of the CMS exist in a directory named "dbadmin" located in the "intranet" directory. Various directories and ASP files exist in "dbadmin" that work with all the tables in the CMS via the web. The following directories and files constitute the site architecture of the administrative views of the CMS. See www.library.gsu.edu/intranet/dbadmin.

- **adminareas/** this directory provides administrators with global access for assignment of individuals to sections of the CMS.
- **cms/** this directory provides administrators with the ability to assign individuals to sites, create new sites, and get usage reports.
- **ld/** this is the liaison database directory, and all Research Guide administrative files are located here.
- **ld/index.asp** the main interface for administration of a CMS research guide. See Figure 4.5.
- **ld/books.asp** add or maintain book lists.
- **ld/databases.asp** add or maintain subscription database lists.
- **ld/links.asp** add or maintain lists of web links.
- **ld/ejournals.asp** add or maintain journal lists.
- **ld/media.asp** add or maintain lists of VHS, DVD, CD, or other media.
- **ld/news.asp** add a link to a library blog to the guide.
- **d/pages.asp** add or maintain HTML-based custom web pages.

Functions and include files handle processing, adding, updating, or deleting records from the database. Active server pages (.ASP) can determine which guide to administer by getting the associated ID of the guide from the URL. Administration links pass a specific variable for "action" so that each page knows whether to display content for a specific guide, add new content, update existing content, or delete content.

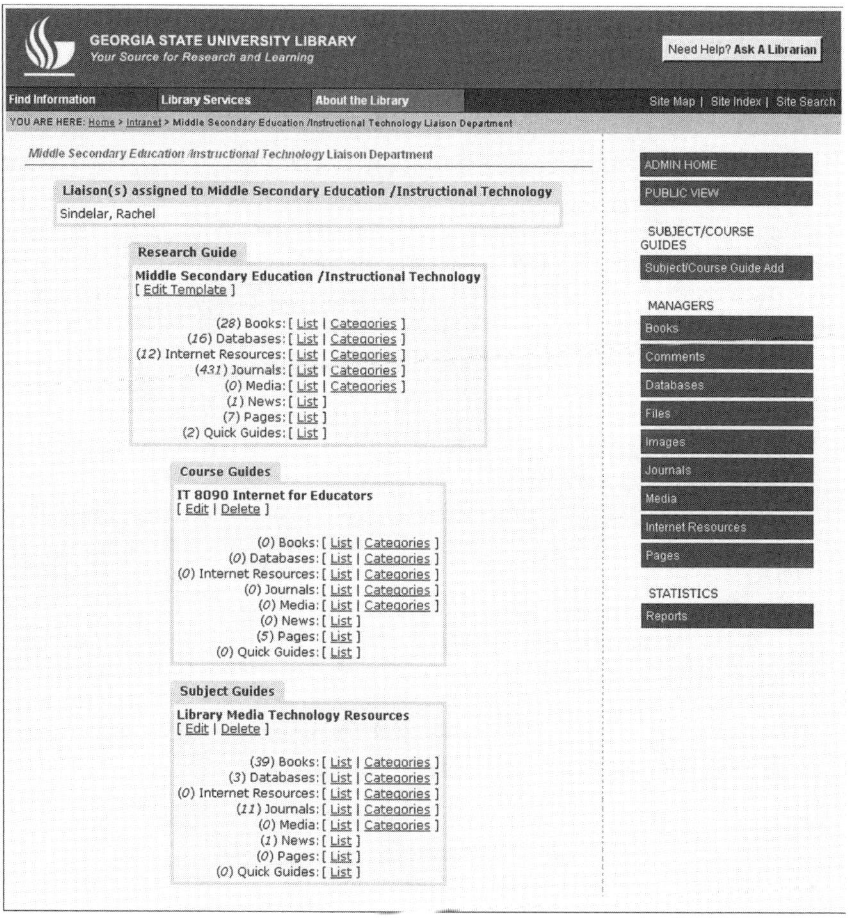

Figure 4.5. CMS interface administrative view.

For example, the full URL to add a web link to a course guide for a marketing course would look like: /intranet/dbadmin/ld/links.asp?action=select&guideID=448&ldID=52&resourceID=1

- **links.asp** determines that the online forms presented for site administration will connect to the CMS tables for web links
- **action=select** determines that a new record will be added to the table
- **guideID=448** determines that this record will be associated with the course guide
- **ldID=52** determines that this record will be associated with the parent (business) research guide
- **resourceID=1** determines that this is a website link record

By using variables for administrative actions and manipulation of database records, a single ASP file page with online forms can manage an entire CMS library of resources for all guides.

PUBLIC PRESENTATION OF INFORMATION FROM THE CMS

A group of ASP files work together as templates for the web page display of Research Guides or other content served out of the CMS. The ASP files pull data from the MySQL database in real time to construct and present any of the hundreds of web pages and lists of resources or research guides, on the fly.

The following files constitute the site architecture of the public view, or template, of the research guides in the CMS:

- **liaison.asp** is the main template file for the research guides, not including the resource lists.
- **resources.asp** is the template file used exclusively for lists of resources in the guide such as books, journals, web links, and subscription databases.
- **one library-wide style sheet (.css)** for font, color, and branding control.
- **various include files** for working with the database, processing record sets from the database, handling variables, and date formatting.

In the heading of both liaison.asp and resources.asp files are a series of include files that carry out various functions.

```
<% 'include file to connect to the CMS database %>
<!—#include virtual="/includes/inc_db_cms_connect.asp" —>
<% 'include file with common functions %>
<!—#include virtual="/research/inc_functions.asp" —>
<% 'include file to format dates %>
<!—#include virtual="/includes/inc_convdate.asp"—>
<% 'include ADO constants files—used in the resources.asp file %>
<!—#include virtual="/includes/inc_adovbs.asp" —>
<% 'include file with subroutines and functions—used in the liaison.asp
   file %>
<!—#include virtual="/includes/inc_code.asp" —>
<% 'initialize variables %>
<% p = "main" %>
<% 'include preprocessing—gets variables from URL and sets code and
   variables for resource pages, liaison pages, quick guides, or print pages
   %>
<!—#include virtual="/research/inc_preprocess.asp" —>
<html>
```

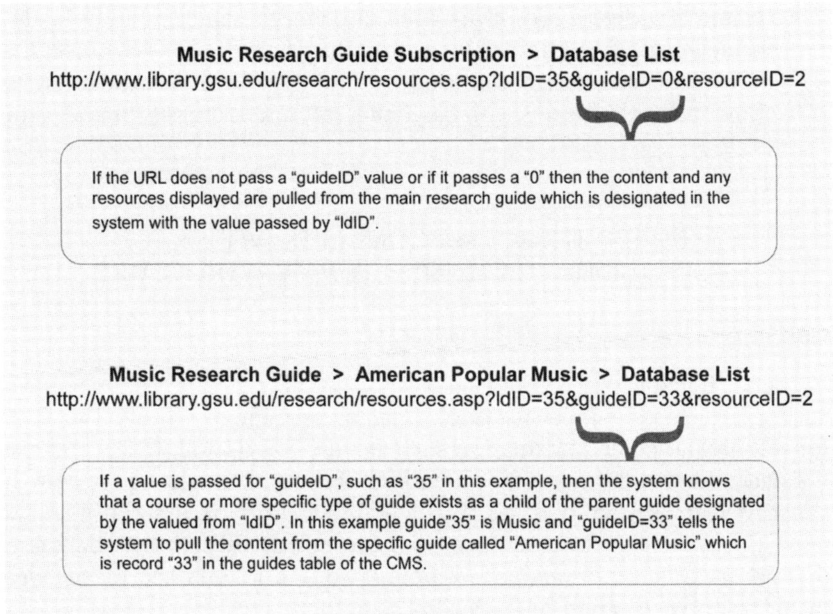

Figure 4.4. Values passed in URLs determine what content to show.

```
<head>
<meta name="robots" content="noarchive">
<meta name="googlebot" content="noarchive">
<title><% = headerTitle %>
<link rel="stylesheet" type="text/css" href="/styles/librarywide.css">
<script language="JavaScript1.1" src="inc.js"></script>
<script language="JavaScript1.2" src="inc_guides.js"></script>
</head>
```

The ASP files rely on variables passed from the URL to execute calls to the CMS database. Once variables are passed, ASP code will retrieve information from the database and assemble it for the viewer in their browser. Figure 4.4 illustrates a URL for a Research Guide.

The three variables passed to the system from the URL are

- **ldID** (Liaison Database ID) is the record identifier for a specific research guide.
- **guideID** determines whether the system displays content from the main research guide or any of the course guides or specific subject guides it contains. If the value is "0" the system defaults to the main research guide located with ldID.

- **resourceID** determines if the content being presented is a book, electronic journal, web link, database, or other type of resource object that may exist in the system. In the URL example in Figure 4.4 the resources shown are subscription databases that fall under the resourceID value of "2."

SUPPORTING CMS CONCEPTS WITH THE GSU LIBRARY TECHNOLOGY INFRASTRUCTURE

Content

The MySQL database contains tables for specific types of resource objects such as databases, e-journals, books, media, and Internet links. The fields for resources include information such as title, description, URLs, and also the date added and the numeric identifier of the person adding the data. In some ways the system behaves as a digital repository or digital library system. Most resource content, such as e-journals or subscription databases that are used by all librarians, are populated and maintained by the electronic resource librarian or CMS administrators.

Librarians, using the administrative interfaces, can select from the collection of existing content to quickly collate resources for a guide or web page. Librarians also enrich the resource tables since they are capable of inserting new records for their assigned websites. Other tables in the database assist in making the system more CMS-like by storing information (descriptive and administrative metadata) about collections of resource objects and descriptions of those collections. Resource objects in the table are tied to the guide's metadata table through join tables in MySQL.

The reuse and repurposing features of the system are used repeatedly and make up a sizeable portion of the website development model of the CMS. Librarians have the ability to add a resource item once, such as a book or journal, and then reuse that item in many research or course guides instead of creating duplicate entries of the resource over time. Librarians can utilize resources added by other librarians in the system as well to help reduce duplication of data.

Control and Customization

The system offers both presentational control and administrative control over the library web presence. Control mechanisms are available to site administrators and also to librarians in their assigned CMS spaces. Librarians have online forms to work with resources and web pages stored in the CMS while site administrators have online forms to edit or add website sections (such as new research guides) and also assign people and authorship rights to those sections.

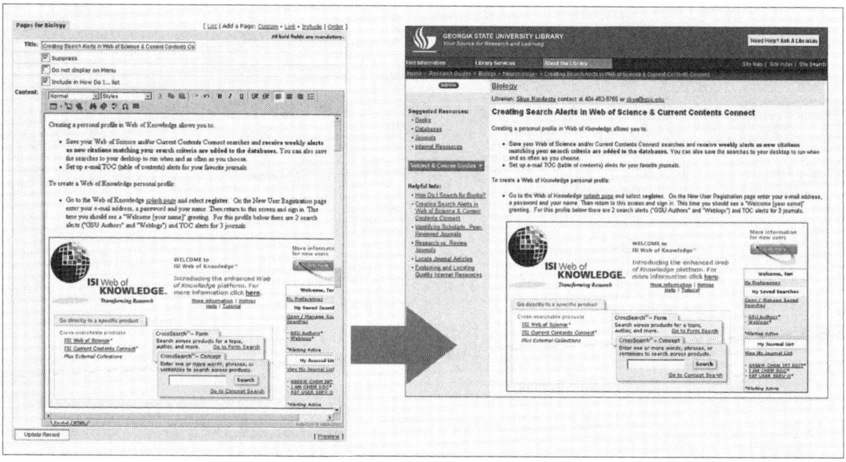

Figure 4.6. Example of web editor showing a custom page in the CMS administrative view and the same content rendered in the template for the public view.

The ASP template and CSS files manage presentational control. These are maintained and developed by the web development personnel to meet functional requirements requested by the liaison librarian web group. Librarians have the ability to customize resource or content presentation within the constraints of the library-wide template system. The most apparent examples of librarian customization are found in the custom descriptions, custom categories, and custom rankings features of the system in addition to the ability to add custom HTML-based web pages.

Custom web pages, like resource objects, are fields in the "pages" table that utilize large field lengths to accommodate the HTML markup needed to store a web page in the database.

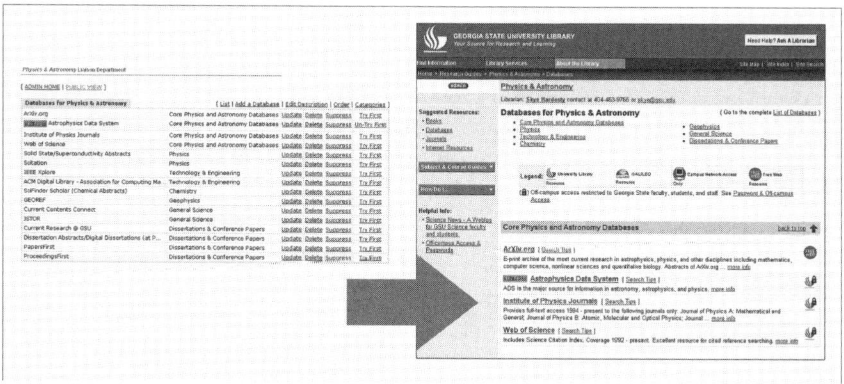

Figure 4.7. Example of subscription database list in the CMS administrative view and the same content rendered in the template for the public view.

Without presentational controls, the system would simply provide alphanumerical listings of resources with universal descriptions applied every time resources were displayed to the user. While simple listings might be sufficient in some cases, customization of resource listings allows for the use of CMS guides in courses or for instructional purposes where objects need to be presented in a particular order to support learning objectives.

Complexity and Context

The Research Guides component of the system is the most complex since it dynamically joins content from many separate tables: information about the assigned librarian(s), the name and collection information of a guide's topic, the individual resources that are present in the guide's collection, and finally, any HTML-based web content that lives in the web page table.

The liaisons' component of the FrontPage site had 14,000 files, hundreds of folders, and was approximately 270 MB in size. In contrast, the entire textual content of the library website now in the CMS amounts to less than 100 MB. The FrontPage research guides that were composed of thousands of HTML pages are now represented by less than a dozen ASP files that create pages on the fly. The database system affords better statistics and reporting on the numbers of guides, resources, which resources are used in which guides, and more. Broken link checking in FrontPage was a project that never got off the ground due to the laborious task of checking and editing thousands of HTML page files and repeatedly updating broken links that may have been copied from guide to guide. In a CMS all links can be checked, their associated use in guides identified, and then all of those associated pages can be updated with a single update to an objects URL in the resource table.

DESIGNING A USABLE CMS RESEARCH GUIDE TEMPLATE FOR STUDENTS AND LIBRARIANS

Just as the development of the CMS was an evolutionary process, so was the development of the template that would standardize the research guides. A temporary transitional template was used for several months until the content from the guides was migrated to the CMS and a new template could be globally implemented. The temporary template consisted of a sidebar menu with standardized labels and links for books, databases, Internet resources and journals, and a text area that was simply copied from the FrontPage version of the guide. The liaisons could add unlimited additional links to this sidebar menu and could edit the main text area without restrictions.

Throughout the template development process the liaisons (first the informal team, then later the more formalized task force) examined the research and subject guides of other libraries to identify common or best practices regarding content, layout/templates, and navigation. While some guides organized content into broad format categories (books, journals, databases, websites), others had items grouped by function (dictionaries, encyclopedias, and indexes), regardless of whether they are print or online, licensed or free. This grouping allowed all encyclopedias to be displayed together, whether they were print, licensed databases, or freely available websites. In a format-based system of organization, like that used for most existing FrontPage guides, the encyclopedias would be displayed on three separate lists. While having one place to look rather than three may be simpler, changing the resource lists would have required the liaisons to recategorize thousands of data elements and would have significantly delayed the CMS transition and migration. The choice to build the CMS database tables around existing data categories (books, databases, journals, Internet resources) was based on manpower, time, and the liaison's desire to limit the reworking of their guides. While recategorizing all the data was not feasible, the programmer developed pages that allow the liaisons to select from all of the formats/tables and combine print and electronic resources into custom lists.

As far as layout and navigation, some of the library guides the task force examined were arranged as a single scrolling page of resources, thus providing immediate access to resources. Others were broken down into secondary pages linked to the main page for the guide, similar to most of the existing GSU research guides. Although the task force wanted the research guide template to provide immediate access to information, our existing guides contained far too much information to be presented on a single scrollable page. Since the liaisons were concerned over the perceived loss of flexibility and autonomy and having to rework all of their guides, the template would have to accommodate existing content. The solution was the creation of a template that highlighted and provided direct access to a few core resources with linked pages for the resource lists, subject and course guides, and custom pages.

The template (Figure 4.8) consists of a sidebar menu and a formatted main section that follows a stepwise progression. The first step (1. "Start with . . .") requires the liaison to list no more than four core resources that can be accompanied by custom descriptions. The next step (2. "Try more resources . . .") provides an area for a second list of up to four additional sources of information and comments. In the third step (3. Contact . . .), a default sentence with the liaison's contact information is provided, along with some optional free-text space to describe their services. In addition to limiting the number of resources, the number of characters for resource annotations and the free-text space are also limited, thus allowing the three steps to be visible on a single screen. In the area following these steps the liaison is provided with unlimited free-text space that is often used to include specialized materials that did not easily fit within the defined template.

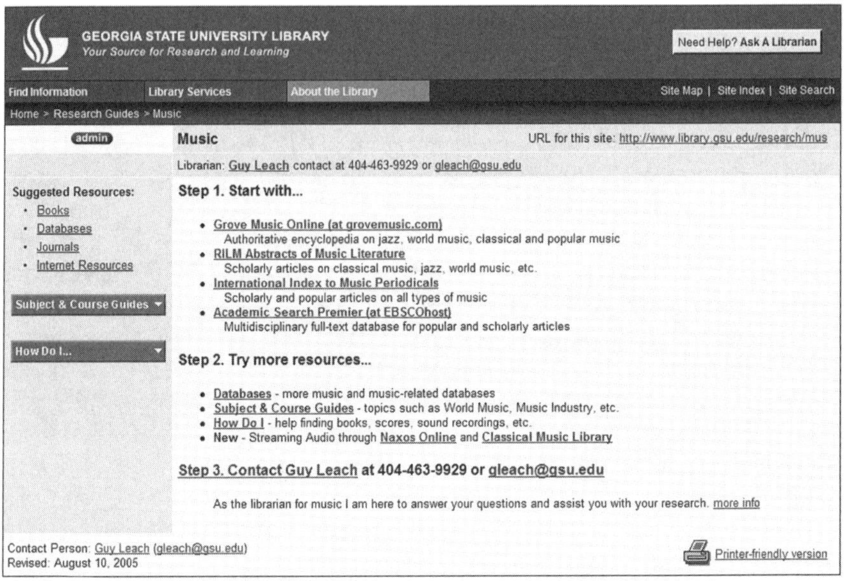

Figure 4.8. Public view of a research guide dynamically displayed from the CMS.

Where the main section focuses on core resources, the sidebar menu provides a uniform display for resource lists, subject and course guides, custom pages, and miscellaneous helpful information. The resource lists ("Suggested Resources") for books, databases, journals, and Internet resources are required elements for all research guides. The subject and course guides and tutorial/custom pages ("How Do I?") are available through drop-down menus. The drop-down menus were a solution to the previous display of this information as a long list of links.

This template accomplished several goals of the task force. The required elements ensured that every research guide offered some baseline resources to help a user get started with research, and the limits kept the required, standardized content visible on the first page. Although the research guide template contains many required elements, it still offers a fair level of customization for the liaisons. They can annotate their selected core resources, organize their "Try more resources" section, and take advantage of the free-text space and utilize the numerous optional elements in the sidebar menu.

As mentioned earlier, the template was initially only applied to the research guides. Despite their initial resistance to the idea of a template, the liaisons expressed their acceptance and approval of the template by requesting that it be made available as an option for the subject and course guides. It should also be noted that the template was designed to serve all of the liaisons for their disciplines: sciences, humanities, and social sciences. While this "one size fits all" approach was largely successful, the template was still flexible enough that some modifications could be made to accommodate unique needs of several librarians.

The template was introduced in August 2004 with the understanding that usability testing would need to be completed. That fall, a usability study was conducted to evaluate the structure, layout, and labeling of the research guide template and data elements. While the study identified many small improvements that could be made to the existing template, the study also revealed that the basic layout of the template did not achieve the desired result, which was to make a variety of research resources readily apparent to the users. In general, the usability study subjects focused on the resources in the main content area of the guide and almost ignored the resources listed on the sidebar menu. As of this writing, the template is being revised to better utilize the geography of the page and to improve navigation. The sidebar menu may be removed and its content incorporated into the main body of the page. The layout and labeling changes will be managed globally through the CMS. The liaisons will have to make some decisions about content changes that cannot be globally updated. Once the revised template is ready, usability testing will be conducted with students to ensure that the changes demonstrate a significant improvement.

In addition to the research guide home page, templates were also required for the pages of books, databases, journals, and websites linked from a guide home page. The templates standardize the layout of these pages but still provide the liaison with the flexibility to create categories to group the resources on a particular page. Liaisons can order these categories and the resources within each category, and they can prioritize selected resources by marking them with a "Try First" icon (Figure 4.9). The liaisons also have the freedom to add custom descriptions for categories and individual resources. These descriptions provide context to the resources within a particular guide. For example, the history and the music liaisons may refer users to the same database but describe the database differently for the benefit of their users. Creating categories, ordering and prioritizing resources, and writing custom descriptions provide valuable information for the users of the guides, whether they are students, faculty, or librarians.

While the CMS provides a variety of tools for organizing content, the liaisons are responsible for supplying the content and manipulating those tools. To assist the liaisons with the new system and templates, the task force created a "best practices" checklist for reviewing each research guide template and the accompanying linked pages. The checklist review provided the liaisons with positive feedback as well as areas that could be improved. While the checklist identified content or layout issues that either did not comply with library web policy and the research guides' mission and purpose, it also highlighted content that could be displayed and formatted better using some

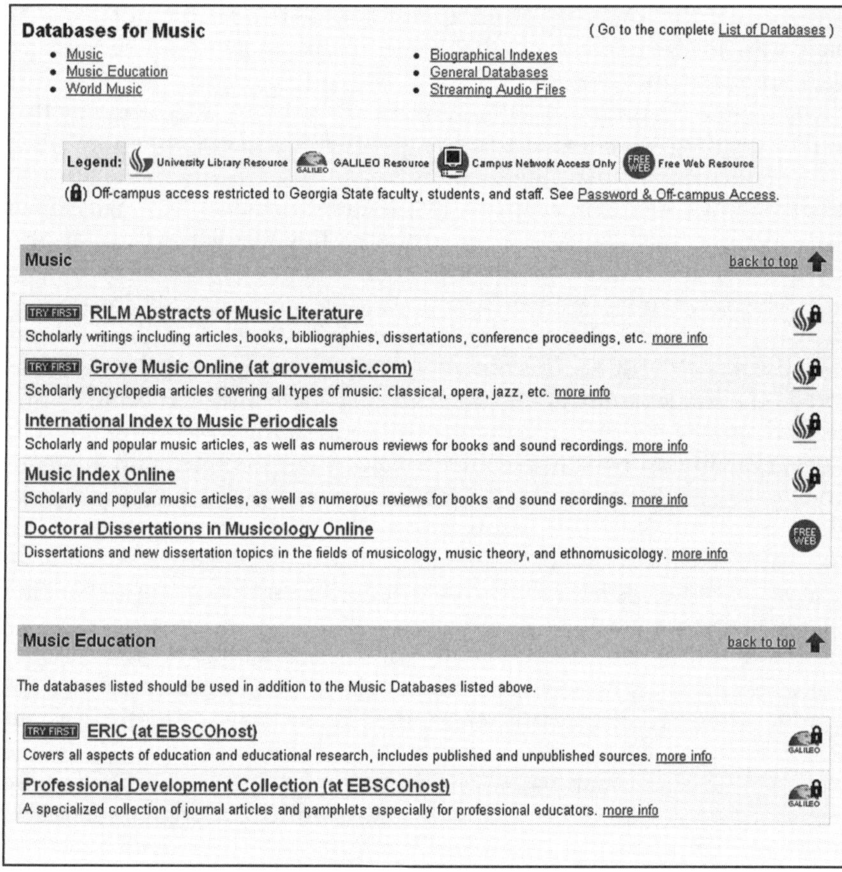

Figure 4.9. View of resource list in a guide showing the "Try First" icon.

of the advanced features of the CMS. For example, some liaisons, having worked in a FrontPage HTML environment, resorted to creating custom HTML pages in the CMS. Often, the content of these HTML pages could have been entered into the CMS resource object table to automate the process of creating lists of resources instead of hand-coding HTML.

Completing the checklist review of the guides highlighted the limitations of the task force. The group had been formed to guide/oversee the liaison's web presence. The group was not formed as an editorial board that monitored and reviewed the guides, nor did the members have formal training in web page development and architecture. The task force was created to assist in the development of the liaisons' web presence and web templates. The templates have provided a uniform structure to increase standardization across all the guides.

The system itself, however, is not the complete solution. There is an ongoing need to train the liaisons on utilizing the diverse and developing features of the CMS as well as to provide them assistance with learning user-centric website development practices and information architecture. Creating and nurturing a culture of learning that combines formal training sessions and workshops with more informal information sharing among content creators will help ensure that the library and librarians get the most out of the system in place.

ASSESSING THE LIAISON MIGRATION TO THE CMS

The development of the CMS was a highly collaborative endeavor involving library web development personnel, the liaison web task force, and the liaisons as a group. The web development librarian and web programmer solicited and implemented task force and liaison feedback throughout the development process. This collaborative approach contributed to the CMS having numerous features and functions that allow for a high level of customization. Since the web development personnel listened and responded to their concerns and requests, the liaisons were able to participate in the process and maintain a sense of control over their guides—making the transition a little easier.

In June 2005 the authors, in partnership with the task force, surveyed the liaisons concerning their experience with the CMS. The goals of this survey were to evaluate the transition process, to identify areas for improvement regarding the training and documentation for the CMS, to develop new features in the CMS, and to improve the interface used for adding, editing, and formatting content. The twenty-question survey was a mix of questions requiring a textual response and those that could be answered by selecting strongly disagree, disagree, no opinion, agree, and strongly agree. Of the twelve respondents (out of thirteen who received the survey), two had joined the library since the CMS migration and therefore had not created guides in FrontPage at GSU.

All of the respondents indicated that the reason for migrating to the CMS was clearly communicated. While all the respondents identified standardization as one of the reasons for the transition to the CMS, roughly three quarters of the respondents also mentioned ease of use. While almost all of the liaisons indicated that the CMS was easier to use than FrontPage or Dreamweaver, a few disagreed or had no opinion. In response to what they liked about the CMS, the respondents mentioned ease of use for both entering data and using existing data. Some respondents also mentioned that they liked the templates, which allowed them to concentrate on content and not worry about format. As far as what they liked about FrontPage, the respondents identified specific features as well as flexibility, having more control, and the ability to customize layout.

Regarding the transfer of content from FrontPage to the CMS, the vast majority considered the transition to the CMS fairly smooth and the support from the systems office to be excellent. The systems office was praised for doing most of the work, listening to the liaisons, and meeting one-on-one to make sure the transfer of information was accurate. A recurring complaint about the transition was formatting constraints and having to rework guides or portions of existing guides to fit the new template. When asked about what additional technical support is needed, some respondents want more assistance with maintenance and clerical tasks. Others mention the need for guidance concerning the architecture and organization of their information.

The respondents had mixed opinions on the documentation and training provided during the transition. Since the CMS was continually changing, providing accurate and current documentation was difficult. Once the CMS had reached a level of stability, documentation was created. During the migration liaisons received individual and group training on the basic features of the CMS. Many respondents were satisfied with the level of training while some indicated that they would like more. When asked what topics could be addressed in additional training, suggestions included many of the more advanced features: building custom pages using the internal HTML editor, using the features of the system to combine all types of resources into single-page formatted lists, and maximizing use of the resource manager where the resource lists are accessed.

The final questions of the survey covered the interface used for creating and maintaining guides in the CMS. While the majority of the liaisons find it fairly logical and easy to use, numerous suggestions were given for improving the functionality of the CMS, many of which the task force was already aware. The feedback provided by the survey identifies successes as well as areas for improvement. (See Appendix A for this article located at www.library.gsu.edu/scholarship/articles/2005/goans/ for detailed survey results.) Migrating to a new system is always a challenge, but the process is much easier and more successful when there is communication and collaboration among the parties involved.

While a CMS equalized HTML skill dependencies, the survey and anecdotal evidence reveals a crucial gap among librarians' understanding about website information architecture and writing for the web medium. When publishing on the web, the librarian is responsible for the organization of content for the web medium. The CMS model, which usually separates content from presentation, may differ from the environment or tools in which the librarian was trained. Many librarians coming from an HTML background with tools such as FrontPage or Dreamweaver may not possess web development or information architecture competencies needed to fully utilize a CMS or other web publishing tools effectively. Libraries, especially those with decentralized content contribution, should consider providing library personnel with information and training on writing for the web.

SURVEY OF CMS ACTIVITIES IN LIBRARIES

After a year of working with the in-house CMS, planning activities began at the systems level for updates. At this time it was decided that a peer survey was in order. Along with other assessment activities, this would help inform future decision making and to gauge the library's activities in relation to peers in the field. The authors also felt that such a survey would offer a more accurate snapshot of current CMS activity among academic libraries than relying solely on the journal literature. Sixty-three peer institutions were identified as potential participants in a survey on CMS adoption and usage. The list was assembled from the Peer Institutions page at Georgia State University's Office of Institutional Research (www2.gsu.edu/~wwwire/peer/) and included the Urban 13 group, GSU's current and proposed peer institutions as defined by the state's Board of Regents, the Southern University Group, and the ASERL academic libraries (www.aserl.org/). An email was sent to the web librarian or closest equivalent at each location, explaining the purpose of the survey and inviting them to participate. Sixteen librarians responded that they wanted to participate, and they were sent the email-based survey in March 2005 that asked the following questions:

- Are you using database driven technology?
- Are you using a CMS?
    - If not, then what do you use for web publishing, and what is your process?
    - If yes then . . .
        - What parts of your site are CMS driven?
        - What CMS product do you use?
        - What is the status of your CMS implementation?
        - What is the process for publishing content with your CMS?

The variety of responses received indicates that content management systems are still an emerging and not yet universally adopted technology. Six of the sixteen respondents reported CMS usage at their libraries, with one library using a CMS to run their entire website and the rest reporting use of CMS technology to run parts of their website. Three of the six libraries built their system in-house, while one used Macromedia Contribute, one used

Zope, and the remaining library used DBMan. Among the ten respondents who reported that their libraries were not using one, three libraries are "fully considering" moving to CMS technology, while seven libraries are not. (See Appendix B located at www.library.gsu.edu/scholarship/articles/2005/goans/ for detailed survey results.)

When the participants were asked about their website publishing processes, their answers reflect the potential strength in content management systems as enabling wider librarian contributions while affording better mechanisms for site administration and editorial control. Of the ten non-CMS respondents, seven reported a web publishing process with content funneled through a single person or small group of people, referred to as editors or other content oversight groups. In contrast, the six libraries using a CMS reported multicontributor publishing activities and efforts to further streamline the process within the CMS environment.

Based on this sample, the move toward CMS migration among academic libraries is neither universal nor is it moving at the same adoption rate even among the libraries who are implementing CMS technology. Although all of the responding libraries are using database-driven technology for certain resource collections like databases and journals, there was no similar consensus on CMS adoption. Using CMS technology to develop more efficient or collaborative publishing processes seems to be present and is viewed by CMS adopters as a benefit to the system over traditional web publishing models.

CONCLUSION AND FUTURE DIRECTIONS

The move to a CMS has been a positive experience and a success due to the collaboration between web development personnel and the liaison librarians. The web development librarian and programmer were able to work with the smaller team of librarians to redesign and revision a large and content-rich subject liaison web presence. Library liaisons and web development personnel were able to leverage the skills and knowledge present in each group to create a system that serves the working objectives of both parties, to the benefit of users.

While the liaison department is the largest group of contributors to the GSU library website, they are by no means the only department that has benefited from the CMS. One of the primary goals was to create a system that could ultimately be expanded to other departments. The CMS makes up the vast majority of the library's website infrastructure and is also being used for committee websites and other sections of the intranet. Plans are under way to further enhance the system and migrate content from departments not yet utilizing the CMS. The need for further training as identified in the liaison survey will also be addressed.

Templates, the primary CMS component that currently presents content to users, are only one part of future development. As technologies evolve to support a more content-based "remix culture," users will tap into the library's raw content to use in their environments and applications. Future assessment and development activities will be directed to keep the CMS poised to meet these changes.

ACKNOWLEDGMENTS

The authors wish to thank programmers Robert Tairas and Jackey Hong for their invaluable work on the GSU Library's content management system. They also want to thank the GSU Liaison Librarians (past and present) who have been involved in this project.

Elements of this paper were the basis for two poster sessions, the first at the American Chemical Society National Meeting in August 2004, the second at the National EDUCAUSE Conference in October 2004, www.library.gsu.edu/scholarship/posters/.

REFERENCES

Bills, L., R. J. Cheng, and A. J. Nathanson. 2003. Subject web page management without HTML coding: Two approaches. *Information Technology and Libraries* Vol. 22, No. 1: 4–11.

Boiko, B. 2001. Understanding content management. *Bulletin of the American Society for Information Science and Technology* Vol. 28, No. 1: 8–13.

Fichter, D. 2005. Is it time to convert? Migrating static pages to database-driven websites. *Online* Vol. 29, No. 1: 51–53.

Ingersoll, P. 2005. Distributed web content management. *Internet Reference Services Quarterly* Vol. 10, No. 2. Preprint accessed at www.haworth.com/dx.doi.org/10.1300/J136v10n2_01.

McKeever, S. 2003. Understanding web content management systems: Evolution, lifecycle and market. *Industrial Management & Data Systems* Vol. 103, No. 9: 686–692.

Mescan, S. 2004. Why content management should be part of every organization's global strategy. *Information Management Journal* Vol. 38, No. 4: 54–57.

Mosley, P. A. 2003. Re-creating a web of service at TAMU with a content management system. *Texas Library Journal* Vol. 79, No. 1: 16–19.

Thamaraiselvi, G. 2002. Concepts of content management. *SRELS Journal of Information Management* Vol. 39, No. 4: 363–370.

5

CMS/CMS: Content Management System/Change Management Strategies

Susan Goodwin, Nancy Burford, Martha Bedard, Esther Carrigan, and Gale C. Hannigan

Texas A&M is the fifth largest public university in the United States. The University Libraries serve more than 45,000 undergraduates, graduate students, and faculty. Developed by Texas A&M researchers and sponsored by the Association of Research Libraries (ARL), the LibQUAL survey has been used as one way to assess user expectations and satisfaction with library services (LibQUAL 2005). LibQUAL measures the "gap" in users' expectations and perceptions of library services. Prior user surveys and the results of subsequent LibQUAL assessments indicated that library resources were difficult to navigate electronically and that users wanted to be more self-sufficient. Those results were not surprising—each of five libraries had developed its own website, plus there were departmental sites and personal sites. Not only was there no standard design to brand the sites as belonging to one organization, library sites were not linked nor was basic information about services and hours consistent, accurate, or complete among them. The University Libraries' electronic presence did not reflect a coordinated, integrated organization, but rather a diverse collection of parts that identified with the whole to varying degrees. Was this merely an outcome of early web development enthusiasm, or a reflection of fundamental (dis)organizational characteristics?

METHODOLOGY

The formulation of an explicit strategic initiative and the allocation of state funds to purchase a sophisticated content management system (CMS) provided the authority and means to make developing the University Libraries' web presence a priority. The effort, from purchase of the software to implementation of the website, was organizationally broad-based and inclusive by design. Early on, the Web Implementation Team (WIT) was formed and given the following charge:

> The Web Implementation Team is responsible for the overall management of the University Libraries website. WIT has the authority to make decisions regarding the content, selection and integration of new products, navigation and presentation, and workflow. WIT is open to new ideas for content and will look for ways to encourage innovations. Content selected for inclusion will be sustainable, able to integrate into the web environment, and meet organizational priorities.

Previous organization-wide initiatives often stalled when people refused to participate or appealed to the next level of authority to intervene on the behalf of local or historic priorities. To avoid this predictable pitfall, WIT's members were selected based on their organizational positions of authority and/or roles as change agents (see Figure 5.1).

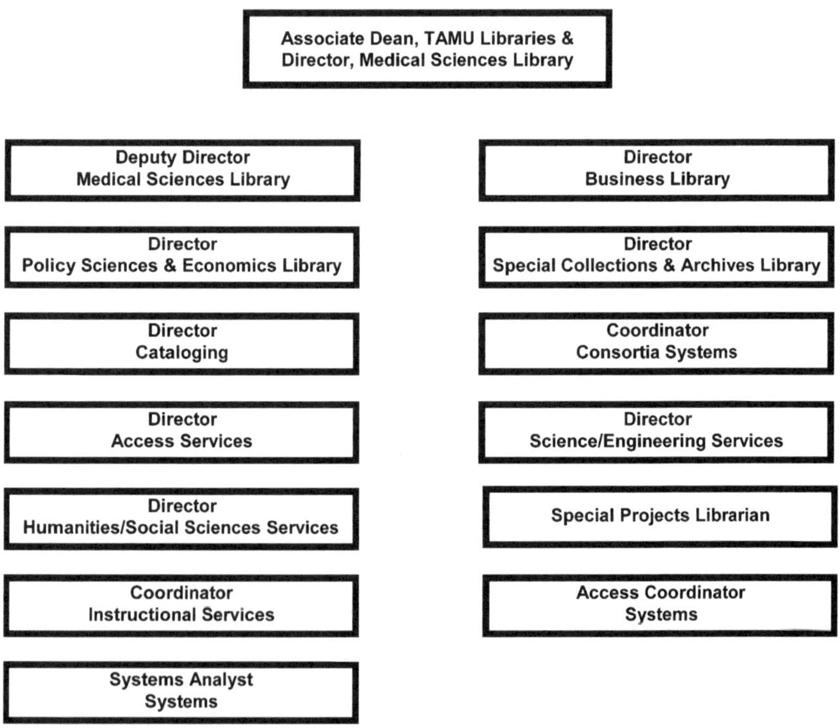

Figure 5.1. WIT organization chart.

Technical expertise alone did not determine membership. WIT had both the mandate and the authority to get its job done.

Since the purpose of this article is to focus on management issues, key accomplishments WIT has overseen are briefly summarized in the Appendix. WIT continues to guide the development of the library's web presence. In the process, the group learned much about the organization, ourselves, strategies that work, and those that don't. The recommendations that follow are the result of reflection on this team's experience from a management perspective.

REFLECTIONS AND RECOMMENDATIONS

Developing the library's web presence is too important and complex a task to delegate exclusively to only systems personnel. For a growing number of users, the library's website is their main point of entry. Our LibQUAL™ survey indicated that primarily undergraduates value the library as a physical place; increasingly, more people use the library virtually. How the library appears and functions electronically is now every bit as important as its physical arrangement. A project this significant needs direct participation of upper management for authority, subject specialists for content, collection managers for organization, in addition to people who understand the software and its capabilities. Over time, numerous committees had attempted to develop a unified library web presence. Their efforts provided recommendations but not progress. In retrospect, the lack of a decision-making chain of responsibility and authority for these groups can probably be blamed for the lack of success. **Recommendation:** For a big and far-reaching project such as the implementation of a CMS, upper level management involvement and support are needed to insure that decisions are made, implemented, and communicated.

The effort of developing a unified web presence reveals where the organization itself lacks unity. WIT's goal was to present library resources and services under "one virtual roof" for an increasingly interdisciplinary user group. Geographic distance, management hierarchies, and narrow discipline-based thinking often presented barriers and resistance from within. For example, library websites gave travel directions to the library from different points of origin; services and policies were different at different locations and these needed review. **Recommendation:** Use the opportunity of building the library's virtual presence to examine what the library communicates to its public and how that presents (or doesn't) a unified organization. This is an opportune time to uncover outdated, inaccurate, and inconsistent information.

Effective use of a content management system requires an organized and comprehensive consolidation of library resources, which emphasizes the need for a different organizational model and culture—one that promotes thinking about the library as a whole, sharing, and collaboration. Some users (and staff) identify strongly not only with their physical discipline-based library but also with its virtual presence as well. For example, the team heard complaints when discipline-based journal lists were replaced with the ability to search all of the libraries' journal titles. Fortunately, the CMS allows both consolidation of holdings and subsequent development of subject pages. Novices can be guided to discipline-based, customized resource pages, interdisciplinary searchers can search the entire collection, and experts can populate their own portals with commonly used resources. **Recommendation:** Expect to justify and illustrate the value of the "bigger picture" of the library—for both users and staff. External factors, such as the increase in interdisciplinary research, will help with justification. Evaluate your organizational structure and reward system as a framework for collaboration and unity of purpose. Be mindful of mixed messages and systems that undermine collaboration and unity. Promote a culture that recognizes the importance of parts contributing to the whole, encourages sharing versus protecting, and values a unified view of diverse components.

It is easy to become mired in and exhausted by relatively minor issues on the way to achieving the bigger goal. For example, discussions about the "right font," size of banners, layout, or colors could go on indefinitely. There is no dispute of individual taste. Consensus about details may not be possible or worth the effort. **Recommendation:** Make decisions based on existing data about usability and move on with the commitment to reassess later if necessary. Development is an iterative process and requires a cycle of continuous improvement. To rephrase Voltaire, the best is the enemy of the good (enough for now) (Columbia World of Quotations 1996). Recognize and seize this opportunity to move your entire organization ahead on the continuum that leads to a culture where risk-taking is encouraged and where we learn from our mistakes and move on.

It is a paradigm shift to change from an internal organizational focus to a user focus. In the past, a user looking for information on a topic basically had to understand the overall structure of the catalog and the libraries' physical organization, or depend on a librarian guide. Now there are more options; users can still get personal service from departmental liaisons or guidance through subject pages, but they don't have to. The move toward increased user self-sufficiency has made some library staff anxious about the vanishing role of information gatekeeper. For some, the very core of their identity is in question. **Recommendation:** Don't minimize the impact of this change. Pay attention to, empathize with, and actively engage staff while encouraging them to focus on the importance of improved access for all users. Challenge all staff to flex their "customer service" muscles, not just those directly involved in or impacted by the implementation of the CMS. For example, one of our successes was the creation of a "workflows" group to create and refine the processes needed to manage and present electronic resources on the web. Staff from acquisitions, cataloging, documents, and systems banded together to share their individual expertise and perspective in handling electronic resources. Participation in this group drew them into the website implementation process, provided a pathway between their traditional responsibilities and new roles, and emphasized the user focus as a shared frame of reference. Their "users" or customers were not only the typical external users but also internal (library) staff.

Don't expect change without affecting roles and responsibilities. Virtual change will drive organizational change. For example, subject/departmental liaisons will need to think more broadly about their roles, which may now include developing web-based subject guides or class materials for faculty and students they may not work with in person. Considering a more interdisciplinary audience, subject specialists will need a better understanding of how their materials fit into a larger context. They may be responsible for updating information in the CMS. These tasks require new skills and new workgroups. Not allocating adequate time and training to develop new competencies is unfair to employees and will most likely result in service degradation and dissatisfied users. Employees and their supervisors should formally acknowledge changes in performance expectations. In WIT's organization-wide effort, the role of middle management was most affected, with some management responsibilities reassigned. Some middle managers abdicated responsibility for making the effort a priority. Again, job expectations had to be explicitly made part of job descriptions and performance reviews. **Recommendation:** Be prepared to rethink and change assignments. Establish the expectation that using a content management system is a new required skill for scholar librarians. Allocate adequate time for training. New job responsibilities and expectations need to be documented and included in performance reviews, which should prompt overall position reviews.

Redesigning a website is a change process and involves all that change management requires. A "soft launch" of the website (a preview of the new site) was meant to give librarians a chance to use and explore the website before it was finalized. But librarians did not react until the actual public release, suggesting that they were in denial about the project's reality. If we were able to relive this part of the project we would have taken more care to encourage and clearly establish the expectation that librarians would use the site before users did. **Recommendation:** Make this your mantra: Redesigning a website is a change process and involves all that change management requires. Review the change management literature and sharpen your change management skills. Don't forget that you are leading significant organizational change, not just redesigning your website.

Communicate, communicate, communicate. WIT meetings are weekly, one-and-a-half-hour, face-to-face gatherings of eight to ten well-paid people. WIT members, by position, are able to speak with organizational authority, but implementing change throughout the organization requires broader buy-in, based on understanding and willingness to assume new roles. LibQUAL survey results made the case for change based on user perspectives. WIT formed a Usability Committee that recruited faculty, students, and library staff to evaluate the website's navigation and terminology. Interactions were electronically captured and then analyzed. Library staff was shown video clips and comments to illustrate why changes in the website were needed. **Recommendation:** Communication is a continuous process, critical to the success of both the website implementation and the change process. Use external and internal feedback mechanisms for "reality checks" about what really is or is not working as expected.

Are we there yet? No. After three years, the authors consider themselves still in the early stages of developing the University Libraries' web presence. Updating and claiming content assignments are variously adhered to. WIT has barely addressed the need to tag content and better understand metadata and classification. Users demand even more online access and "shortcuts" to reserve materials, through external programs such as WebCT. Not all first attempts were wholly successful. **Recommendation:** Be prepared to work hard, make mistakes, admit them, and try again, hopefully with even more confidence and "buy-in." The core group that initiates needed change must not get discouraged just as everyone else is beginning to understand and benefit from that change. A balance between optimism and realism is necessary. Forge ahead, with an ear to the ground and an eye on the goal.

SUMMARY

The selection and cost of a content management system—or any software—is an important, but not the most important, aspect of developing the library's web presence, unless one views the library's website as a bucket crafted by technical or public relations staff into which content can be poured. Like the automation of the card catalog before it, developing the library's web presence represents a major cultural change for libraries, but one that is even more far-reaching. The transition from card catalog to online catalog followed a charted course that was marked and plotted by a long-standing tradition of cataloging codes, metadata standards, and information-sharing protocols. Website development is much more a journey through uncharted waters. The use of a content management system can help define the shorelines and smooth some rough waters, but the course is still left to be charted by the clarity of organizational vision and priorities.

REFERENCES

LibQUAL: Defining and Promoting Library Service Quality. 2005. Available at www.libqual.org [accessed 1 September 2005].

The Columbia World of Quotations. 1996. Available at www.bartleby.com/66/2/63002.html [accessed 1 September 2005].

APPENDIX: WEB IMPLEMENTATION TIME LINE

09/1999–08/2001
- Libraries' Systems Department researches CMS options and system requirements

09/2001
- RFP developed and released in late fall
- WIT formed and began to meet weekly (late fall)

01/2002–06/2002
- Review of RFP responses for shortlist (early spring)
- CMS selected and negotiations begin (late spring)

07/2002
- CMS contract signed

07/2002–08/2002
- CMS technical training begins
- WIT identifies individuals for development of library-wide staff training

09/2002–01/2003
- CMS implementation and staff training begins
- WIT identifies content for new website and devises initial organization

01/2003
- "Soft launch" of new "TAMU Libraries" website

05/2003
- "Hard launch" of new website
- Three search boxes added to home page for searching electronic resources (find databases, find e-journals/e-books, and simultaneous searching of the two library catalogs)

06/2003
- Added home page link to deliverEdocs (digital document delivery and interlibrary loan service)
- Removed simultaneous catalog search box from home page
- Changes made to header and footers to make more visible

07/2003
- Changes made to layout of portal page

08/2003
- "Quick Information" drop-down list added to home page (includes nine links to "important" information)
- "Quick Help" links are added to bottom left portion of home page
- Links to both library catalogs added to website header
- Subject searching capability added to database search box

09/2003
- Color scheme of home page changed and graphical header added; header and footer bolded to further increase visibility

10/2003

- "Quick Information" name changed to "Frequently Requested Links," and some links removed while others are added
- New Subject Guide index page created with individual guides
- Computers and Printing subpage created for In-Building Services

01/2004

- "Find Five Articles Fast" added as link under home page search boxes
- "Frequently Requested Links" now up to 12 links

03/2004

- AskNow virtual reference link added to home page
- "Frequently Requested Links" now up to 14 links

05/2004

- Single citation matcher link added to home page

06/2004

- "Frequently Requested Links" now up to 15 links

07/2004

- "Giving to the Libraries" added to navigation tab on home page
- "Frequently Requested Links" now up to 16 links

09/2004

- "Browse Databases by Subject" link added to home page
- "Frequently Requested Links" now up to 17 links

02/2005

- Video tutorial portlet with links added to home page

04/2005

- Changes made to functionality of search boxes on home page

05/2005–08/2005

- "Frequently Requested Links" renamed to "Quick Links," reordered, and cut down to 11 links
- LibCat, Chiron, and Other Catalogs links pulled from "Quick Links" and put into separate portlet on home page
- "deliverEdocs" link on home page renamed to "Interlibrary Loan/Document Delivery" and relocated to center of home page to increase visibility
- "Help" tab added to navigation tabs, Collection & Exhibits renamed Collections, Research Tools & Advice renamed to Research Support

6

Untangling a Tangled Web: A Case Study in Choosing and Implementing a CMS

Terry L. Huttenlock, Jeff W. Beaird, and Ronald W. Fordham

This chapter is a reflective case study of the experiences of a library's systems department in choosing and implementing a content management system (CMS) for the library website. A reflective case study was chosen because it allows an examination of an issue using reflection as a means for telling the story. Libraries today are faced with the challenge of an expanding online environment. The need for a solution is therefore not unique. By reflecting on this process, it is hoped that others will be helped as they look for solutions and face similar situations.

In 2003, the systems department in the library at Wheaton College, a small liberal arts college, was faced with multiple challenges: a legacy web environment, the need to make maintenance quicker and easier, as well as a need to position the website for future development and expansion. The Systems and Technological Services Department is made up of a faculty librarian who is also the department head; a computer operations supervisor, responsible for the server environment; and a computer support coordinator, in charge of managing and supporting PCs. This is their story.

THE STORY

As in many small libraries, the website started out merely as static pages connected to the larger institutional site, containing basic information about the library. The architecture was flat, the design unsophisticated, and the coding very simple, devoid of advanced elements such as templates and style sheets. Because patrons still relied primarily on print resources, the website was not required to be more than a purveyor of basic information.

As electronic resources increased and database access moved from CDROM to Internet-based, however, the structure and function of the website became focused on accessing online resources. As with many libraries, the website development trail was not very well marked, and the conflict between print holdings versus electronic access continued to cause tension when allocating time for development. The maintenance of the site was little more than a sideline and, at times, changed at whim. As more and more importance was being placed on using the Internet for access, the next phase in the site evolution was to establish a committee in an attempt to apply real web design principles and information architecture. But the prevalence of individual preferences over usability principles continued to dominate the core elements.

In 2000, with the arrival of Eric Morgan's MyLibrary[1] portal software, it was realized that a dynamic environment could be developed with little effort, which would ease the maintenance issues associated with adding more and more electronic resources. Using the MyLibrary philosophy and the underlying database to create pages for the site offered multiple access points to the online resources while maintaining data consistency across the pages. As the site became more complex, the need to have both a test and production environment became evident. With two servers now deployed, one for testing and one for production, there was finally an environment where there could be experimentation and application of new ideas and products. There was also the need to institute other types of consistency and usability design features such as navigation, colors—"look and feel." To this end, a primitive CMS was written in-house to apply templates to pages and to implement a workflow that facilitated staging pages in the test environment and moving them to production.

This homegrown system helped, but not enough. Creating and maintaining pages as the web presence grew was still a lot of work for a small department of 2.5, which balanced web development with many other responsibilities. With the increased reliance on the website for accessing all types of resources, it was time to look for a true CMS in hopes that: (1) through the separation of content and design, content creation could be distributed to nonprogrammers while still maintaining site consistency; (2) links to the electronic resources could be generated dynamically from the databases already being used; and (3) whatever coding was done on one part of the site could be reused, as necessary, on other parts of the site.

The search for the perfect CMS started in spring 2003. It began by analyzing, installing, and demoing open source CMSs. Open source was chosen because the library's track record with this type of software had been very positive—today, with the exception of the library catalog, it runs or supports nearly every application offered. While some CMSs were simple to install, others were more difficult. Likewise, first impressions of the CMS offerings varied widely. First impressions were often an important factor, as many of the systems were given merely cursory looks due to the many other issues requiring attention. In fact, the CMS finally chosen did not initially make the short list, as installing it was more work than installing many of the others and some of the end use seemed obtuse. Additionally, the design on the demo site (now since revamped) was a bit off-putting.

After nearly a year of looking at quite a few products, there were seven that stood out and required further attention. By March of 2004 time was running out—there was a need to decide on a product if conversion was going to occur over the summer. Therefore, the decision was made to sequester the systems department in a conference room over spring break to make a final choice. The library had decided to completely redo the current site, so the summer seemed an opportune time to implement the new site by way of a new CMS. The site could be coded in the new system and, hopefully, enforce some standardization and systematization by way of the system.

Once the department sat down to make a choice, it was realized that a somewhat formalized rubric was needed on which to base it. First, it would ideally be open source, for the reasons mentioned above, and because, as in other small libraries, there is a need to accomplish much without a lot of money. It should also offer a relatively easy migration, or inclusion, of data from the old website. The system should not be too complex or overly proprietary, should use standard languages, and should boast a well-installed user base. The product should be well documented, should allow the crafting of a site that could look any way someone wanted it to, should be pleasing from both a content manager's as well as a developer's standpoint, and should be an established product, not in a first version release. It should be secure, be extensible, and, finally, be a system that could be implemented in a limited time frame, preferably in one summer. Not too much to ask.

As one may well imagine, sitting in a conference room for a week, doing nothing but testing and analyzing CMSs, was neither an easy task nor the way anyone wanted to spend their time. It quickly became discouraging for a number of reasons. Many of the products tended to offer, in the absence of complex customizations, only cookie-cutter designs. Some included their own proprietary scripting languages, which required a steep learning curve and could present problems if the need ever arose to change systems. Some didn't seem as finished, as Wheaton needed a site that would be dependable. And, perhaps not surprising, though not encouraging, many of the products started to look the same. No matter which CMS one chose, one could easily create the same boxy site with approximately the same amount of work. Even with a multifaceted rubric, it was determined that the most important factor was finding a product that could easily use the existing database structure. There was neither the time nor the desire to recreate or convert the existing databases. The MyLibrary database was designed by librarians for the purpose of presenting library resources to library patrons, and it had served well in that capacity. Though this was only one element in the rubric, and not initially at the top of the list, it quickly became apparent that the ability to query the MyLibrary data and easily display results was one of the highest priorities. Based on this criterion, one product stood out from the rest—WebGUI.[2]

So just what is WebGUI? Plain Black, the company behind WebGUI, describes it as "an application framework that handles content management." WebGUI also manages database connectivity, sessions, and security. It also provides a framework for building reusable objects (which WebGUI calls "assets") that may be deployed within the WebGUI framework. Many of these assets are provided with WebGUI, such as forums, FAQ, polls, etc. Third-party developers add their own assets to create a well-rounded system. Through the use of these assets a true separation of style and content can be achieved.

So why was WebGUI chosen? Primarily because it was so easy to reuse the MyLibrary data; the querying and display of the data was little more work than writing an SQL query. Also, WebGUI's platform and language were standard: Apache, Perl, and MySQL. Sites designed with WebGUI can look any way you want them to, due to a very flexible, templated design environment. The user base is active and broad, including nonprofit groups, large corporations, government departments, and web-hosting environments. Though it is an open source product, paid support is available. Even though WebGUI did not initially appear to be as easy to use as other systems that were tested, as one began to understand the system it was pleasing to discover that it followed standard programming and design principles. The WebGUI APIs, though occasionally in flux, are published, allowing for a fair amount of third-party development. The installed base comes with almost anything one would want in a modern website including a calendar, an FAQ generator, forum, syndication, and a shopping cart. Finally, as was underscored at the first WebGUI user conference in October of 2004, the user community is active, industrious, very creative, and international. The lead developers and the community push and adhere to an aggressive development schedule; since installing the system in 2004 there has been one major revision and continual minor releases. Another major revision is due in fall 2005.

Installation of the product was relatively uneventful. The only drawback was a lack of experience with the configuration and use of mod_perl, which is *highly* suggested as the only way to get a usable site out of WebGUI. The installation instructions in *Ruling WebGUI*, the official, paid-for documentation, were easy to follow, once it was decided to follow them. It was advantageous to have had experience configuring and installing open source software. This probably made the installation easier than would otherwise have occurred. What took the most time, though, was learning to use the system. This can be the case for many open source products, where the end user has to learn how to use the system mostly by experimentation; WebGUI is no exception. *Ruling WebGUI*, though purported to be indispensable in the use of the system (and found to be very helpful in the installation and securing of WebGUI), actually contained very little guidance on how to use the system—especially in regard to how various elements relate and interact. In the words of one of the systems staff, learning often occurred in the manner of "lightbulbs going on after first blowing a few fuses." This process was frustrating at times. In retrospect, it is not a recommended process for the unwilling or anyone who lacks the time to dig in and try to figure things out. Eventually, though, after gaining an overall understanding of the CMS in relation to the site being designed, WebGUI makes it very easy to quickly design and develop the environment. A solid knowledge of HTML is recommended as well as, for those using external databases, SQL.

With the software installed and the servers ready to go, it was time to begin to learn the system. The initial testing server ran cumbersomely slow in CGI mode, necessitating the switch to mod_perl. Macros that had been left out of the initial installation base had to be added; this required learning how to include them in the configuration files. Writing the new site progressed very quickly while a new server, including an upgrade to Apache 2.0, was being built. In hindsight, doing a major upgrade of Apache while simultaneously learning how to configure and make use of mod_perl presented the typical challenges associated with installing multiple products at the same time. This was not ideal. At times there were questions about how WebGUI worked; a collaborative effort proved successful in resolving most issues. Performance tips from the WebGUI user community's listserv proved very helpful, and regression testing was used to maximize performance. After attending the first annual WebGUI user conference in the fall of 2004, the system was fine-tuned based on suggestions and ideas gleaned from conference sessions. Overall, the biggest issue was learning how to use and navigate the system. This was accomplished with a lot of trial and error and determination. Persistence, and an overall desire to make this work, produced a working site in very short order.

In the beginning of the actual site design a "hunt and peck" method was used to get the first templates to look acceptable. Though template variables were well documented in the system help pages, there was a need to figure out how they functioned in the HTML templates. Due to time constraints, the new website design meetings were occurring simultaneously with the installation and learning of the software. The specifications for the new site therefore did not take into account many of the system's capabilities. Ultimately, it was found that the flexibility existed to create almost any "look and feel" and that the design was not constrained by the system. Special features such as macros and SQL reports were also not easy to figure out. A bug in the SQL reports was discovered in the first version installed. As one may imagine this was a major setback, given the need to query databases and create dynamic pages. At one point the decision to go with WebGUI was questioned, but persistence prevailed as posts on the forum pointed to an easy resolution of the problem by upgrading to the most current release. In retrospect, it is important to take into account the capabilities of the CMS when designing a site, since many of the features can enhance usability. Fortunately, even after the site layout was completed, additional features as they were discovered were easily incorporated by demonstrating how they would improve the site.

The first year running WebGUI was uneventful. There were no performance issues, no unscheduled downtime, and the site was well received. After attending the WebGUI conference, security issues with an incorrectly configured directory structure were discovered. This was quickly changed, and the system was made more secure. Development during this time constituted an immediacy philosophy, a continuation of the summer redesign, but adding pages and making changes was very simple. At times it seemed as if the development process had taken a step backward, as changes were made and work was being done in real time; it was disconcerting to not have a test and production system. The complexity of moving data from one server to another made it difficult to have a dual system like the one that had been available before. Everyone had confidence in the system, and many felt that a dual environment was not necessary; the system did not crash. This does not eliminate issues of hardware failure, and this is being addressed with a new text/production environment that will have a basic type of redundancy and a way to test and learn new releases before putting them into production.

With the installation of WebGUI, site updates were so simple that they could be distributed to anyone in the department who had the time to make the change. Data management of form input was now handled outside the department. The site had a consistent "look and feel" based on templates, and new pages could be added very quickly. Reusable objects existed for repeating data or functions, and pages were being dynamically generated with simple SQL queries. The foundation was laid for future site expansion.

THE UPGRADE

Winter 2004 brought the announcements that not only was WebGUI releasing a new major upgrade but also Eric Morgan was planning a complete redesign of the MyLibrary database to create more flexibility and apply metadata standards. It was going to be another hectic summer.

After installing the new version, it was discovered that while the installation was relatively straightforward, the attempt to convert the old data broke the site. Warnings had been issued that this might occur due to the new APIs and new philosophy behind some of the objects, especially SQL reporting. The entire system had basically been rewritten in this new version. So began the hard work of figuring out why things broke, learning the new user interface, understanding how to get around in a new layout with a new philosophy, and comprehending the rewritten objects.

After learning how to navigate through the new system, the next step was to create a site that looked identical to the existing one. The goal was to make the conversion appear seamless to the end user. This was necessary in order to counter the common perception that, when one does an upgrade, the appearance of things changes to the detriment of the user. The point of the upgrade was not to rewrite the site, but to upgrade the infrastructure, thereby positioning the site for future upgrades and development. Many users did, in fact, ask "What did you do all summer?" which was both frustrating in that the users did not fully appreciate all the work that had been done and at the same time rewarding as the goal of a seamless conversion had been accomplished.

As is typical, given the multitasking nature of systems work, revisions in other major components of the infrastructure were occurring while the WebGUI revisions were taking place. Of particular concern were the latest updates to the MyLibrary database structure, which had also moved toward a new philosophy. It was critical to incorporate the MyLibrary changes; otherwise, the SQL reporting code would have to be rewritten twice over the course of a single summer. This created the unenviable position of trying to quickly adapt to yet another paradigm shift. It seems that, for the systems department, the only constant is change.

ISSUES

Similar to the struggles with initially getting up to speed with WebGUI, another learning curve had to be negotiated in order to comprehend the concept of assets and how everything related within that construct. Although the new look and feel of the administration module incorporated a richer interface, it was not intuitive. Error messages were generic, and the same message could be generated for any number of underlying reasons. While the WebGUI developers had warned the user community well in advance that there was the potential for issues to occur when moving to this major release of the software, tracking down the source of problems with the converted pages proved to be quite time-consuming and exasperating. In several instances, it was more efficient to just simply rewrite the page in question rather than try to figure out why the page did not get instantiated properly in the new version.

While this conversion resulted in more work, new users who initially start out using a more recent version of WebGUI should not experience the same difficulties. New users can be further encouraged by the fact that WebGUI releases are almost always delivered on schedule and, in those rare instances in which a release is delayed, a detailed explanation of the reason for the delay is provided along with a firm new delivery date.

In hindsight, there may have been better ways to do the upgrade but, once it was completed, it resulted in a much better working knowledge of WebGUI and a greater appreciation of what it can do. It was worth the struggle. Among other features, the new release provides the user with a "drag-and-drop" environment along with an enhanced WYSIWYG editor. As with anything new, it takes a while to learn the intricacies of these new features. Once they are mastered, however, updating a site can proceed in a timely manner. In this case, the conversion of the website was completed in about a month, which was similar to the amount of time required to get the initial implementation of WebGUI up and running.

EXPERIENCES

The decision to attend the initial WebGUI user conference, which was held in fall 2004, proved to be a wise investment of time and resources. The conference provided a forum wherein both the developer and user communities could interact and provide input into the future direction of WebGUI. The exchanging of both ideas and experiences was encouraged, and the resulting synergy was felt by all participants. While the developers had an idea of where they intended to go with the product, they remained flexible and open to suggestions as to what the future roadmap should look like and what path to follow as they moved forward. Everyone was excited about the future, knowing that everyone was headed in the same direction. The seemingly boundless energy of the developers, combined with the global perspective of the WebGUI community, reaffirmed the belief that the choice had been a wise one and that WebGUI was in good hands.

WHAT'S NEXT?

There will be an upgrade to the latest gamma version that has been released since the completion of the conversion this summer. An intranet site will be developed that will enable the staff and various departments in the library to take advantage of many of the information-sharing features that are now available. New content will continue to be added, and work will proceed toward distributing content creation through the use of the new approval system, which will be incorporated into WebGUI later this fall. The dual server environment will be reestablished, so that new releases can be tested and there is redundancy in the event a problem occurs with the production server. New features will continue to be tested, so it can be determined how well they meet library users' needs. Opportunities to share these experiences with others will be sought to provide insight into the many possibilities inherent in WebGUI, along with suggestions to hopefully help others avoid some of the difficulties that can be encountered.

WHAT COULD HAVE BEEN DONE DIFFERENTLY?

Reflecting on the project brings the realization that there is a need to not underestimate the magnitude of such a project, and the importance of communicating this to others as the extent of the accomplishment can easily be downplayed. As one is allocating staff and structuring a timetable, it is necessary for others to understand how much work a project like this is going to entail. Most people only see the tangible product—a new "look and feel," a new website—and during an upgrade they may actually see no changes. It is difficult in the initial installation to represent the overall flexibility, maintainability, and expandability that results from all the hard work put into this kind of project. During the struggle to learn and implement the system, several things could have been done differently, including (1) making more use of the user community as far as trying to understand how all the pieces fit together from a user's standpoint; (2) setting a more reasonable timetable and being more diligent about staying on task; (3) expecting the unexpected; (4) anticipating having a large learning curve and making mistakes; and (5) being willing to change benchmarks because of the learning curve and the unknown. No matter what open source system one chooses, learning and experimenting is an integral part of the open source community, as it is an environment where "creativity is the mother of invention."

In conclusion, usability is more than just how easy a system is to use, it is based on the context of the actual tasks that someone will need to use it for (Shneiderman 2004). This may differ in different settings, as an academic setting may be different than a corporate one. Therefore, when choosing a system, it is important to analyze not only the intended users and what they know but also the tasks that need to be accomplished by the system. In reflection, the ultimate success of this project relied on finding a system that would meet the library's unique needs, using the existing underlying database structure. An error was almost made by "judging a book by its cover" when WebGUI was discounted the first time. Its initial look may not have been ideal, and it may not have been the easiest system to learn and use, but it met the needs. This is not to say that libraries will have the same needs, but it stresses the importance of finding what is usable for each unique environment, keeping in mind that what works in one setting may not work for another.

NOTES

1. dewey.library.nd.edu/mylibrary
2. www.plainblack.com

REFERENCE

Shneiderman, Ben. 2004. *Designing the user interface: Strategies for effective human-computer interactions*. Boston: Addison Wesley.

7

Building a Local CMS at Kent State

Rick Wiggins, Jeph Remley, and Tom Klingler

BACKGROUND

The first generation Kent State University Libraries & Media Services (LMS) website was a small accumulation of static pages. The second-generation site, in place from the late 1990s through the early 2000s, responded annually to millions of page requests. In the early 2000s, the web team, a subset of the Systems Department staff, began to realize that the site had a long way to go in terms of data consistency, presentation consistency, and automation. The team began to hatch the idea to build a new, fully automated site. A better site needed better control over presentation to achieve a more professional, consistent look. Better control over staff data input would eliminate poor quality HTML. A better site required optimized management of data that tended to appear in multiple places in various stages of currency. And, a top need was better content description for more flexible retrieval and presentation. Feeling that metadata was driving the future of the web, the team knew that it needed to build a site that exploited metadata for the organization and retrieval of both research data and basic operational library content.

Each page on the second-generation site was made up primarily of static HTML pages coded in Macromedia's Dreamweaver. Content providers for the site were a small (but growing) number of LMS staff members with varying levels of HTML experience. To create a new page, a staff member would typically copy an existing page, save it as a new page, delete the content of the former page, and then create their new content. Staff who didn't know how to edit web pages would send their edits to staff members with more experience (typically the site's webmaster).

With the number of staff content providers on the site growing, most of whom had only a basic understanding of HTML, the integrity of the site's overall look and feel started to degrade. The site was formed with a series of nested tables, with many layers of tables for overall page layout, navigation options, and other components like page headers, content areas, and footers. The problem with the practice of copying existing pages was that in deleting areas of the former page's content before entering the new content, the author would often delete too much code, or not enough, which would result in a broken page layout of broken tables. Many times the staff didn't know how to fix it, or didn't pay any attention, and so the errors were left in place. Over time the pages on the site that were supposed to have a consistent structure actually started to look more and more different. For example, the footers began to stretch over different areas of the bottom of the pages, and the site logo in the upper right-hand corner of the pages began to shift position from one page to the next. The team clearly had a fundamental problem with the structure and the editing process for the site.

In addition to accidentally breaking a page's layout, some staff started to go their own way with their pages. Some altered page layouts by removing or changing the navigation bar that was supposed to be consistent on all pages; others changed font faces and colors, bringing a whole new level of undesired "creativity" to the site. With different staff straying from the original design, the LMS website started to look less consistent and less professional.

Another problem inherent to a site full of static web pages was the need to make sitewide updates. There were times when a new item needed to be added to the navigation sidebar or the contents of the footer needed to be updated. There were times when an update was needed to the overall look and layout of the site to bring it back to a more consistent structure. Attempts to perform sitewide find-and-replace code corrections were difficult or impossible because staff had made changes to the code, sometimes intentionally, sometimes accidentally. An attempt at a global update to the code would reveal that many pages would still have to be individually updated. And, even this approach assumed these pages could be located by clicking through the site and randomly coming across the errors. Sometimes a page's code didn't get updated as intended, continuing to break the integrity of the site. All of these problems provided more evidence of the site's fundamental structural problems.

The team also discovered hundreds of stray and duplicate pages; pages that were considered "deleted" just because there were no known links to them; pages that were older versions of a current page; entire directories with no known links into them; duplication of data on different pages, sometimes with one instance of the data being current and the duplicate out of date. It was clearly time to plan a new site that would be built and managed by a new method.

BEGINNING TO PLAN

At the start of planning for the new site, a web committee of LMS employees was formed, composed of interested staff members from various departments. The committee decided the site should be recreated from scratch, content should be easier to publish, and the site should be easier to maintain and update. It quickly became apparent that the new site also had to offer improved features. The committee very much wanted the new site to be based on the needs and feedback of our users—the students, faculty, and staff. It was widely felt that the old site was built by librarians for users who, to navigate the site successfully, would have to think like librarians.

One of the first important steps with the new web committee was to meet with focus groups and conduct usability studies to find out what they did and didn't like about the existing site, how they used it, how difficult the site was for them to use, and what they wanted in a new site. Rather than restricting what types of users should be listened to, the committee ensured that the focus groups were a mix of students, faculty, and student library employees. After completing release forms, the participants were asked questions about the current site, were asked to compare it to other sites, and were allowed to offer any concerns and requests that had not already been considered. Participants in the focus groups were fed pizza and soda and were given $15 each on their university ID spending account. Usability studies were conducted as well, with individual participants completing assigned tasks using the current site and speaking aloud about whatever thoughts or problems they might be experiencing. Usability study participants were also each given $15 on their accounts. The pizza and money turned out to be just the right enticement; just the right number of participants were involved, and they were genuinely interested in helping the committee work towards a new and better site.

GENERAL GOALS AND REQUIREMENTS

In order to improve the usability and ease-of-maintenance of the new website, the team established a set of general goals for the new site. This list of goals became the foundation upon which the more detailed requirements for the site and for a CMS that would be used to manage it were built.

Edit Content Using Web Forms

Instead of using web content editing software like Dreamweaver or BBEdit, the staff would do all editing in the CMS using web forms. This approach would reduce the need for special software purchases, installation, and training. Staff would be able to edit web content from anywhere they could access the CMS with a browser. In order to allow for what-you-see-is-what-you-get (WYSIWYG) editing, special software would be purchased and installed into the CMS to provide this functionality in a web browser. But, in order to maintain a clean separation of the content from the presentation of the pages, many of the typical HTML features that people would expect in such a tool would not be made available. For example, the selection of fonts, font colors, and font sizes would not be made available. More radical, the typical HTML table editing tool available in web content editing software packages would not be made available. This decision would prevent the use of tables for layout, making the website more ADA-compliant.

Staff would not need to know how to write HTML to edit content and would not be given the ability to write raw HTML. The CMS and WYSIWYG editor would allow them to create content without ever seeing the underlying HTML being generated. The creation of the HTML would be done dynamically and would rely heavily on the use of Cascading Style Sheets (CSS) for the description of the presentation.

Organize Pages Using Metadata

The traditional hierarchical organization of the earlier sites now seemed too arbitrary and inflexible. In time, any newly invented hierarchy would no longer make sense but would be deeply embedded into the structure of the website, making widespread changes problematic. Instead, the team wanted to use metadata to organize the pages on the new site. By allowing the staff to add classification terms to the pages they created, the team could create dynamic indexes of page links, provide a more focused search capability, and easily generate a site index. This approach would allow patrons to use various methods of locating content. To provide a rich enough set of terms, the team worked with the web committee and the catalog and metadata librarian to create a controlled vocabulary of functional terms—those related to library functions (e.g., overdue fines). Additionally, they agreed to allow the use of Library of Congress Subject Headings (LCSH). While LCSH terms would be more useful for pages like subject guides, they would also be available for use with any page. For more specific groupings of pages, a set of uncontrolled "special" terms could be added to any page. In all, then, three types of metadata were defined: functional terms, LCSH terms, and special terms.

This classifying of pages would also support a metadata search of the site. While many sites provide a keyword search, the committee felt that a metadata search would produce better results since these terms are specifically selected by the library professionals to describe the content of the page. The use of controlled vocabularies also would allow for the display of a dynamically generated site index. Each functional term and LCSH term in use would be displayed in the site index with a list of all pages that had been classified with that term.

Store Tabular Information in Database Tables

In order to provide a single location for common information (e.g., library hours), it was agreed that all tabular information would be stored in actual database tables. This information would be made available for display on any page in the website. The CMS would allow for the creation of new database tables, the addition of new table fields, and the editing of table data.

Within a page, the CMS would allow a staff member to specify which table to use, which fields (columns) to display, and which records (rows) to include. Using this technique, a staff member would be able to create a table of information without the use of an HTML table-editing tool. Again, keeping an HTML table-editing tool out of the hands of a wide variety of staff would prevent inconsistent looking pages and pages with broken formatting caused by broken tables.

Make the Website Able to Be Indexed by Spiders

The web pages created using the CMS would be dynamically generated and would not have a hierarchical directory and filename structure. In order to make these pages able to be indexed by spiders (e.g., Google), the URL used for displaying content could not include parametric information.

Create Draft Copies of Pages for Editing

Staff would create draft copies of pages when editing. This workflow would allow previewing of draft page content via the intranet before the draft was published to the public website. Staff would be responsible for their content and would not require any approval before publishing their content, but they could ask their colleagues to review their content before publishing it.

CMS REQUIREMENTS

Initially the team had hoped to identify a commercial or open source CMS that could be used for the new site. As this section will show, the team specified its requirements for such a product, reviewed quite a few of them, and eventually reached the difficult realization that only a locally written CMS could come close to satisfying all the goals and requirements.

The general requirements for the CMS fall into five basic areas:

1. Content Creation
   1.1 Integrated authoring environment: Does the tool provide the ability to create all of the types of content needed?
   1.2. Separation of content and presentation: Is the content created independent of the presentation?
   1.3. Multiuser authoring: Can many users be editing content simultaneously without overwriting each other's work?
   1.4. Content re-use: Can a single copy of an item of information be displayed in multiple locations with different views?
   1.5. Metadata and cataloging information creation: Can metadata and cataloging information be created and maintained for indexes, searching, and site mapping?
   1.6. Link management: Does the system prevent internal links from breaking?
   1.7. Nontechnical authoring: Can content providers create content without knowing HTML?
   1.8. Ease-of-use: Is the user interface intuitive and easy to learn?
2. Content Management
   2.1. Version control and archiving: Does the tool allow previewing of new content and roll back to previously published content?
   2.2. Workflow: Can default editing permissions be set on a group level, and is there an approval mechanism for approving changes to content?
   2.3. Security: Will the tool integrate into the existing local security infrastructure?
   2.4. Integrated with external systems: Will the tool work together with other existing systems?
   2.5. Reporting: Does the tool provide an extensive set of reports—both retrospective and proactive—and allow for customized report creation?
3. Publishing
   3.1. Style sheets: Is the final appearance of the content controlled through style sheets?
   3.2. Page templates: Is the overall page layout controlled by templates, and can new templates be easily added?
   3.3. Extensibility: Is there a method to incorporate non-CMS managed content into the website?
   3.4. Support for multiple formats: Can the tool publish content in multiple formats (e.g., HTML, PDF, WAP, etc.)?

        3.5.1. Personalization: Does the tool allow for presentation based on user profiles or user preferences?
        3.5.2. Usage statistics: Does the tool provide reporting on page hits, most popular pages, daily usage, and search terms being used?
4. Presentation
    4.1. Usability: Is the presented content easy to understand and use?
    4.2. Accessibility: Does the presented content conform to the W3C Web Accessibility Initiative?
    4.3. Cross-browser support: Is the presented content viewable with all popular browsers on all popular platforms?
    4.4. Limited client-side functionality: Does the presented content require additional client-side technology (e.g., Java, JavaScript, or Flash) to work properly?
    4.5. Speed: Is the content presented with a minimal page size to make page loading quick?
    4.6. Valid HTML: Does presented content conform to the current HTML specification?
    4.7. Effective navigation: Does the presented content include consistent, comprehensive, and usable navigation aids?
    4.8. Metadata: Does the presented content contain sufficient metadata to allow effective indexing and searching?
    4.9. Search engine access: Are the site pages accessible to spiders and crawlers so that the site will be indexed by engines like Google?
5. Contract and Business
    5.1. Training: Does the vendor provide training materials for both the administration and use of the CMS?
    5.2. Documentation: Is there adequate documentation of the CMS for users, administrators, and developers?
    5.3. Warranty: What is the warranty period for the product?
    5.4. Maintenance agreements: What maintenance options are available and at what cost?
    5.5. Resources required: Does the product require hardware or software resources, which LMS does not currently have or could not easily acquire?
    5.6. Skills required: Does the product require employee skills that LMS staff do not currently have or could not easily acquire?
    5.7. Cost: Is the cost of the product fixed or per-seat? Is it within reach?
    5.8. Scalability: How well will the product scale without requiring the acquisition of additional hardware or software?
    5.9. Reference sites: What other sites are successfully using the product?

CMS PRODUCT REVIEW

To begin the product review, the team established a simple spreadsheet matrix with requirements along one axis and products along the other. Team members were each assigned a group of products to research. Then, the review content was merged, and several meetings were dedicated to reviewing the results.

Lists and Reviews

The review of potential CMS products was helped by these comprehensive CMS product listing and review sites:

List of CMS at Wikipedia
en.wikipedia.org/wiki/List_of_Content_Management_Systems
CMS Watch Vendor List
www.cmswatch.com/CMS/Vendors/
The OSCOM CMS Matrix
www.oscom.org/matrix/index.html
CMS Ratings at OpensourceCMS
opensourcecms.com/index.php?option=content&task=view&id=388&Itemid=143
CMS Review
www.cmsreview.com
Overviews of CMS products at Hartman Communicatie BV
www.hartman-communicatie.nl/extra/tools.htm
tools.hartman-communicatie.nl/overzicht.html

Sample Products

Listed here is a sampling of products that received some consideration. This list is not meant to be exhaustive or evaluative but to show the breadth of products and environments that were considered.

Apache Lenya: cocoon.apache.org/lenya/ An open source CMS
Bricolage: www.bricolage.cc/ An open source CMS
Drupal: www.drupal.org/ An open source CMS
IVia: infomine.ucr.edu/iVia/ An "open source internet portal and virtual library system"
Midgard: www.midgard-project.org/ An open source CMS
OpenACS: openacs.org/ An open source website tool kit
php website: phpwebsite.appstate.edu/ An open source CMS

Typo3: typo3.org.com/about/typo3/ An open source web content management framework
WebIdeaTree: www.webideatree.com/ A commercial CMS
Zope: www.zope.org/ An application server environment for building a tool like a CMS

Promising New Projects and Products

Well after the project was under way and the local CMS was nearly finished, the team discovered these projects/products of interest. The team has not evaluated them thoroughly but encourages anyone starting a product review to add them to their list of products to review.

LibData: libdata.sourceforge.net/ An open source CMS from The University of Minnesota
HyperContent: hypercontent.sourceforge.net/ An open source CMS from Columbia University
Caravel: www.caravelcms.org/ An interesting new open source CMS

THE FINAL DECISION

The team realized early that the vast number of products in the CMS arena made it impractical to review them all. Consequently, it acknowledged early that the perfect product might simply be missed in the review process. In spite of this challenge, the team proceeded with its systematic review. In most cases, charts, lists, descriptions, and reviews were used; in some cases software was downloaded and tried.

Some products didn't offer enough metadata control. Others didn't offer the desired editing control. Others didn't offer the internal link maintenance desired by the team. Some were too difficult to use. Others didn't offer flexible re-use of database table content.

Many products were far too expensive. The team leaned early toward seeking an open source solution. They had no desire to spend a big chunk of money up front that would be followed by endless annual maintenance charges.

Also important in the decision process was the fact that the team already had significant infrastructure in place. The existing intranet was vibrant and heavily used. It was built in a UNIX, Apache, MySQL, and PHP environment. The team wanted to be able to integrate the new CMS product into the intranet as another staff-working tool, and they wanted to be able to exploit their proficiency in PHP/MySQL with the new CMS.

In short, none of the low-cost or free products that were reviewed satisfied all of the new site and CMS requirements. After a thoughtful process, the team came to the difficult decision to write its own CMS in-house. The library's management team, recognizing the central importance of a strong website to the library's future, made the strategic decision to dedicate the staff resources to the project.

ENVIRONMENT: HUMAN

Beyond the web team, the local environment included a wide range of staff. Staff in diverse departments like Reference, Circulation, Interlibrary Loan, Reserves, Branches, Audiovisuals, and Teleproductions would all be contributing content to the new site. In the case of resources like research databases, staff from various departments would be contributing information about a single resource. For example, a reference librarian would input database descriptions and URLs and describe the appropriate subject metadata for that database. At the same time, a technical services librarian would input availability restrictions for that resource, like whether the library's license permitted remote access to the database. Plans like these were laid in place to capitalize on staff throughout the organization.

To make these plans efficient, the CMS would have to provide a variety of updates to staff. For example, staff would have to receive an email update when a new resource was added so that they could complete their portion of the work of describing it or so that they could point to it from one of their content pages. In short, the human environment also supported the decision to build a local CMS because only a local system could be customized enough to include alerting services tailored to the work, the content, and the local staff's division of duties.

ENVIRONMENT: TECHNICAL

The LMS environment consists of both Microsoft Windows and Unix servers. The websites are supported by Apple Xserves running Mac OS X Server—a flavor of FreeBSD Unix. The web server is the open source Apache server. Almost all coding is written in PHP, an open source, server-side scripting language. The back-end database is the open source MySQL server. Mac OS X Server comes with Apache, PHP, and MySQL already installed.

The server architecture includes a Windows file server, which allows sharing of the non-database web content, i.e., HTML pages and PHP scripts, between the production web server and the test web server. The web servers connect to the file server as a client using the Network File System (NFS) protocol. They are connected via a private local area network using a gigabit Ethernet switch. Since the file server runs standard Windows 2003 server software, staff can connect directly to this server using native Windows file sharing (SMB). While it is possible to run Samba on the Mac OS X servers to provide SMB services, the web team has found that having Windows desktops connect to a real Windows file server allows them to control access more easily using Microsoft's Active Directory services. This also means that user accounts do not have to be created on the web servers for staff use, thus reducing administration requirements. As Mac OS X's support for Active Directory matures, the file server might be able to be replaced with a Storage Area Network (SAN) device.

Having a separate test web server with access to the full set of HTML pages and PHP scripts allows thorough testing of software updates and changes to applications without disturbing the production website. Once testing of these updates and changes is complete, they can be safely applied to the production server.

The LMS intranet website provides a central point for information needed by the staff. Many staff tools, including the CMS, are now web-based and accessible via the local intranet. Access to the intranet is via the secure HTTP (HTTPS) protocol. Access to the public website is via standard HTTP protocol.

The staff uses both Windows and Macintosh desktop systems. In order to provide a WYSIWYG editor for staff to use in our CMS, the team needed to find something that would work on both platforms. They chose the Editize editor from SitePoint Pty. Ltd. Editize is written in Java and runs inside both Windows and Macintosh web browsers. However, Editize did not work properly in Internet Explorer (IE) on some staff Windows desktops. Unable to determine why this was occurring, the team decided to offer DevEdit, a product from Interspire Pty. Ltd., as a Windows IE-only option. DevEdit does not use Java and so does not present the same browser problems as Editize.

DEVELOPMENT PLAN

The committee wanted the new website to go live at the start of the next fall semester, only 14 months after the decision to write a local CMS. This tight time line made a development plan very important. The team had to work quickly, breaking down what modules to build, what prototypes to test, what focus groups to conduct, and the like, and then lay out a time line in which all of these needed to occur. Because there were so many different aspects of the project, some could take place at the same time. Others had very specific prerequisites. With a team working on the overall project, the workload could be divided. The basic content creation code was written first. Then, content creation started while the team finished writing the remaining content creation pieces and the public display code.

Prototypes for the design of the new site were being developed while the CMS was still being coded. Because all content was stored within database tables, and because CSS was being used to separate content from style, the layout and design of the site didn't have to be completed before the contributors started developing the content. Sketches for the new site were created based on Focus Group and Usability Study feedback on the original site, as well as on the new features the committee wanted to add to the new site. Although the sketches and prototypes of the new site weren't functional, they were adequate to describe intended functionality to the focus group participants and get their feedback, finding out what features they didn't feel the new site needed, what was missing, and what needed to be changed. Two rounds of prototypes were presented to focus groups, with the second round of sketches having a tighter focus based on the feedback from the first focus group.

There were many features that the participants loved and/or felt were long overdue, such as a field on every page to search the library's online catalog and the link on the home page that takes users directly to their account login for renewing books and the like. The idea of simply reducing the amount of content on our home page received some of the best responses from the participants.

Some features of the new site they disliked, such as redundancy of information and links on the new home page. This input really helped the team pare down the content and streamline the home page. The focus groups also helped in cleaning up some of the design issues on pages that were too busy in their layout or background colors. Site developers were also reminded by the focus groups to keep the terminology on the site simple and clear.

Sometimes, hearing how the new features could help them in new ways, they changed their minds and decided they would like the new services, such as the thin space dedicated to their link history (also known as breadcrumbs), or the added space dedicated to the Media Services portion of Libraries & Media Services. Some Focus Group participants felt the navigation tabs across the top of the page should remain "on" after a user clicked on one of them and went to the designated page. After they learned the site wasn't nailed down with a rigid hierarchy and that there were numerous ways to get to a page depending on the user's needs, they understood that leaving a tab's background color in the "on" state could be misleading.

There were some instances when services the participants continued to feel weren't needed were kept in the new site due to the requirements laid down by the web committee, such as the "What's New" section on the home page, which they felt they never viewed and took up valuable space. It turns out that the focus groups consisted mostly of library patrons who found out about the study from the "What's New" list, so even though they felt "What's New" didn't warrant the space, they were using it!

Based on the time line to date, the content editor had to be one of the first things developed so that staff could begin adding content to the site even as the CMS was continuing to be developed. In addition to general text, images, and links to other sites, resources (e.g., links to databases, journals, and websites) were also an extremely important aspect of the new site. Since resources were to be incorporated into the content of many pages, the resource editor had to be built at the same time the content editor was being developed. The programmers were on a tight schedule to get the CMS editor built as quickly as possible while making it as reliable as possible. Once the most basic parts of the CMS editor were constructed, staff could be trained and set to work on stocking the CMS databases with site content.

TRAINING AND DOCUMENTATION

Once the content editing tools were functional, at least the text, image, resource, and table building tools, staff training began. At no time before were so many LMS staff prepared to develop pages on the website. Multiple training sessions were required to reach all the staff who were being assigned responsibility for their departments' content. Most seemed quite enthusiastic to learn the new tools, some were intimidated, and others felt restricted by a system that didn't let them design whatever they wanted and have direct access to the HTML. In time, though, they all found the new system helped maintain a more structured, polished looking website.

The staff was able to train on a test version of the CMS, building as many pages as they wanted without affecting what the public would see. They could build pages with any content just to learn the system, or they could build rough drafts of pages they wanted to later publish to the public site, getting a feel for how they wanted to present their information while still learning the CMS. At first they had to do this without even knowing what it would look like to the public. Focus-group feedback on the prototypes had not yet been completed, and construction on the public version of the site was far from complete. These practice exercises also helped the staff learn that this new CMS stored their information in such a way that any later change to the look of the site would not result in a loss of their content.

The staff was first taught how to build standard content pages—text, links, and images. For many this was a brand new concept. Additional training sessions were set up just for the librarians who would be working with resources and other sessions just for those who needed to create tables.

Considerably later, a refresher on table creation was included with the form-building training session.

During the summer, as the programmers were coding the CMS and public site, and as staff were just starting to learn how to use the CMS, two student employees were hired to also thoroughly learn the system. They followed the programmers along to classes and individual staff training sessions and used the test version themselves. Their job was to learn the system as if they were the developers and the staff using the CMS and to write up the documentation for it. Two different approaches to documentation were used. One student was to write up a training manual for the CMS that would be accessible online so staff could refer to it rather than going to the programmers with each question. The training manual included step-by-step instructions on how to use each tool built into the CMS and included screen shots with every section.

The other approach was to build in context-sensitive help. The other student worked on a glossary of tool tips, so that staff could click on a section of the CMS they were using and get the tips and defining terms for that specific section of the tool. This context-sensitive help throughout the CMS proved to be very valuable and well received by the staff. In building this documentation, the students were able to take an outsider's point of view on the whole system and recommend ways to improve the usability of the CMS to the programmers, as well as visit individual staff who still needed one-on-one help with creating their pages.

DATABASE SCHEMA

Considering the complexity of the CMS, a lot of energy was initially spent on determining the overall database schema. The team knew there was a risk of getting part way into the project and realizing that something vital just wouldn't work because of an overlooked content or storage requirement. This team of programmers had not previously attempted a project of this scope, and so quite a bit of consideration went into developing an extensive, extensible, thorough, and reliable schema. Schema planning was based on previous experience with less complicated projects as well as the desire to implement and combine all the desired new features of this CMS and website.

CONTENT CREATION

When the staff logs in to the intranet and enters the CMS to begin work on a page, the CMS home page presents details on her/his 20 oldest pages. The left column of the CMS provides links to all of the available tools: page editors, table tool, resource editor, file and image tools, reports, subject headings lists and tools, preferences, help, and an enhancement submission tool.

Page Overview and Navigation

A page on the new site typically uses a standard template. The template page is broken up into three basic rows of content, and each of those can be broken into subsections. A typical page includes in the top row a header with navigation, a Quick Jump navigation tool, and breadcrumbs; in the middle row, the main content area with a left side column, a center column, and a right column; and in the bottom row, a footer.

The header includes logos and two search fields—one for searching the site's content and one for searching the online catalog. The "Search our site" tool allows a patron to enter search terms, which are matched against metadata terms for pages and resources on the website. If no results are found, the patron has the option of performing a keyword search against the complete page content of the website. Additionally, since many patrons were attempting to do catalog searches via the "Search our site" tool, an option to send the keyword search terms to the online catalog is provided.

Beneath the logos and search fields, but still in the header section, are the navigation tabs. These tabs break out some of the subsections of the site, but the content isn't necessarily restricted to any one of the tabs. Because the team avoided enforcing a rigid hierarchy on the content, the tabs don't remain "lit," or selected, once the user has clicked on one of them.

Beneath the tabs (and still in the header) is a Quick Jump drop-down menu including some of the most popular links within the site. Next to this are the breadcrumbs, which let a user track back through their path of visited pages in the website as an alternative to using their web browser's back button.

The Site Index tab displays a dynamically generated list of all pages and resources organized by metadata terms. An alphabetical list of all metadata terms in use by any page or resource is displayed. The patron may select the initial letter of the terms to display. Only controlled vocabulary terms are included in the Site Index.

Beneath the header section is the main content area, which is divided into three columns. The page editor shows the three columns available for content: left, middle, and right. The left column is always present by default. The author of a page may choose to turn the left column off, but the web committee recommends that our staff keep it viewable unless turning it off is absolutely necessary for the content of their page. In this way users won't be confused by the changing upper-left starting point of the page content as they navigate through the site. The middle column, or more appropriately "the main column," is where page authors put most of their content. The optional right column is rarely used, but it can be handy when an author wants to provide additional information or links that they feel might need to stand out from the main content area. In early discussions of adding RSS feeds, this right-hand column has been considered as a location. The optional left and right columns are each fixed width, and the main/middle column expands to fill the remaining space. The style sheets for the left and right columns scale down the content to be proportional to the smaller space. Fonts are smaller; space between paragraphs is decreased.

Each page has a footer, which starts with a text-only version of the tabs across the top of each page. Next comes the Icon Legend/Key, which shows the icons that may be found on any page and what they stand for (off-site links, PDF files, required form fields, etc.). Since some of these icons are dynamically displayed on the site, based on links and content provided by the staff, the key for all icons is consistently displayed on all pages. After the key are left and right columns of information, containing when the page was last updated, a privacy statement link, copyright information, the option to email a link to the page, and a contact link for the page.

Simple URL

Because the site URLs contain only page numbers, they can be difficult for patrons to remember. In order to provide an easy-to-remember URL for pages, the CMS allows staff to assign a word to the page that can be used with the URL. For example, this page: www.library.kent.edu/page/10562, which contains information about how to find articles, can also be accessed using this URL: www.library.kent.edu/articles. This "Simple URL" is stored along with the soundex value for it. If a patron enters a Simple URL that is not in the database, they see a list of Simple URLs with similar soundex values to what was entered.

Getting Started: Text and Images

As the programmers started to build the presentation modules, first came the module for the most basic parts of the website—the text and image areas. The third-party WYSIWYG editor that was licensed and integrated into the CMS editor pages allows the author to add and edit text, to mark text as headers or regular content, and to make links to other pages and images. It also provides standard editing features such as bold, italics, ordered and unordered lists, and text alignment.

Image Tool

Staff may insert images, but the images must first be uploaded using a tool that allows the image to be given a name and description. Staff may use images uploaded by other staff, and they have the option to preview all the uploaded images, including the graphic, the file name, and the description. The image tool restricts what file types the staff can upload to the JPG, GIF, SWF, and PNG formats, as well as limiting the file sizes that can be uploaded. This restriction assures that the staff does not upload files that might be too large and therefore too slow for a person using a dial-up connection to download at home.

In addition to images, a restricted list of other file types may be uploaded to the CMS, including text files, spreadsheets, PDFs, PowerPoint presentations, and videos (DOC, TXT, RTF, PDF, XLS, PPT, MOV, MPG, and AVI). These files can then be embedded in a page or linked to from the page. These uploaded files also have a restriction on their file size, but special exceptions can be made for larger files if necessary.

Table Tool

On the old site, HTML tables were often misused to create the layout of a page or to hold images in place. Web development in general is moving away from this practice and instead using Cascading Style Sheets for the positioning of content. It is becoming more clear that tables should be used as they were originally intended—for tabular data. To help correct the tendency to misuse HTML tables, the team deactivated the option to create them in the WYSIWYG editor and built a much more powerful tool in its place. The table tool allows the staff to create database tables, name the tables, set up the fields (columns) of data in the tables, and define what type of data (characters, dates, yes/no, etc.) will be stored. Staff can then add a table section to their pages using the data from a table they created or data from a fellow staff member's table. A single table can have its data displayed on multiple pages or multiple times on a single page.

Staff can create database tables, stock them with content, and then choose how that content is displayed in their pages, intermingled with the text and image sections. The table data can be sorted to display in any order and can have the display of its content restricted by criteria set by the author (e.g., only display data within a certain date range, only display data with certain text, or only display data if checkmarked, etc.).

When displaying content from a table, the staff member chooses from a series of options to determine what content will and won't display, what order it will display in, and how it will display. The table data can be displayed in the expected gridlike table format, or it can be manipulated to display as a bulleted list. Table title and rows may be displayed, and when appropriate, table rows may be numbered. The table's location on the page may be given an HTML anchor, and its position on the page may be centered and have a set width or the browser may use the default settings. There are times when an author only wants to display a limited number of results from the table, so this option was built into the tool. The display of data can be date-dependent, so that a record can be set to display within a particular date range.

Multiple pages can use data from the same table, reducing the need to enter the same information on multiple pages, which in turn reduces the amount of outdated information across the site. For example, if a staff member's name and department are pulled from the staff directory table and listed on more than one page, updates to the information in the staff directory table will be reflected on all the pages.

When a table is added to a page, the author may choose to limit which records are displayed based on criteria. Using the table display tool, they are essentially building an SQL query with which they may require fields to contain certain data, such as be less than, greater than a certain number, be compared to a date, etc.

If the data coming out of a table has limitations on what will be displayed, and if those criteria result in no data actually displaying on the public page, the staff member can be sent an email message letting them know their table is displaying "zero rows" and that they might want to go back and adjust these limitations. The code checking for zero rows is automatically run nightly. It's possible, especially in the situations where a date is used in the limitations, that a table displaying content today may stop displaying any content at a later date. Or perhaps a page author is displaying records from another staff member's table, and the original table is edited in such a way that it no longer displays any records on that author's page. In situations like these, an email is sent to the author, letting them know that their table display is empty.

Calendar Tool

After the table tool was developed and the site was getting closer to production, a tool was needed to display calendars/service hours on the site. Since many of the departments and service points have different schedules that change based on variables like the day of the week or the week of the semester, and since the coordination and display of these schedules is overseen by the Library Dean's Office secretary, a tool was created so that she could enter the data for each department, setting date ranges that spanned weeks at a time if needed. For example, hours could be entered for all Monday through Friday ranges,or for a specific date range or only for the Circulation Desk. Once all this data is entered and approved, it can be changed from draft to published status and made available to the public. The public can see this data in a monthly calendar grid for one department or can see a day-by-day listing of hours for all departments at once—all pulling from the same database tables. The calendar information can also be exported to a PDF displayed in a specifically formatted, printer-friendly page layout, matching the original format used for many years by all the public service points.

Form Tool

Once the site went live and all the major components were built, the team could go back and fill in some of the gaps, such as giving staff the ability to create forms on their web pages. So that staff wouldn't have to ask a programmer to build a specific data-collecting form, the form tool was created as an overlay of the table tool.

The staff may create their own web forms, first by building a table to collect the data gathered in the web form and then by using that table's fields as the fields in the web form. The web form is built in the same way as a standard text and image area. Only staff can use tags in the format: [field:fieldName] as placeholders for the form's fields. At the time the form is displayed to the public, those tags are converted into the appropriate field type, as set up in the original table and with options in the form tool. The character width (columns) and number of rows in a field may be set by the staff as well, in case they need specifics like a small single line field, a multiline text area, or the like. Fields may be single line text entry, multiline text entry, date pull downs, checkboxes, or selection lists. Any data collected by the web forms is stored in the original table, and the staff has the option to have that data emailed to themselves as well.

In other words, after the creation of a table in the CMS, a form can be built based off the table. All fields in the original table are displayed as options to include in the form and may be marked as required if the page author feels this is necessary. Required fields are marked with a red asterisk when displayed in the public form Fields may be pre-populated with default values. Selection lists (created as common-delimited lists in the original table) display as pull-down lists of options in the form.

To set the position of a field in the form, the author can copy CMS-specific tags into the WYSIWYG editor. Fields may be marked as required, be displayed in any order desired, and may even be not displayed to the public (for example, the date the form is filled out). At this point, the form builder is the only place in the CMS that allows staff to use HTML tables, since they are one of the best ways to lay out a form with its headers, fields, and descriptions.

Page Index

When constructing a page, the page author can include a section that is a page index, a list of related links within the site. When an author chooses to include a page index, s/he chooses words from the predefined list of descriptive terms, LC subject terms, and special terms that are used to describe every page in the CMS. When a person views this page index, a dynamically generated list of the pages matching the terms is provided, with links to each of those pages. A page index may be sorted alphabetically or chronologically by last published date by the viewer of the page. This sorting is dependent on the viewer's session ID, so two different users of the page could choose to sort their view of the page index differently.

Resource Editor

Resources are a very important component of the new site content. Resources can include anything from research databases to websites. Staff decides what constitutes a resource and adds the information for the resource using the CMS resource editor. The metadata available for classifying a resource includes: title, description, Library of Congress Subject Headings, format (e.g., journal), URL to content, URL to other information about the resource, access restrictions, coverage, full text availability, catalog record number, and audience (e.g., scholarly). Resource descriptions can also be added on a per-department basis. Additionally, weightings (e.g., core) can be added by department or department course. This department and course metadata can then be used to dynamically create subject guides and course-specific pathfinders.

The extensive resource metadata description built into the system, combined with personalization, also on an ambitious development agenda, may prove to be core to future developments like an online reference interview function and an option for classroom faculty to enter resources and resources descriptions themselves to make course-specific resource pages.

Resource Index

Resource indexes are similar to page indexes, but instead of specifying a list of related pages on the site to display, the staff member selects from a series of complex options (e.g., subject, format, discipline, department, etc.) that specify a list of resources to display. Recall that a "resource" is an intellectual item like a database, a website, or a journal article that has been described in the system with the resource editor. The Resource Index editing tool in the CMS allows the staff member to display resources that match criteria like department, course, and weight (from "core" to "may be of interest") that makes it easy to create pages that list course-specific resources.

The CMS as it stands today offers the staff member a rich set of tools to build pages, build forms, describe resources, and display content in specific ways. A year-and-a-half past its launch date, the CMS is proving to be stable and capable for the needs of all of the staff members in the organization.

ADMINISTRATIVE TOOLS

Reports and Statistics

From day one of the planning, the team wanted the CMS to provide rich reporting tools as well as rich maintenance tools. To date, the list of reports in the system is rather extensive, including reports on data like broken links, terms used, and pages per contributor.

Link Maintenance

Currently the website has more than 4,500 links, including internal and external links. One objective of the new website is to minimize the number of broken links. This objective becomes increasingly difficult as the number of links in the website grows. To achieve this objective, two steps have been taken. First, internal links, which are links to other pages on the website and links to images and files on the site, cannot become broken because the CMS prevents pages from being deactivated or images and files from being deleted if there are any links to them from elsewhere on the website.

Second, every external link in the website, including those in pages, resources, and tables, is checked every night to ensure that it is accessible. If a link is inaccessible, a counter is incremented. Some links will be inaccessible for short periods of time due to network problems or website maintenance; the CMS accounts for this fact by simply tracking a broken link for five days before taking any action. Once a link has been inaccessible for five days, an email message is sent to the page, resource, or table editor indicating this problem status. A second message is sent once a link has been inaccessible for ten days. Once a link has been inaccessible for 15 days, an email is sent every day reminding the staff member of this fact. A report of the current broken links is also available in the CMS to all staff members who are content providers.

Site Statistics

The following are generated on a monthly basis: monthly hits per page statistics, monthly sessions per page, monthly visits duration per page, all pages totals, and referrers list. These figures include the total of last year's hits and each page's percentage of a month's hits. If a visitor views the same page more than once in a visit, each hit to the page is counted.

Month-by-month sessions per page, including totals for the previous year, and each page's percentage of a month's sessions are also recorded. If a visitor views the same page more than once in a visit, only the session is counted.

The cumulative amount of time spent on each page in a month is tracked by the use of session cookies. Nevertheless, the total figure is a rough estimate, since literal time spent on a page cannot be recorded if a visitor closes their browser or goes to an off-site link.

A report called "All Pages Totals" displays boiled-down information from the other statistical reports, such as the grand total hits and sessions for a page, when that page was last visited, how often that page was the first or last page visited in a session, and how much time was spent on the page since its creation. This report is proving to be very valuable to staff members as they evaluate the use of their pages.

The Referrers List report counts the number of visitors from external websites to the new site. This report can help the committee evaluate where users come from and therefore decide how and where to focus its efforts; for example, on the addition of links to the site on external sites. For example, the fact that four times as many users get to the new site from the university home page (www.kent.edu) than from the faculty/staff/student portal (flashline.kent.edu) might be important. Also important might be the fact that so relatively few users get to the site from the online catalog (kentlink.kent.edu).

Future enhancements to the statistics will include a report of the most common paths through the site. This report will allow the web committee to track, for example, the most popular links off the home page. It will also allow the study of how efficiently (or not) users find certain information on the site.

FUTURE ENHANCEMENTS

During the focus group sessions, the team heard from patrons that they would like to be able to personalize their interaction with the website. Some patrons preferred a more graphical interface, while others a more minimal interface. The option of giving patrons more control over their experience with the site is a high priority on the project enhancement list. Because the site is dynamically generated, creating a customizable interface will not be a difficult goal to achieve. To date, the chief limitation has been the lack of a centralized authentication service on campus. There is no desire to create another username and password for a patron to remember. Nor is there a desire to use the patron's online catalog log-in, as this still uses the patron's social security number.

Recently Kent State University has implemented a Lightweight Directory Access Protocol (LDAP) server, which could be used as an authentication server. At the same time, work is under way to implement the Shibboleth system (shibboleth.internet2.edu/) as a single-sign-on service. A Shibboleth implementation would rely on the local LDAP. The team plans to wait until Shibboleth becomes available on campus and use it as the authentication method for the website personalization project.

Another potential enhancement involves the Resource Editor and the Resource Index. Since these tools are used to describe resources and to present customized lists of resources, and since several of the variables in each are items like course, department, weight, and discipline, it takes only a small leap to envision classroom faculty across campus being trained to input their own resources for a page that is specific to a single course.

One of the most exciting enhancements envisioned for the system is an online reference interview that takes advantage of the extensive resource description included in the site. A series of questions ranging from subject, to course, to department, to scope of assignment could be presented and result in the display of a customized list of resources appropriate to the particular project at hand. Combined with personalization, single-sign-on, and integration with the university's student portal, this reference interview could be sophisticated enough to welcome the student at sign-on, present them the list of their current courses, and begin the interview by asking them which of the current courses has prompted the current reference question.

CONCLUSION

Several years into the project, the web team at the Kent State University libraries has built a local CMS that includes functionality that is very helpful to libraries. One of the most important of these functions is the extensive metadata description that is created for every resource on the site. Another is the extensive provision for the reuse of content. Another is the rich array of editing tools and their separation of content from HTML and site presentation. Still another is the suite of link maintenance tools and statistical reports for the site. Overall, staff and management feel that the personnel investment in the project has more than paid off in terms of site quality and efficiency.

REFERENCES

Dahl, M. 2004. Content management strategy for a college library web site. *Information Technology and Libraries* 23(1): 23–9. http://www.ala.org/

Han, Y. 2004. Digital content management: The search for a content management system. *Library Hi Tech* 22(4): 355–65.

Kiryakov, A., B. Popov, I. Terziev, D. Manov, and D. Ognyanoff. 2004. Semantic annotation, indexing, and retrieval. *Web Semantics: Science, Services and Agents on the World Wide Web* 2(1): 49–79.

Li, X., and J. P. Fullerton. 2002. Create, edit, and manage web database content using active server pages. *Library Hi Tech* 20(3): 285–301.

Litke, J. D. 2001. Strategic implications for future content management systems. *SMPTE Journal* 110(1): 23–7.

Powel, W., and C. Gill. 2003. Web content management systems in higher education. *Educause Quarterly* 26(2): 43–50. www.educause.edu/ir/library/pdf/eqm0325.pdf

Sennema, G. 2004. Creating an internal content management system. *Computers in Libraries* 24(1): 8–13. www.infotoday.com/cilmag/jan04/sennema.shtml

Somani, A., D. Choy, and J. C. Kleewein. 2002. Bringing together content and data management systems: Challenges and opportunities. *IBM Systems Journal* 41(4): 686–96.

Wales, T. 2005. Library subject guides: A content management case study at the open university, UK. *Electronic Library & Information Systems* 39(2): 112–21.

Westman, S. 2002. Building database-backed web applications: Processes and issues. *Information Technology and Libraries* 21(2): 63–72. www.ala.org/ala/lita/litapublications/ital/2102westman.htm

White, M. 2002. Content management from vendor selection to successful rollout. *Online (Weston, Conn.)* 26(6): 20–2, 24.

White, M. S. 2002. Managing content management system selection. *EContent* 25(7): 42–3.

Wu, Y. D., and L. Mengxiong. 2001. Content management and the future of academic libraries. *Electronic Library* 19(6): 432–9.

Yu, H. (ed.) 2005. *Content and workflow management for library websites: Case studies.* Hershey, PA: Information Science Pub.

8

Migrating a Library's Website to a Commercial CMS within a Campuswide Implementation

Tom Kmetz and Ray Bailey

Up to this point, the body of literature, which covers the implementation of content management systems in libraries, is small but varied, focusing on particular technological tools and organizational issues. This case study conforms to this model but is distinguished in one way—it may be the first examination of a library's effort to participate in a larger campuswide initiative to implement a commercially available system.

Holly Yu recently wrote:

> Although the rapid proliferation of commercially available content management systems makes it easier to find a vendor that might have the right solution, many available content management products do not provide the functionality aimed at library functions and services. The cost to purchase a commercial WCMS application is beyond the reach of the majority of libraries. Building an in-house system or application using open source technology is becoming a trend. (Yu 2005)

Actually, Yu might have taken it a step further to say that the cost is not just beyond the reach of most libraries but also beyond the reach of most universities. Only a handful of CMS vendors presently have sufficient interest in the academic market to provide realistic price quotes. Also, the web server traffic at a college or university will almost always be greater than a comparably sized company. While businesses have employees and customers who may use their website extensively, few will have anything comparable to a student body placing daily, heavy demands on the website. Finally, and this may be a debatable point, it seems that even a medium-sized school such as Morehead State University is probably more organizationally complex than a comparably sized company. For these reasons, some commercial systems may not scale smoothly to an academic environment.

So Yu is correct about the trend of homegrown and open source systems. But this trend could easily be reversed in the future, after the CMS vendors have picked over the low-hanging fruit of large corporate customers and begun to perceive academia as a viable market. If they tailor their systems and their pricing to the needs of academic institutions, then it is likely that homegrown systems in academic libraries will be swept away just as completely as homegrown OPACs have been. It would be the rare library that would desire, insist on, or be allowed autonomy in the face of a campuswide implementation.

DESCRIPTION OF THE PREEXISTING LIBRARY WEBSITE

In the summer of 1996 the Camden-Carroll Library at Morehead State University launched its first website. Its primary purpose was to provide a link into the web interface for its catalog, which had previously been accessible via telnet. At that time, the library offered a few periodical indexes, which could be accessed after entering the catalog system. Also included on the website was some basic information about the library such as its hours and its departments. The site was contained in a single directory and consisted of about 140 html and gif files and was housed on the campus web server maintained by the university's Office of Information Technology (IT).

By midsummer of 1998 the website had been retailored. Links into the index databases now resided outside of the catalog, and the website was organized under five navigational categories: Catalog, Resources, Services, Directory, and Other. A subdirectory structure was created to mirror these categories. In the years since, only a couple of top-level subdirectories have been added with numerous subdirectories proliferating inside of them.

The librarian with primary responsibility for the website has used FrontPage to maintain the files on his hard drive. He uploads them to the campus server with tools provided by the IT office. On the verge of its transition to a CMS, the website stored on his hard drive contained a total of 932 files. Additionally (and not included in that file count), there were more than a half dozen library staff members with the need, the skill, and the desire to create and maintain pages for their own areas. In July of 1999 each was provided with one or more subdirectories to which they could upload files directly to the server. Although a basic style guide was created to regularize some aspects of these subdirectories, it was established from the start that librarians and staff controlling their own files would have the freedom to design the pages in ways that would best suit their purposes.

Technologically, the site has become more complex, but the foundation has remained static web pages maintained in FrontPage. For example, authentication for the databases involves a combination of server redirects, EZproxy server software, and LDAP into the campus administrative system. When it came time to implement online reserves, the IT office provided the library with the ability to secure a subdirectory with LDAP. This secured subdirectory was also useful as a place for things needing to be behind a password, such as alternative database authentication using the referring URL method and passwords for particular purposes such as downloading specialized client software, e.g., SciFinder Scholar.

Organizationally, the library has not changed much since 1996. There has been only minimal turnover in the ranks of the librarians, and the same director served from 1986 to 2004. On the other hand, the Office of Information Technology has split itself into several different units by function. Within IT there is now a subunit that deals with academic computing and another with telecommunications. A separate Office of Institutional Research & Computer Applications has been established. And finally, with the decision to pursue a CMS, the responsibility for the content of the university's website came to reside in the Office of University Marketing (UM) which employs a Web Marketing Director and a Web Content Architect. Fortunately, all of this organizational reshuffling did not result in any noticeably high turnover, so the key people supporting library functions have remained accessible over the years.

The driving and shaping force for the library's website has been the productive relationship between the library and the campus IT offices. When attending conferences and hearing the stories of other libraries, it became apparent that a typical relationship between librarians and a campus IT staff is often much less communicative and much less positive than Morehead State University has been. Because of this relatively smooth collaborative spirit, a librarian was invited in 2003 to participate in the selection of a CMS system.

FUNDING AND SELECTING THE CMS

Each year, when new money is added to the budget, it is tied to a committee process. The University Planning Committee's primary function is to rank budget requests based upon how well a proposal might support the university's strategic plan. Any faculty or staff member can submit a budget request. Then, after a process involving the committee, the provost, and the president, the top ranking proposals are funded with whatever money is available in the pool for that year. In 2003 the Assistant Vice President for

University Relations requested nonrecurring money for a web content management system. At the end of the process the proposal, ranked third overall, fell easily above the budgetary cutoff.

In October of 2003 a CMS Work Group of eleven people was formed to oversee the Request for Proposals (RFP) process and consult informally during the implementation period. The work group consisted of college-level web authors, a librarian, and a representative from the IT office, and it was chaired by the Web Content Architect (WCA). The WCA was a skilled server administrator who had previously worked in the Office of Information Technology and took on the challenge of the new position, the primary task of which was to implement the new system.

The RFP produced price quotes from eight vendors for a first-year startup cost ranging from $27,750 to $76,465. The typical annual maintenance cost was around $6,000. This range represents the least expensive tier of vendors in the industry (a listing of vendors can be found at www.cmswatch.com/). The reality of the market at the present time is that the vendors perceive that corporate customers with relatively deep pockets are what will sustain them. Of the eight, four were invited to demonstrate their products either by visiting our campus or telephonically. In discussions after the demonstrations, it became clear that a vendor named Ektron (www.ektron.com/) had the greatest desire to blaze a trail into the academic market.

CAMPUSWIDE IMPLEMENTATION

Because MSU is Ektron's first sizable and campuswide academic customer, the campus has been serving very much as a beta test site for them. As one would expect with any beta testing situation, things do not always go smoothly. During the fall semester of 2004 the UM office took on the Herculean tasks of server and software installation, establishing new subdirectory and interface structures, policy revisions, and campuswide training for departmental web authors. Any problem in one area, of course, had an effect in another area. For example, a delay in getting a properly functioning server configuration meant that some of the scheduled training sessions had to be conceptual rather than hands-on. Other things were accomplished with surprising ease. For example, several years ago an attempt to gain approval for a set of campuswide web publishing regulations resulted in controversy and proved ultimately fruitless. This time, however, a five-page document was circulated, commented on, and approved without too much difficulty. It is currently available at www.moreheadstate.edu/daa/uar/ and is numbered UAR 701.01.

An original goal was to use the existing IBM hardware and Linux server to keep much of the architecture open source. During the installation, Ektron's technical staff recommended that a Microsoft array of software and server products be used. The campus followed this recommendation, regretting that the preference for an open source server would not be implemented but hopeful that a partnership between Ektron and Microsoft would prove to be an advantage. On their website Ektron states,

> Ektron is proud to have attained Certified status in the Microsoft Partner Program. . . . It's a sign of Ektron's commitment to and success in building software solutions that support organizations that utilize Microsoft technologies. Our solutions are designed to run on the Microsoft Windows operating system and integrate with other Microsoft technologies . . .

So the main technology underlying MSU's implementation is Active Server Pages (ASP) on a Microsoft SQL Server.

In their case study Rodriguez and Osburn write:

> The new Website coexisted with the old Website. However, all new content was to be added only to the new site using the WCMS. This proved helpful in two aspects. First it helped ease the library employees' resistance to moving to a new Website since the old site was quickly becoming outdated (2005).

This was the basic approach that was followed. A cutover can be handled in a number of ways. For example, the library system at Indiana University Bloomington reports that they found it necessary to implement an interim CMS to meet a tight deadline (Dallis and Ryner 2005). Regardless of the method used to ease the transition, the essence of a launch date is that whichever domain names are currently in use must be transferred to the new server. At that point the new system must be ready to assume the web traffic burdens of the old.

Because the library was an early adopter, the official launch date of November 29, 2004, did not present a problem—essentially the library was ready to go. Being in the loop, the library knew that most of the units on campus, however, had not migrated their content. So the first deadline served as a way to focus people on the task of migration. In that sense it worked. On the 29th an announcement was made that many units needed additional time, so a new deadline was set for February 7, 2005. What occurred on that date brings to mind the subtitle of Art Spiegelman's *Maus II* —"and here my troubles began." Within minutes of going live and experiencing the real demands of campus web traffic, the website crashed. The old site was promptly restored. After the crash was diagnosed, a re-launch date was set for a month later (March 7). On that date the site crashed just as quickly and completely as it had the month before.

At this point one might imagine a general feeling of unhappiness prevailed on our campus concerning the CMS. And one might further imagine that the relationship between the university and the vendor was somewhat strained. Since then, a more complete diagnosis over a period of several months uncovered several contributing factors. These included hardware issues and programming issues with ASP.net. The original recommendations from Ektron concerning the hardware were based on their experience handling the loads typical in the business environment, so they had not initially realized what kind of traffic a university might see. There was also a problematical string of code for which Microsoft indicated that there were no problems they could see with the script. The implication was that MS's implementation of ASP.net was not handling this particular piece of code the way it should have been. With these issues addressed, the IT office has conducted vigorous load testing of the new configuration and has found it to be satisfactory. This might have led to a summer re-launch. Unfortunately, the Web Content Architect was needed for an even larger migration project involving the campus administrative systems. So his vacant position has only recently been filled. The person hired had served previously on the CMS project as an assistant to his predecessor, so he was quite familiar with all the work done thus far. Now his task will be to first reassure the campus community that a re-launch will not crash, and then to re-launch the system without it crashing again. When that happens, the library will be ready to take up where it left off on its own migration.

LIBRARY-WIDE IMPLEMENTATION

Another quote from Yu:

> Although the needs and benefits of WCM are apparent, it remains difficult nonetheless to move from the realization of its importance to the establishment of Web content practices in the library (2005).

In the Camden-Carroll Library case, no major obstacles to "the establishment of Web content practices" have yet been discovered, because the technical failures of the server postponed efforts to engage the staff in the formulation of policies and procedures for the future maintenance of the website. The authors can only report on how the library reinvented their website in anticipation of such practices.

Fortunately, more than half of the librarians have HTML skills. For that reason technophobia was never much of a barrier to change. Even if it had been a factor for the library, however, it would have been overcome with relative ease because a well-designed CMS will move that dynamic in the opposite direction. The developers of a CMS in the library at CSU Sacramento report that in the first year of its use, the number of people involved in the creation of web pages tripled from seven to 21 and that, "Most of the new web page creators had very little experience with HTML and were the ones who were the most excited about this newfound capability" (Rodriguez and Osburn 2005). Web-authoring within Ektron's system is a much easier proposition than using traditional web-authoring tools. If a person understands the concept of logging in with a password and has some basic word processing skills, then (s)he can create and maintain content on the website. Librarians and staff were not resistant to being trained on the new system, regardless of their previous skill level, and were able to move content from the old system to the new with remarkable speed and ease.

That training involved some very specific tools such as a calendar provided by the system and some fairly advanced form-handling capabilities. But the general concepts conveyed in the training can be summed up briefly. The key elements of the system are:

content blocks—instead of .html files, the system uses content blocks. When text is pasted in from a web page or a word processor all previous formatting tags are stripped from the code so that only formatting allowed by the system's templates may be applied. Each content block is assigned a number by the system. So the tail end of a URL will look like this:

/index.aspx?id=1934

instead of this:

/index.html

As an aside, redirects are used to create cleaner-looking URLs at the unit level.

subareas—essentially a subarea is the same as a traditional subdirectory with some important differences. In this implementation, a subarea can have its own navigation bars (both a header and a footer) as well as its own banner graphic. Importantly, the UM staff will only assign permissions at the subarea level and not at the more granular content block level.

syndication—using a JavaScript client-side include means one can insert content blocks inside other content blocks.

eWebEditPro—a browser-based web editing tool that takes the place of client software such as Dreamweaver or FrontPage. The user will log in to modify a content block and be presented with eWebEditPro.

Any experienced web designer understands that regardless of the technology employed there are two structures that must be created and maintained and which are dependent on one another. First, there is the file and subdirectory structure that underlie everything (above all it must be well tailored to the working habits of the people who maintain the site). Second, there is the structure of the interface that is presented to the users (above all it must be easily navigable). To end up with a resilient and enduring system these two structures should be created in tandem and be married to each other in the holy bonds of technology. Yet the forces that shape them are, and should be, separate matters.

THE UNDERLYING STRUCTURE

In the above paragraph, the phrase "file and subdirectory structure" when referring to the new system should actually be "content block and subarea structure." In the recently published *Encyclopedia of Information Science and Technology*, it states that:

> Content management in organizations is deeply intertwined with organizational work. Therefore development of content management should include the aspects of organizational work on which content is used and produced (Honkaranta and Tyrväinen 2005).

The directory structure on the preexisting site was created to be maintained by a single person, and at the top level looks like this:

/dir/ [i.e., directory]
/images/
/includes/
/other/
/res/ [i.e., resources]
/secure/
/ser/ [i.e., services]

Within those seven subdirectories are 40 additional subdirectories put in place since 1998 to organize more than 900 files. Only one person has ever dealt directly with this structure. Fifteen additional subdirectories were controlled by other people.

> per—govdoc—learntechnology—reserves—secure/ereserves—accservices—technology—cat—inst—acq—colldev—collections—records—excamser—ill

In rethinking this structure there were two primary considerations. The policy at the campus level was to assign all permissions at the level of the subarea. Understandably, the UM staff did not want to be assigning permissions for individual content blocks. So any person tasked by a supervisor to maintain a particular content block would have the access necessary to edit any other content blocks residing in the same subarea. The practical implication of this is that overall security of the library's site would be enhanced with a greater number of subareas. Of course, there are other safeguards to accidental or deliberate mishandling of content. The system maintains a history for each content block, allowing for easy reversion back to an earlier draft. Also, approval chains could prevent content from being posted to the live website until after review by a supervisor. At MSU, however, approval chains have been viewed as somewhat stifling and potentially draconian, so they have not been activated. The second and more important factor that shaped the new underlying structure was the idea that each librarian has two basic roles. Each is responsible for a functional area in the library and for liaison duties with one or more academic departments outside of the library. It would not suffice to assign a subarea to an individual librarian and say that it could house content blocks for both purposes because these roles can frequently shift. A structure such as that would quickly become tangled as people leave and arrive, move to a new job within the library, or trade liaison duties. The structure that emerged is based on the functional roles so that whenever the people filling those roles change the structure can remain the same. It consists of numerous subareas.

List of Library Website Subareas

/calendars/	Calendars: Library Calendar; Classroom; Seminar A; Conf. 2; Conf. 3
/databases/	Databases Lists: alpha lists, descriptions, syndication list, date added list
/libraryinfo/	Library Information: general files not associated with a particular area or academic department reside inside /libraryinfo/
/news/	Library News
/access/	Access Services
/acq/	Acquisitions
/auto/	Automation
/cat/	Cataloging
/coffee/	Coffee Shop
/dean/	Dean of Library Services
/ekhsin/	Eastern Kentucky Health Sciences Information Network
/excam/	Extended Campus
/instruction/	Instructional Services
/ill/	Interlibrary Loan
/ltl/	Learning Technology Lab
/pergov/	Periodicals & GovDocs
/records/	Records Management Program

/ref/	Reference & Online Services
/res/	Reserves
/collections/	Special Collections
/aef/	Accounting, Economics, & Finance
/ahs	Agricultural & Human Science
/art/	Art
/bes/	Biological & Environmental Sciences
/ci/	Curriculum and Instruction
/clah/	Counseling, Leadership, Adult and Higher Education
/dct/	Communication & Theatre
/eflp/	English, Foreign Languages, & Philosophy
/ggh/	Geography, Government, & History
/hps/	Health, Physical Education, & Sports Sciences
/iet/	Industrial & Engineering Technology
/imagingsciences/	Imaging Sciences
/irapp/	Institute for Regional Analysis & Public Policy
/is/	Information Systems
/iwsp/	Interdisciplinary Women's Studies Program
/mcs/	Mathematics & Computer Science
/mmr/	Management, Marketing, & Real Estate
/music/	Music
/nursing/	Nursing
/physsci/	Physical Science
/psych/	Psychology
/sswc	Sociology, Social Work, & Criminology

Presiding over this much larger structure will be two librarians instead of just one. Both authors of this paper were assigned permissions for the entire library site. Working together on some tasks while specializing in others will allow the librarians both to be more efficient and also more ambitious in planning. The hope is that all librarians will find the new ease of creating web content a spur to what they are willing to create and maintain in both their functional areas and in their liaison areas.

THE STRUCTURE OF THE INTERFACE

As the subarea structure was being created, a subcommittee of the library's Web Committee was assigned to create a new design for the library website. The old design, shown in the screen shot below, is a direct reflection of its own underlying subdirectory structure.

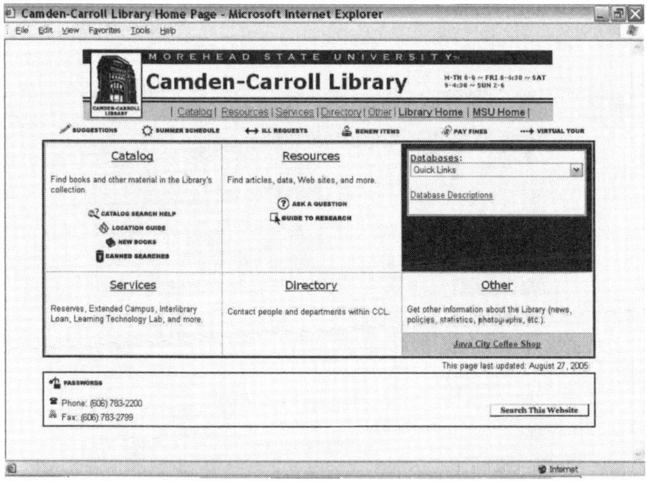

Figure 8.1. Old design of Camden-Carroll Library website.

In contrast, the navigational elements in the new design are not organized to correspond with the underlying structure. This was necessary because the substructure can no longer be thought of as being behind-the-scenes. Its audience is not just the library staff web authors but also the broader audience of campus web authors who will be able to easily view it using the CMS. Because the subarea structure must make sense to as large a number of authors as the university hopes to enlist, it cannot mirror the structure of the public interface, which obviously must make sense to as large a number of users as the library hopes to serve.

Within the parameters of the CMS, the headers, footers, and main university navigation bar are constant on all pages. Individual web designers control subarea navigation bars and the main body of the page. Therefore, the subcommittee's task was to construct a well-organized website with relevant content.

The subcommittee agreed upon a few basic principles to guide the creation of this new interface:

- The new site should be as intuitive, simple to use, and as free of jargon as possible.
- The design and structure of the new site should mirror the dominant needs of our users.
- The new site should be efficient for the experienced user but also provide extensive assistance for the novice user.

With these goals in mind, the subcommittee created the design shown in the following screen shot.

Figure 8.2. Current design of Camden-Carroll Library website.

In contrast to the previous design, the home page de-emphasizes technical terms (*catalog, database,* etc.), and these terms are explained contextually when they do appear. Instead of jargon, the subcommittee employed more ordinary labels—such as "Find Books" or "Find Articles." The main categories reflect what the users are typically looking for when they visit the website. The internal navigation bar (which appears on every page in a blue band directly under the banner graphic) mirrors the main categories and provides a link back to the home page. Thus there are quick and easy paths to all of the most popular services and resources from anywhere within the site.

With this design, users who are familiar with the site should be quickly able to gain access to the tools they need, while newer users can benefit from the logical layout and the comprehensive "Get Help" section. The authors believe this new design will make the website more useful, more easily navigable, and more intuitive for the widest possible audience.

NEGATIVES AND POSITIVES OF THE NEW SYSTEM

Naturally it is frustrating to miss deadlines and be thwarted by technical failures, but time, effort, and a bit of luck can turn these problems into mere memories. The authors, however, have a couple of concerns that may persist even after a successful launch.

Librarians are typically ideologically more inclined to support free or open source initiatives. Pragmatically, their lower cost is certainly desirable. Only time will tell whether proprietary or open source will ultimately dominate academic CMS implementations.

Often a campus unit will become reliant on a single vendor, e.g., a distance-learning office with its courseware system. Academic libraries have been fortunate in the web environment in having multiple systems that, while integrated, will not collapse en masse if one of them fails. If the link resolver is down for a few days, it is definitely annoying, but one can still search the databases. The authors do worry that they are moving more in the direction of being too dependent on a single vendor. For all of its drawbacks, static HTML, when it is well written, does have the advantage of being a fairly reliable technology. For example, in the new system, the authors have experienced some instability with the JavaScript client-side includes, which needs to be addressed before a new launch because the library would very much like to make extensive use of them. But these are the sorts of things that must be dealt with when moving from a relatively simple technology to a more complex one.

Outweighing these concerns and despite the setbacks that are probably unavoidable when one serves as a beta site, the authors remain enthusiastic about Ektron's system. While FrontPage or Dreamweaver are certainly more powerful than eWebEditPro, it was surprisingly easy to leave them behind. Many of the superior features that they offer deal with manipulating the look and feel of the page. But with a CMS (any CMS) the look and feel are handled by templates. In this case, the library was included in the discussions concerning the templates, so the end result was not too far off the mark from our ideal. When a person is learning HTML, most of the fun is in exploring all of the options, but if you are no longer a novice and have the responsibility of maintaining an organizational website, then the effort to maintain some measure of consistency in the look and feel of the pages can become a tedious chore that is not easily delegated. What could be a happier event than for that chore to be transferred to someone at the campus level? For the experienced website developer, it is much more fun to spend time thinking about new ways to develop content than it is to spend time considering (or policing) fonts, colors, and graphics. In the library's case, the UM office has worked closely with the library in developing the site's look and feel.

There is one remarkable aspect of participating in a campuswide implementation, which the authors have not found mentioned in other case studies—because nearly all of them are library-wide implementations. With the way that the system is built there is neither the ability nor the need to maintain back-up files on your PC. Back-ups of the database that drives the system are handled at the campus level. There is no set of HTML files with which to be concerned. If there is no HTML and if the library is not the one directly responsible for backing up the database, then what is there to store on a hard drive? Really, the only things left are miscellaneous documents relating to the library's other systems, e.g., the OPAC or EZproxy or a link resolver. Though this realization is jarring at first, it becomes quite easy to adjust to after realizing that one can edit the site from any networked computer located anywhere.

The reality of one person maintaining the majority of a static HTML site is that most of his or her energy is devoted to keeping the databases running smoothly and receiving documents from others in the library to post to the site. For example, it makes perfect sense for the Dean's secretary to send out a paper memo with the updated telephone list and have that serve as the signal to the site maintainer that the telephone list on the website should be updated. Multiply this times the number of informational items that it would be desirable to have on a website. That one person soon becomes bogged down in the minutia of routine maintenance tasks when instead he or she should have that time to explore new possibilities and to strategize. A CMS makes it possible for people to perform the tasks easily on the website that they would perform naturally outside of it. Additionally, there is a happy by-product of the fact that there no longer is the need for one person to maintain an authoritative copy of all the HTML files. With the CMS, any number of people can have the highest level permissions. In this case a two-person team is proving sufficient, but larger libraries could give sitewide rights to several librarians.

Probably most institutions with traditional web servers have outdated content for which they are uncertain who is responsible. Wiping the slate clean and starting over with a new system at our institution has allowed the Web Content Architect to keep a much more current and accurate list of who controls what. Sharing that list with everyone on it can promote a spirit of cooperation. The system's architecture can do the same. After logging into a page and updating it with WebEditPro, there is the option to click further into the system and enter what is called the Work Area. The Work Area contains advanced options and is used primarily for navigating the subarea structure of the entire campus. This presents the possibility of more tight integration with content from other campus units.

CONCLUSION

The UM office reports that Ektron has incorporated into their newest releases many of the lessons learned thus far from this experience, and a new launch date has been announced. With luck, MSU's CMS should be operational before this goes to press. The authors can imagine that together they are laying down pavement on a lonely country road, which perhaps in the future others will choose to travel and which may eventually be widened into several lanes.

ACKNOWLEDGMENTS

The authors would like to thank April Nutter and Drew Henderson for reading a preliminary draft and providing helpful commentary.

REFERENCES

Dallis, D., and D. Ryner. 2005. Indiana University Bloomington Libraries presents organization to the users and power to the people: A solution in web content management. H. Yu (ed.) *Content and workflow management for library websites: Case studies.* Hershey, PA: Information Science Pub.

Honkaranta, A., and P. Tyrväinen. 2005. Content management in organizations. M. Khosrow-Pour (ed.) *Encyclopedia of information science and technology.* Hershey, PA: Idea Group Reference.

Rodriguez, J. C., and A. Osburn. 2005. Developing a distributed web publishing system at CSU Sacramento Library: A case study of coordinated decentralization. H. Yu (ed.) *Content and workflow management for library websites: Case studies.* Hershey, PA: Information Science Pub.

Yu, H. 2005. Library web content management: Needs and challenges. H. Yu (ed.) *Content and workflow management for library websites: Case studies.* Hershey, PA: Information Science Pub.

9

Building a Collection Development CMS on a Shoestring

Regina Beach and Miqueas Diál

A STATEMENT OF THE PROBLEM

It was becoming increasingly important—at many levels—that collection development efforts needed to change at Texas A&M University, Kingsville (TAMUK), a small comprehensive university of approximately 5,000 students in South Texas. There was limited participation and cooperation by teaching faculty at the Kingsville campus and virtually none by the faculty at the System Center in San Antonio. Additionally, changes were needed in the library's technical services department that would more fully embrace technology and better support student and faculty needs in the twenty-first century.

Much thought was devoted to finding a solution to these problems. The primary author participates in many library-oriented listservs, and content management systems (CMS) had been a discussion topic on a few. In this article, the authors describe the need for a collection development CMS, necessary changes in library technical services, and the process in developing a working prototype.

Content Management Systems allow anyone with authorization to enter information onto a web page without knowledge of hypertext markup language (HTML) for purposes of updating a website. Also, information may be entered on a web page form for sharing or distribution. All of this may be done at any time of the day or night at the user's convenience. The more this model was considered, the more it seemed the answer for better support in building physical and electronic collections both local and from a distance with teaching faculty input.

The seeds were planted for the idea to develop a content management system for collection development during the summer of 2004, when library services and collections were found to be deficient at the Texas A&M University System Center, San Antonio, by the respective accrediting agency, Southern Association of Colleges (SACS).

The System Center is a partnership between the Texas A&M University System and the Alamo Community College District in San Antonio to offer third- and fourth-year classes. It came to fruition to further the higher educational needs of residents of South San Antonio, an underserved area. Classes have been held since the 2000–2001 school year on the campus of Palo Alto College (PAC), one of the Alamo District's community colleges. Library services for System Center students are largely provided by George Ozuna Jr. Learning Resources Center at PAC; that is, the library services have, to date, largely been provided by the community college campus where the System Center classes are held.

In the fall of 2004, a faculty member (the second author) was asked to join the project to gain the perspective of teaching faculty and to aid in database construction and design. This worked out very well, when the true size and scope of the project became a reality.

LIBRARY SUPPORT FOR DISTANCE EDUCATION

To successfully deliver library resources for distance education, technology resources need to be integrated. Not only should the integrated library system (ILS), website, and electronic resources work together, but they also should have a common interface. Many university libraries have achieved this level of sophistication in their support for distance education or have made significant strides in this direction. The challenge for small universities is to find staff, staff time, and resources to do this while carrying out very basic library functions at the home campus. The reference desk needs to be staffed, books bought, and books cataloged. The need of the student standing in front of you is very pressing and very real, while the need of a student at a remote location is much more of a concept than a reality, until one of them calls or sends an email.

Moments of reflection and reports from accreditation entities make the plight of distance education students, where the home campus is also small, very real.

> Neither students nor faculty feel that library holdings at PAC are commensurate with the intellectual rigor desired for competitive scholarly work. There are very few holdings in the library specific to academic programs. On those limited occasions in which faculty are given the opportunity to order materials,

> they claim to receive no follow up concerning the status of their orders. A liaison from the Kingsville campus has the responsibility of working with the faculty, informing them of new additions and collections in the Jernigan Library, and apprising them of the arrival of new books.[1]

Of additional concern is the long-term effects of the inadequacy of library resources upon the lives of students when faculty are forced to teach "down" to the library resources that they have access to.

> Some faculty at the TAMU-K System Center campus reported streamlining assignments based on limited library resources, which raises further concerns among the faculty about the level of competitiveness of their students upon graduation. The library is inadequate to support research and instructional support services. Similarly, students feel constrained by what they consider to be inadequate library/information resources. The PAC library is not seen as an appropriate resource, due in part to limited hours of operation and variable holidays. Moreover, computer labs and study rooms in the PAC library are sometimes inaccessible.[2]

A CMS for collection development rectifies the process for ordering books by making it accessible to any faculty with a computer and Internet connection (this has been a challenge as well) at any time, night or day. The order form on the CMS essentially replaces the physical order card. Records in the online public access catalog (OPAC) inform the inquirer where the physical item is located (or not) within the ordering and technical services processing workflow.

Part of the vision in developing a CMS for collection development was the longer term goal of integrating it with course-management software, such as WebCT or Blackboard. Increasingly, librarians are focusing less on pathfinders and are developing library course pages in collaboration with distance education faculty. Library resources are being delivered more commonly via course-management software. Integrating collection development into that process is only one step beyond it.

Administrators, faculty, and students have a great deal of resources devoted to integration of libraries and course-management systems. It is regrettable that many are not aware of this and of the price involved as time passes by in quality of education suffered by students and in wasted time, money, and opportunity. Students will simply go where it is available.

> "Several years ago, the librarians here at UNT decided to view each student as a potential distance learner. In doing so, we vastly improved our ability to assess our library resource offerings and to make decisions as to how to modify the system in order to fully service our distance education students," says librarian Frances May of University of North Texas.[3]

Also at issue is the closeness in adherence to the Association of College and Research Libraries (ACRL) recommendations in its "Guidelines for Distance Learning Library Services." The originating institution's support "should provide ready and equivalent library service and learning resources to all of the institution's students, regardless of location."[4] Integration of library services, collections, and collection development by making use of course-management systems would go far towards meeting this goal.

TECHNICAL SERVICES WORKFLOW

An additional goal in developing a CMS for collection development, that probably will be a long time in coming to actual fruition, is the concept of entering bibliographic data one time only. Instead of technical services staff both in acquisitions and cataloging entering bibliographic data a multitude of times, it is entered one time by the requester. While this will not entirely come to pass with our prototype, we will come close to this ideal model.

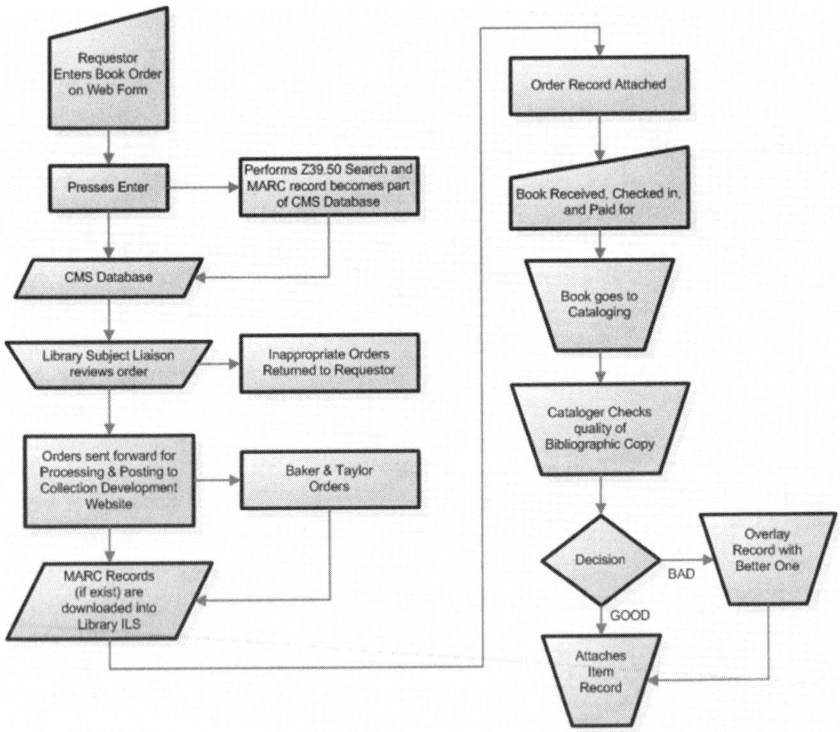

Figure 9.1. Bibliographic information flow.

The above diagram is somewhat simplified (especially in the acquisitions details) in order to show the flow of information. Approximately 90 percent of TAMUK's monographic acquisitions are placed with Baker & Taylor using their Title Source II product. There are two flows of data possible that are represented in the diagram, one originating from the CMS's form and another from Baker & Taylor's Title Source II. Beginning with fiscal year 2002–2003, faculty have been encouraged to set up carts in Title Source II and utilize it as a part of the ordering process. Title Source II has had very limited use by the faculty. The CMS form is anticipated to have much more higher use, and its full implementation is eagerly awaited by many.

The workflow represented in the diagram, particularly the Baker & Taylor stream, was put into place and tested during the summer of 2005. As of this writing (August 2005), a few of the bugs in the bibliographic record loading process have not entirely been worked out.

Changing the workflow began in earnest with a partial retirement in late January 2005 in the acquisitions department. Change does not occur readily or rapidly at TAMUK. This is true at many libraries, but particularly so at TAMUK in the primary author's experience. With the exception of one individual, all of the technical services staff has been working at the library more than 20 years. The acquisitions assistant, who partially retired, had been working full time for the university for 37 years. Change has to occur in baby steps by introducing a small idea, perhaps allow for some discussion, train as necessary, allow some time for adjustment and assessment, and then begin the cycle again.

For the "data entered once" idea to be successful, a closer alignment between acquisitions and cataloging is required, with the eventual goal that involved processes and staff will become one. A review of the literature indicates that, due to technology, this model is becoming prevalent. There are definite advantages to having a small technical services staff who have worked a very long time with each other. People know and trust each other more in libraries with long-term staff than in libraries with greater turnover since they have taken breaks and lunches together for 20 years as well as having been there while children have been born and grown up. This is the positive aspect of the change process and makes it easier to accomplish when it begins.

In February 2005, in order that business could go forward and invoices paid on time, a copy cataloger was trained in acquisitions. She was completely trained in selecting vendors to order from, placing orders, adding order records to the integrated library system (ILS), Innovative Interfaces, Inc. (III), receiving and checking in orders, and in paying invoices. This was very successful and greatly enriched the individual's breadth of knowledge and perspective.

The rocky portion of the change process occurred during summer 2005 when the primary author took order cards away from the acquisitions production environment. There was literally weeping and screaming. It is incredible that there are so many emotions tied up with a small paper card, but technical service processes have been bound with the staff from beginning to end. Never mind that the information on the order card was duplicated at least once by the library's ILS and usually duplicated once again by Title Source II. Also, during the past nearly four years, there had been complaints from the faculty about having to use them at least once a month during the ordering cycle. This was an intellectual and emotional large leap for staff and a huge change for them.

Unfortunately, TAMUK has never had electronic ordering or invoicing. These options were thoroughly investigated during summer 2005. Due to the age of our III server, using the telnet version of III, and III doing away with BISAC for EDI, TAMUK will not be placing electronic orders using III in the near future. This is a situation that can remain the same due to most of our orders being placed directly with Baker & Taylor via Title Source II for the last three years. Before that time, surprisingly, all book acquisitions were done via letter and/or fax.

The primary author further investigated ways to streamline the acquisitions process, focusing on duplication of effort, the number of keystrokes involved, and keying in of data multiple times. After considerable thought, the most efficient method for verifying receipt and paying an invoice would be scanning an ISBN barcode from an invoice into the ILS. Baker & Taylor does not print ISBN barcodes on their invoices, however, nor does the company seem willing to consider doing it. This turned out to be just as well. Further investigation revealed that with III, check in and payment is a two-step process and there are no other options. In order to pay an invoice, III requires the order record number.

The cataloging department, until recently, had always received cataloging copy from OCLC. For a small library, this is a very expensive practice. Using MARC records from Title Source II saves OCLC charges, saves the acquisition staff from keying a short bibliographic record, and the order and bibliographic information is available much more immediately to the requestor and patron. This is becoming increasingly more important in the distance education environment.

The integration of the above changes in workflow with the changes that will come about as a result of the full implementation of the CMS is anticipated to go smoothly.

THE PROTOTYPE

As noted above, the Book Request database was designed to reduce the paperwork and inconvenience of the faculty and staff who order books through the campus library. Also mentioned is the desire that the requestor's online form entry will eventually be the first—and perhaps only—time that the information will need to be entered into the library's catalog system. Although expected increased use will require that the database be created in a larger programming environment, the prototype was developed in Microsoft Access. It keeps track of the basics: the department, the requesting employee, and the book information. The table relationships are shown in Figure 9.2 below.

Because the different systems within the library are yet to be completely integrated, an interface for the library staff was necessary. Figures 9.3 and 9.4 below show the forms. The fields as shown in the table relationships and the forms were based on the paper order forms, which have been used for many years. As is common in the development of database applications, the fields and forms will certainly be altered after receiving comments from the library staff and the campus employees who order books and other library materials through the system. For example, the library staff may desire more or different reports to be generated. The annual ordering history by person and by department seemed the most logical reports to create first.

The campus employees' web interface is shown in the following two figures. The first is a login page to confirm the employee's identification number and department (Figure 9.5).

The next figure (Figure 9.6) shows a few parts of the longer book order form. The book order web form contains fewer fields than exist in the database. It was determined that the end users—that is, the campus employees ordering books—will be unaware of much of the information. Even with fewer

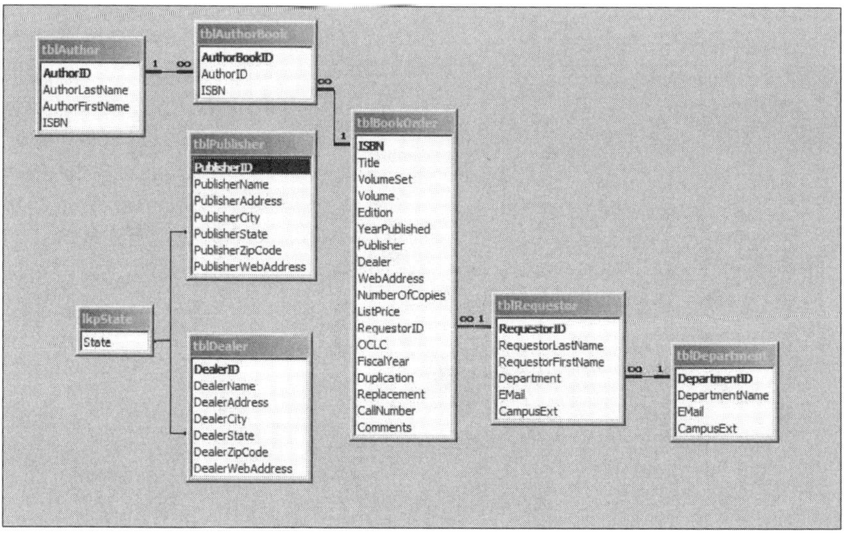

Figure 9.2. Entity relationships of the book request database.

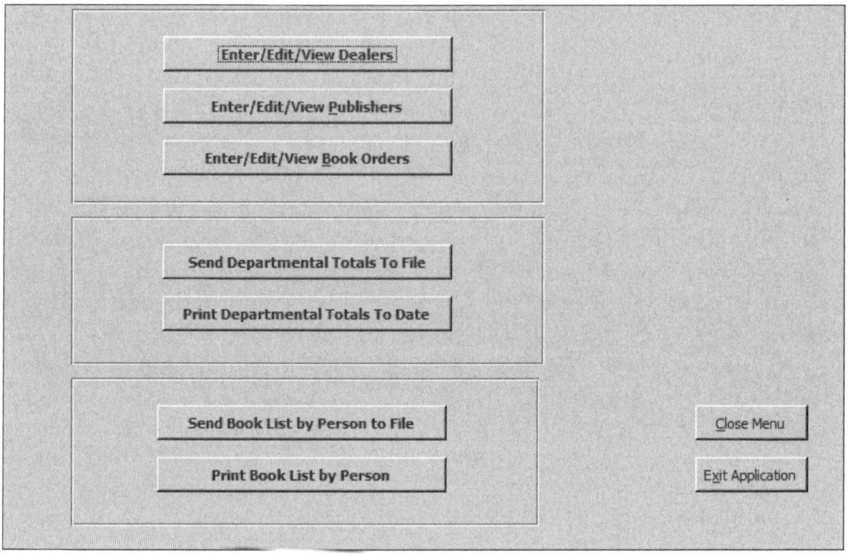

Figure 9.3. Opening menu of the library staff's book request database.

fields on the web form, users are requested to complete the form as much as they can; the remaining information is completed by the library staff.

The technology of this first step in automating the book-ordering process has been rather easy—at least for this simple prototype. The difficulty in developing a long-term system will be twofold: (1) disseminating the information and having campus employees actually use the system, and (2) integrating this ordering process with other library systems—both those currently used and those envisioned for the future.

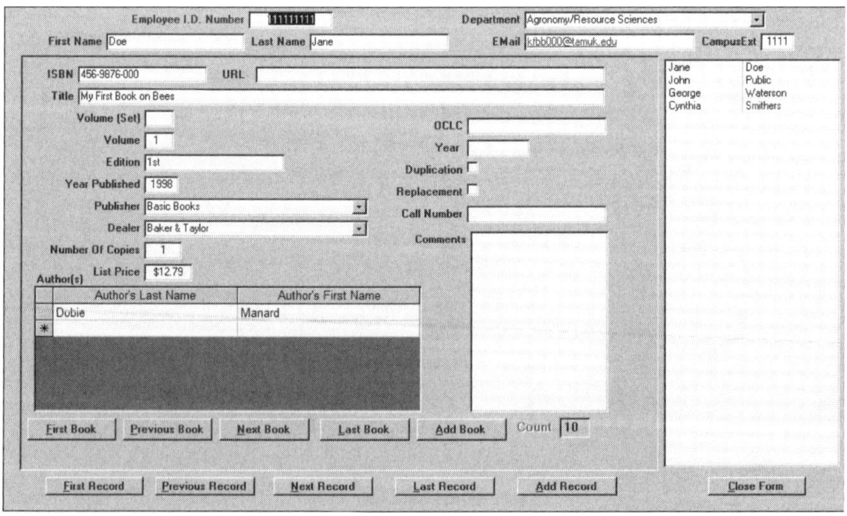

Figure 9.4. Book order form of the library staff's book request database.

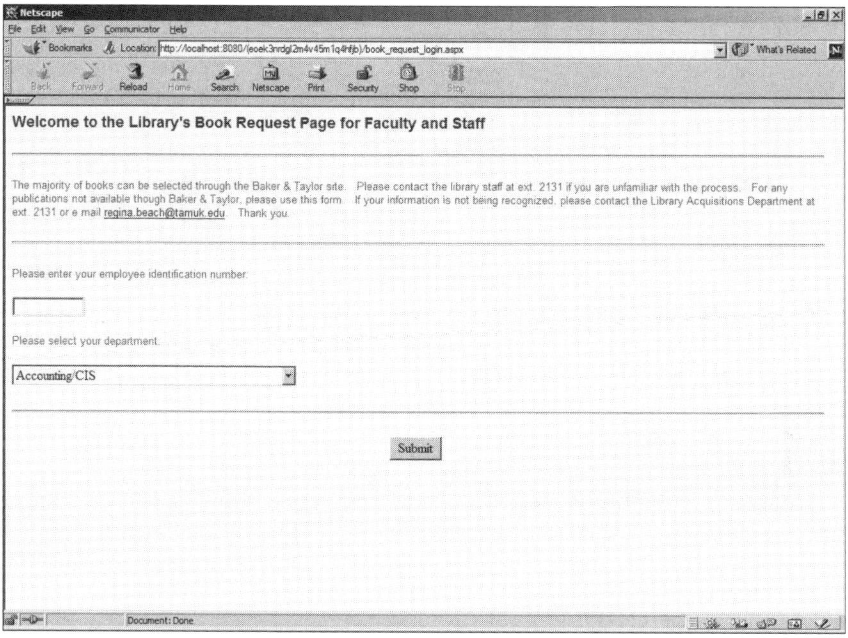

Figure 9.5. Login web form.

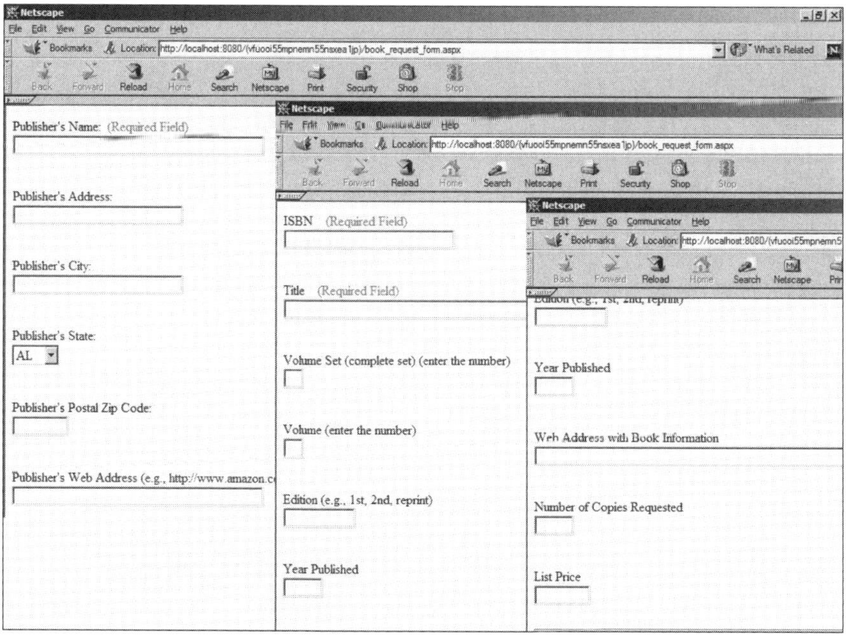

Figure 9.6. Book request web form.

Regarding the first hurdle, perhaps the most important aspect will be receiving feedback from users as to the convenience of the online ordering form and then responding by adjusting and correcting the process. The assumption is that, like all information systems, ease of use will in large part determine the success of the system.

The second challenge—that of integrating library acquisitions with all the current and future library systems—is expected to be a process of years. The primary difficulty will be coordinating matches (or "crosstalk") among systems, which use their own identifiers. Seamlessly matching the primary identifying records of entities such as the Library of Congress, wholesale distributors (e.g., Baker & Taylor, Ingram's), and the campus library's catalog will be a time-consuming endeavor. Included in this challenge is the use of different servers and platforms on which the systems reside—systems that have been purchased and implemented at different times over many years. Integration is possible, however, and there are many ways to achieve this goal.

Envisioning the future, another area to integrate will be the online courses and the preferences of instructors to make available online a variety of course textbooks, journals, other reference materials, online tutorials, and multimedia such as audio and video.

FUTURE PLANS

The original plan's time line included full testing of the prototype during summer 2005 and full implementation for fall 2005. Negotiating security issues within the library, however, was an unexpected problem and one that was difficult and required care with potential political problems as well. As of this writing (August 2005) full implementation may be a moot point. Funds for monographic acquisitions are expected to be small in the coming fiscal year. This will hopefully allow for thorough testing by acquisitions staff and the building of the collection development website as well. Online training will be important to the success of the collection development CMS. There are plans for development of online tutorials as well as the possibility of live training sessions delivered via streaming.

Additionally, the two authors would like to write again about the collection development CMS once it is fully implemented to completely evaluate its success (or not) and assess its value.

CONCLUSION

The content management system for a collection development project has been a thoroughly enjoyable collaboration. However, it is difficult to gauge at this time the full extent of its function and usability without full implementation. It is expected to be well received by faculty making suggestions for library acquisitions based solely on the one fact that manually filling out an order card will no longer be necessary. The future is expected to have some exciting times in store for the library's collection development program.

NOTES

1. *Report of the Substantive Change Committee, Texas A & M University—Kingsville, System Center at San Antonio*, Commission on Colleges Southern Association of Colleges and Schools, April 16–18, 2004.
2. *Report of the Substantive Change Committee.*
3. Susan Gaide, "Integrated Library Services Boosts Online Recruitment and Retention," *Distance Education Report* vol. 8, no. 8: 1–2, 6.
4. *Guidelines for Distance Learning Library Services* [online], Association of College and Research Libraries (2004). Available at: www.ala.org/ala/acrl/acrlstandards/guidelinesdistancelearning.htm

REFERENCES

Bace, M. A., and P. Ratkovich. 2004. Personnel turnover as impetus for change. *Innovative redesign and reorganization of library technical services.* Bradford Lee Eden (ed.). Westport, CT: Libraries Unlimited.

Bailey, S. B. 2004. Navigating toward the future, building on our strengths: Reorganization and change at Emory University Libraries. *Innovative redesign and reorganization of library technical services*. Bradford Lee Eden (ed.). Westport, CT: Libraries Unlimited.

Branton, A. 2004. Successfully merging workflow and personnel in technical services: A management perspective. *Innovative redesign and reorganization of library technical services*. Bradford Lee Eden (ed.). Westport, CT: Libraries Unlimited.

Branton, A., and T. Englert. 2002. Mandate for change: Merging acquisitions and cataloging functions into a single workflow. *Library collections, acquisitions, & technical services* 26: 345–354.

Coats, J., and J. Kiegel. 2003. Automating the nexus of book selection, acquisitions and rapid copy cataloging. *Library collections, acquisitions, & technical services* 27: 33–44.

Congleton, R. 2002. Re-evaluating technical services workflow for integrated library systems. *Library collections, acquisitions, & technical services* 26: 337–341.

Gibbons, S. 2005. Library course management systems: An overview. *Library technology reports* 41, no. 3: May/June 2005.

Glazier, R., and Dr. J. D. Glazier. 2004. Merging departments in a small academic library. *Innovative redesign and reorganization of library technical services*. Bradford Lee Eden (ed.). Westport, CT: Libraries Unlimited.

Greever, K. 2003. Nuts and bolts: Acquisitions and cataloging at Kenyon. *Library collections, acquisitions, & technical services* 27: 147–154.

LeClair, A. M. 2004. Centering technical services: Developing a vision for change at Union College. *Innovative redesign and reorganization of library technical services.* Bradford Lee Eden (ed.). Westport, CT: Libraries Unlimited.

Martin, C. 2004. Workflow analysis as a basis for organizational redesign at McMaster University Library. *Innovative redesign and reorganization of library technical services.* Bradford Lee Eden (ed.). Westport, CT: Libraries Unlimited.

Maurer, M. B., and M. L. Hurst. 2003. Library-vendor collaboration for re-engineering workflow: The Kent State experience. *Library collections, acquisitions, & technical services* 27: 155–164.

Painter, M. A. 2005. Library support for distance learning. *Distance Education Report* vol. 9, no. 12: 3.

Ramsay, K. M. 2004. Technological change and technical services: A case study of a mid-sized research library. *Innovative redesign and reorganization of library technical services.* Bradford Lee Eden (ed.). Westport, CT: Libraries Unlimited.

Tumlin, M. D. 2002. Serials for distance education research projects: What are we missing? *Serials Review* vol. 28, no. 3: 206–212.

Wiegand, S. 2002. Incorporating electronic products into the acquisitions workflow in a small college library. *Library collections, acquisitions, & technical services* 26: 363–366.

10

An RDF-based Digital Library System

Yan Han

THE NEED FOR A TRUE INTEROPERABLE INFORMATION ENVIRONMENT

Libraries, cultural heritage institutions, and learning organizations manage and provide access to vast stores of information. This information is in multiple file formats and has typically been described for a specialized community's needs. Acquired for many years, this structured information would be of enormous value, especially if it could be easily discovered and its meaning would be known across domains. It was noted that libraries have not exploited traditional or emerging tools for *knowledge organization* to their full potential. The report also states that research is specifically needed in how tools of knowledge representation can be used to improve users' experience in searching, navigating, and comprehending digital collections (Caplan et al. 2003). *Interoperability* is essential in this environment. As interoperability moves to the foreground of research topics, the report also notes that "the digital library community lacks a commonly-accepted architectural model" and "interoperability relies on standards, but many of the standards in the digital library arena are suspect in terms of their quality, applicability and durability"(Caplan et al. 14). There is a recommendation that libraries develop architectural models of standards-based, content-neutral repositories to serve as a foundation for higher level standard services (McLean and Lynch 2004).

Digital repositories have become an essential foundation for delivering content, including scholarship, education, and cultural heritage. Some established reference models are beginning to emerge (e.g., Open Archival Information System [OAIS]). This content, however, exists in specific context.

Scholarship such as journal publishing and Electronic Theses and Dissertations (ETD) requires unique features for publishing, searching, discovery, and management. Education such as classroom instruction and distance learning often need their own metadata and workflows to achieve their goals. Cultural heritage programs have their own specific audiences and needs such as registration management. Therefore, all these communities tend to develop their own metadata element sets to fulfill their unique needs. Namely, Dublin Core, MARC, MODS, and METS for the library community, EAD for archives, IEEE LOM and SCORM for the learning community.

The current practice of encapsulating content within a well-defined, purpose-based repository limits its ability to be discovered and repurposed in new and innovative ways. The traditional and current practices of exchanging information across domains and systems include Z39.50 and OAI-PMH. These practices somehow provide simple and easy means to integrate content from different sources and systems. The meaning of the content, however, is described within the context of a specific community and is often bound to a specific application. Although it is possible to locate the information stored within the repository for a new use, it was not facilitated by the repository's architecture or the system. For example, a person searching for "American lion" will not be directly led to content that has been described with the term "puma," which is much more common in a controlled vocabulary set. The user may stumble across this information within the course of the search, but the connection is not facilitated by the current digital library infrastructure. To leverage legacy investments and continue to support needs of specialized communities, it is crucial to create a true interoperability environment where information not only meets the needs of specific communities but also can be shared with others.

INTRODUCTION TO THE JOURNAL DELIVERY PROJECT

The University of Arizona (UA) has been a part of AgNIC (www.agnic.org), an initiative of the National Agricultural Library (NAL), since 1995. The mission of the UA AgNIC project is "to provide electronic access to the full scope of information in the field of rangelands and rangeland management to people everywhere and of all knowledge levels by collecting, creating, evaluating, and organizing relevant resources." The UA AgNIC project team is composed of librarians, technical staff, and rangeland experts from several collaborating units in the UA Library and College of Agriculture and Life Sciences.

In April 2004, NAL announced that funding for small cooperative agreements was available to AgNIC partners to build full-text content, which can be delivered to users through AgNIC. The library submitted a one-year project proposal for digitizing 20 volumes (v.1–20, 1979–1998) of the journal *Rangelands* and providing open access to the journal. The proposal was funded and a working plan was developed, including copyright clearance, digitization standards and process, metadata crosswalk, and development of a journal delivery application.

AN RDF-BASED DIGITAL LIBRARY SYSTEM

The UA Libraries are conducting research on building a semantic digital library system, which can be used by libraries and cultural heritage and learning organizations to provide robust support for specialized applications while simultaneously providing a technical foundation for meaningful access of content across the information structures of specialized heterogeneous systems. In addition, cross-domain meaning will be established by encoding organizational tools such as taxonomies, controlled vocabularies, and thesauri in a machine-readable format so that essential links and crosswalks can be established. The building of a modular application on the semantic digital library system for journal delivery is a part of this research.

For the past six years, this research group has been evaluating and/or implementing several digital library systems to find a single digital library system framework to manage and provide access to our content. Like many libraries, our content is diverse and includes journal publishing and delivery, ETD, learning objects, archival materials, and museum items. The divergence of metadata standards and content formats among these specific domains and communities is necessary to address the specialized business and operational needs of these communities. It will continue to be an important attribute of the whole networked information environment for the foreseeable future. Therefore, there are valid requirements to meet special needs of these communities, but at the same time it is also crucial for users to be able to discover information across the domains and communities without having knowledge of all of the domains' specialized knowledge organization and system structure and services.

The systems that the UA Libraries evaluated and/or implemented include commercial and open source systems such as DSpace (www.dlearn.arizona.edu), Fedora, Greenstone, CWIS (www.grow.arizona.edu), and SiteSearch (jrm.library.arizona.edu) (Han 2004). Systems analysis defined various metadata and systems requirements and specified that a successful system should be flexible and accommodate multiple digital formats and multiple metadata standards with related services and tools to fulfill current needs. In addition, the design must be modular and standards-based so that it can interoperate with other systems and also accommodate future needs. A number of shortcomings in commercial and open source digital library products have been revealed (Fedora 2004). Some products have made progress in addressing some of the issues; however, the following disadvantages were found:

- All products are narrowly focused on specific metadata standards that offer good solutions for specific purposes. Library-focused products usually use Dublin Core (DC), METS, and MODS, while archival digital library systems tend to use EAD.
- Most products have a predefined hierarchical structure that limits users' experience (e.g., discovery, access) and administrators' management (e.g., categorizing, extending the hierarchy).
- Products did not allow for arbitrary, multiple semantic relationships to be encoded for objects and for meaning to be shared across domains and collections.

The UA Libraries discovered the Resource Description Framework (RDF) (www.w3c.org/RDF/) by the W3C. RDF, a core part of the Semantic Web, uses Uniform Resource Identifiers (URIs) to uniquely identify resources and provide a framework to describe a resource in terms of its properties and its relationship with other resources. RDF uses a *graph* of nodes and arcs representing the resources, and their properties and values (W3C 2004b). It is intended for situations in which this information needs to be processed by applications and other software agents, rather than being displayed directly to a user. It provides a common framework for expressing the information to be shared across applications. Since it is a common framework, application designers can leverage the availability of common RDF parsers and processing tools. The ability to exchange information between different applications means that the information may be made available to applications other than those for which it was originally created. As an example, the Dublin Core Metadata Initiative has adopted the RDF model (W3C 2004c).

The UA Libraries are building a system with multiple layers. The system is composed of:

- A storage layer that is standards-based, content-neutral, and metadata-extensible using RDF and RDF Schema (RDFS).
- A metadata management and semantics layer that can be used for metadata management (e.g., support multiple descriptive metadata formats and other types of metadata), ontologies, and taxonomy. Knowledge management such as transferring of meaning across domains is addressed in this layer.
- A common services layer that is standards-based and allows application-specific and heterogeneous access. For example, metadata services such as OAI-PMH, linking services such as OpenURL, and search service.

- An application layer on top of a common service layer that allows different applications to fulfill diverse needs of communities.

IMPLEMENTATION

The journal delivery application is the first step to build a specific prototype application based on the digital library system and work as a concept-proof project. The storage layer is the core part of any digital library systems. Digital library systems such as DSpace, CWIS, SiteSearch, and Greenstone usually have tight connection between systems' functionalities and their database schemas. Since a digital library system usually has its specific system and user requirements such as an intended metadata format, workflow, and user interface, it tends to have its own construct of multiple tables in database (e.g., Oracle, MySQL) to model complex relationship between entities.

Compared to complex relational database schema, entities in the RDF framework are simpler and more straightforward. There are only three entities in the framework: *subject, predicate,* and *object*. A subject or an object is a resource (a thing to be described), while a predicate, an aspect of a resource, expresses the relationship between a subject and object. In the RDF graph model, a subject or an object is a *node* and a predicate is represented as an *arc* in a graph. The three terms form a subject-predicate-object statement (called a *triple,* see Figure 10.1) and consequently multiple triples form an RDF graph (W3C 2004a, 2004b). The powerfulness of RDF lies in its graph model to describe the complex networked information environment.

The UA Libraries selected an open source RDF database, Sesame, as the storage layer for the semantic digital library system due to its popularity, support, and maturity. Sesame is an open source RDF database with support for RDF querying and inferencing. With support of several RDF query languages, it has flexible access API and good support (Broekstra et al. 2002). Building on top of the Sesame RDF database, the database schema has an extremely simple structure (see Figure 10.2), as it has only four tables: resources, triples, namespaces, and literals. Table "resources" stores subjects and objects, while table "triples" contains subject-predicate-object statements (triples). Consequently, the simple database schema also reduces programming efforts whenever there are needs to connect databases to perform queries. Database management issues are also reduced.

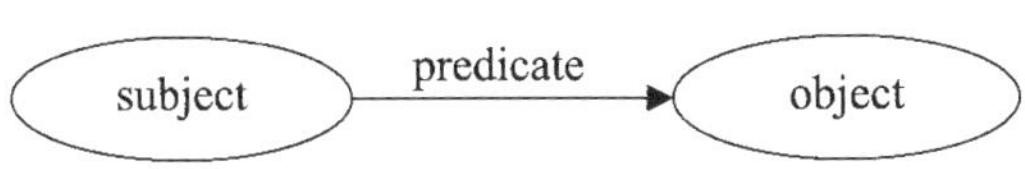

Figure 10.1. An RDF Triple (W3C 2004b).

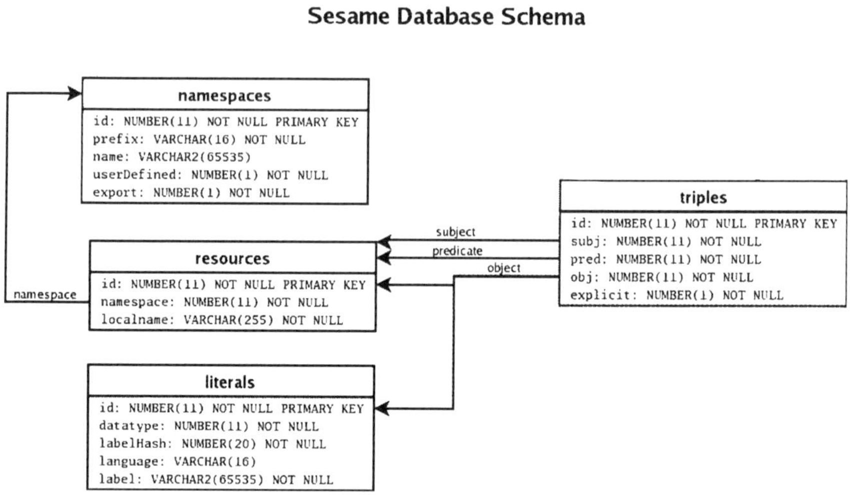

Figure 10.2. Database Schema for the RDF-based digital library.

The metadata management layer might be the most complicated layer in terms of the framework, design, and programming. To be a generic semantic digital library, it must be able to provide supports for multiple applications (e.g., the journal delivery application) by handling multiple descriptive metadata formats such as DC, MARC, and EAD. On the other hand, it may need to deal with other types of metadata such as technical metadata and preservation metadata. In addition, knowledge management requires complicated ontologies, a variety of controlled vocabularies, and multiple taxonomies to work together.

At this moment, a completed product to support multiple metadata formats is not available. Only qualified DC was implemented to handle all the needs of the journal delivery application. Some 1,220 MARC records were received from NAL, each of them corresponding to one article in the journal of *Rangelands*. Since the current metadata management layer is using qualified DC, a simple crosswalk (mapping) is necessary for transferring records in MARC to their counterparts in DC. MarcEdit contains an XSLT script that provides MARC to DC mapping based on MARC to DC crosswalks published by the Library of Congress. It is worth noting that "not all possible MARC fields are included in this mapping, but only those considered useful for broad cross-domain resource discovery" (Library of Congress 2001). The original script misses some important MARC fields, including 246 (alternative title), 300 (physical description), 651 (subject), and 773 (host item entry). These fields are significantly important for the collection and at the same time improve customers' experience in browse, search, and discovery. The XSLT script was modified to meet the need for mapping all related MARC elements.

In the common services layer, modules have been written to enable the current OAI-PMH metadata service and OpenURL linking service. These services will be common services not only for the journal delivery application but also for future applications.

The journal delivery application lives in the application layer. Based on systems analysis, the application must provide basic browse and search functions. For example, it must provide a hierarchical browse feature and search function for metadata fields such as author, title, and keyword. In addition, its user interface should be designed with information architecture in mind. The application is using Java Servlet and JavaServer Pages (JSP) technologies with Model-View-Controller (MVC) design pattern in mind. Since journals usually have a predefined hierarchical structure, the following classes are constructed in hierarchy: article, issue, volume, and journal. Corresponding helper classes are also designed to handle other interactions with the RDF database and display.

The application has been running since April 2005. With respect to UA Libraries' systems requirements, the author believes that the journal delivery application achieved its functionality. Furthermore, the application and its underlying architecture provide a solid basis for integrating other applications for their specific needs. The next step is to build an ETD application, which will handle ETD needs and be in the application layer by using the same storage and metadata management architecture.

SUMMARY

Starting with presenting the needs for a true interoperable networked information environment, this chapter describes some of current issues in current digital library systems and the lack of true interoperability across domains. The chapter reports that the UA Library's approach is to build a semantic, standards-based, and content-neutral digital library system. It is hoped that the semantic digital library system will be able to allow better interoperability. Extensive research has been carried out to investigate an appropriate framework to represent information resources in the system by using the RDF graph model. The system utilizes the RDF database as the core storage layer and allows an upper application layer to build specific applications to meet various needs. Experience shows that the use of the RDF database results in a very simple database schema and reduces programming efforts involving the journal delivery application.

ACKNOWLEDGMENT

This chapter is based on a proof-of-concept project at the University of Arizona Libraries. I would like to thank my colleagues' work and input for the project. Krisellen Maloney and Travis Bowen were very active in the project.

REFERENCES

Broekstra, J., A. Kampman, and F. Harmele. 2002. *Sesame: A generic architecture for storing and querying RDF*. The International Semantic Web Conference, Sardinia, Italy. Available at www.openrdf.org/doc/papers/Sesame-ISWC2002.pdf (accessed 10 August 2005).

Caplan, P., B. Barnett, L. Bishoff, C. Borgman, K. Hamma, and C. Lynch. 2003. *The report of the workshop on opportunities for research on the creation, management, preservation and use of digital content*. IMLS. Available at http://www.imls.gov/resources/resources.shtm (accessed 1 October 2004).

Fedora. 2002. *Mellon Fedora technical specification*. University of Virginia Library, Cornell University. Available at www.fedora.info/documents/master-spec-12.20.02.pdf.

Fedora. 2004. *Fedora, phase 2*. Available at www.fedora.info/documents/fedora2_final_public.html (accessed 1 October 2004).

Han, Y. 2004. Digital content management: The search for a content management system. *Library Hi Tech 22*(4): 355–365.

Library of Congress Network Development and MARC Standards Office. 2001. *MARC to Dublin Core crosswalk*. Available at www. loc.gov/marc/marc2dc.html.

Maloney, K., Y. Han, and T. Bowen. 2005. *A semantic RDF-based digital library system*. A proposal submitted to IMLS National Leadership Grants.

McLean, N., and C. Lynch. 2004. *Interoperability between library information services and learning environments—bridging the gaps: A joint white paper on behalf of the IMS Global Learning Consortium and the Coalition for Networked Information*. IMS Global Learning Consortium and CNI. Available at www.imsglobal.org/digitalrepositories/CNIandIMS_2004.pdf.

NASA—Consultative Committee for Space Data Systems. 2002. *Reference model for an open archival information system (OAIS)*. Washington, DC: NASA. Available at ssdoo.gsfc.nasa.gov/nost/wwwclassic/documents/pdf/CCSDS-650.0-B-1.pdf.

W3C. 2004a. *RDF primer*. Available at www.w3.org/TR/rdf-primer/#intro (accessed 1 October 2004).

W3C. 2004b. *Resource description framework (RDF): Concepts and abstract syntax*. Available at www.w3.org/TR/rdf-concepts/ (accessed 1 August 2004).

W3C. 2004c. *Resource description framework (RDF): Dublin Core Metadata Initiative*. Available at www.w3.org/RDF/ (accessed 1 August 2004).

11

Evolving an In-house System to Integrate the Management of Digital Collections

Marilyn Lutz and Curtis Meadow

LIBRARY ENVIRONMENT

As early as 1991, library staff began creating digital resources, although at the beginning, they did not adopt a strategic plan for the digitization of collections. While choosing a collection for digitization was not entirely serendipitous, it depended largely on the uniqueness of the resources and the availability of funding from grants. Staff did adhere to and adopt standards or "de facto" standards (where none existed) for each project to insure long-term accessibility and the usefulness of resources. Over the course of a decade, this "project approach" to building digital collections resulted in the proliferation of many separate databases, based primarily on varying formats and metadata requirements. Simultaneously, an information technology infrastructure evolved to support access to and distribution of digital content to the university community of users.

With initial success in creating digital resources, the library staff's traditional collection development and management responsibilities shifted to a planned approach in creating digital content, in providing access to digital content the library neither owned nor managed, in preserving and archiving content not accessible to users, and in serving as an access portal. This shift in digital collection development occurred as standards developed and new technologies evolved to support the integration of vast amounts of disparate information. User demands for "one-stop shopping" to meet information needs pushed the envelope. To accommodate this change, the library's information technology environment required a new architecture in which digital objects and metadata make sense within the context of individual projects but also serve as multipurpose "building blocks" for reuse in the context of other services.

Over the course of a decade, the library's digital collections grew, and so did the need for a solution to the "many databases" problem (Figure 11.1). At the University of Maine Library (UML), 14 digital collections had been created and were housed in separate databases structured around descriptive metadata unique to the digital objects managed but largely based on source records (MARC) from the online catalog. Each collection had different attributes that made searching across the collections difficult to achieve. UML needed more effective management of technical information (administrative and structural metadata) about these digital collections and an overarching design for managing metadata that would move away from "many databases" and move towards a more efficient and integrated management system. UML was also challenged by the problem of distributed indexing; a system that is physically distributed but logically centralized seemed difficult to realize. A new design should allow for the construction of collections that are independent of the locations of the documents in the collections. It also would address issues of accessibility over technology changes and more efficient storage management for large objects such as digital audio and video.

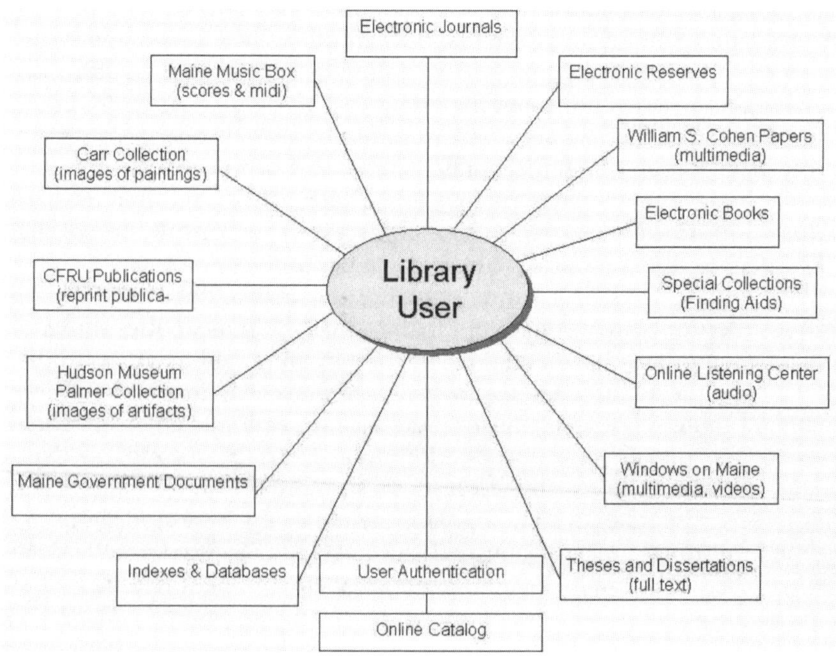

Figure 11.1. Digital Collections.

CMS ENVISIONED

The unavailability of off-the-shelf software and/or its cost led to a plan to develop a system in house, or at a very minimum to build elements of the infrastructure to manage the library's digital resources. "Freely" available software packages were in their infancy (Greenstone 2000; DSpace 2002; Fedora 2003). Budget constraints required the use of already-available resources as much as possible. The CMS that UML envisioned originally was a single database serving as a repository for harvested metadata from the many databases of digital objects, for it solved the problem of unified searching across databases. The CMS as a central repository had the added advantages of URN or DOI resolution; rights administration; and providing an access point for other metadata harvesters, in particular the Open Archives Initiative protocol (OAI-PMH).

While the CMS was originally envisioned as a repository for harvested metadata, the design was developed with the goal that the CMS would be the primary repository for new digital collections, thereby eliminating the need to build separate, standalone databases. With this in mind, the CMS was designed using the following broad goals:

1. It should be flexible enough to store multiple metadata schema about any digital object, including objects yet to be defined.
2. It should be able to present a meaningful end-user display of metadata for all types of digital objects.
3. It should be capable of indexing and retrieving different classes of objects in a manner appropriate to each class.
4. It should be able to provide information-sharing services with other information systems.

UML had a relational database management system RDBMS (Microsoft SQL Server 2000) with good full-text search capabilities, and given the economic constraints, UML used SQL Server to structure a content management system that would manage processes for digital resources; that is, capture, organize, and publish metadata about physically distributed collections. Features of the system included the ability to automatically import metadata directly into the underlying database using a metadata harvester and to validate data; remote entry and editing of metadata records from a web browser interface; mapping metadata to the Dublin Core standard; and authorization.

PILOT PROJECT (2002–2003)

Special Collections Finding Aids Database: Mapping XML Documents to an RDBMS Structure

From 2002–2003, working with Special Collections staff, UML developed a prototype system to manage digital objects using the EAD-encoded finding aids for Special Collections, and in particular, the finding aid for the William S. Cohen papers (Figure 11.2), an extremely lengthy (roughly 1MB) finding aid to both multimedia and paper content. Early on UML developed a template for encoding finding aids and storing them in a SQL Server database. Special Collections had over 100 other EAD-encoded finding aids to various Maine-related collections. While many of the finding aids are small enough for comfortable browsing, several are large enough that search facilities are required in order to use the finding aids effectively. As XML documents based on a standard document type definition (DTD), the finding aids were amenable to searching with XML Path Language (XPath) and XML Query (XQuery).

At the time, however, XQuery existed mostly as an incomplete specification, and direct browser support for XML was poor at best. Providing XPath search facilities would have required a computationally intensive process in which the XML parser executes a search specified in XPath and returns results in XML, which are then transformed using XML Style sheets (XSLT) into HTML that is viewable with the browser. Additionally, UML did not have a native XML database for storage of documents. Along with the tech-

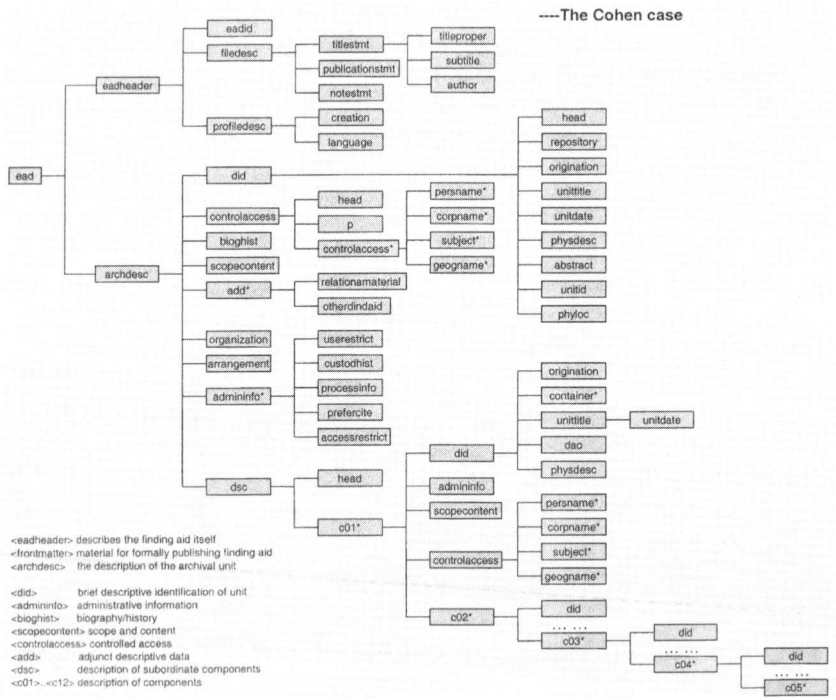

Figure 11.2. EAD structure brief overview.

nical difficulties of this approach, the limitations of XML for search purposes (XML documents, unlike a database, are not indexed; XML parsers offer no full-text search facilities) influenced the decision to map the searchable text in the XML documents into a relational database management system (RDBMS) with full-text search facilities (Figure 11.3).

The SQL Server database was designed to capture all the searchable information from the EAD-encoded finding aids using several sets of tables that correspond almost directly to certain elements of the EAD DTD, and a specific table that contains data to be indexed by the full-text search engine (Microsoft SQL Server 2000). A finding aid loads processed maps-indexed data into the database using two XSL Schema files and a series of transformation programs that alter the finding aid format to one that corresponds directly to the database structure. Searching the finding aids documents uses the RDB indexes and SQL. A document ID links search results to an XML filename, and XSL Style sheets (XSLT) are used to present the HTML contents.

In addition to the finding aids, a "digital objects" database was constructed as a searchable resource for finding and viewing digital objects associated with the Cohen collection. The finding aid itself indexes both the digital resources and the large quantity of paper documents included in the collection. The digital objects database essentially indexed only the DAO (Digital Archival Object) elements from the finding aids. The digital objects database was expanded to include other collections maintained by Special Collections, such as state government documents. The net result was a database covering multiple collections that could easily be searched with a single query. The digital objects database, based on the EAD structure, was viewed as the prototype system that might be expanded into a larger content management system with an associated metadata repository.

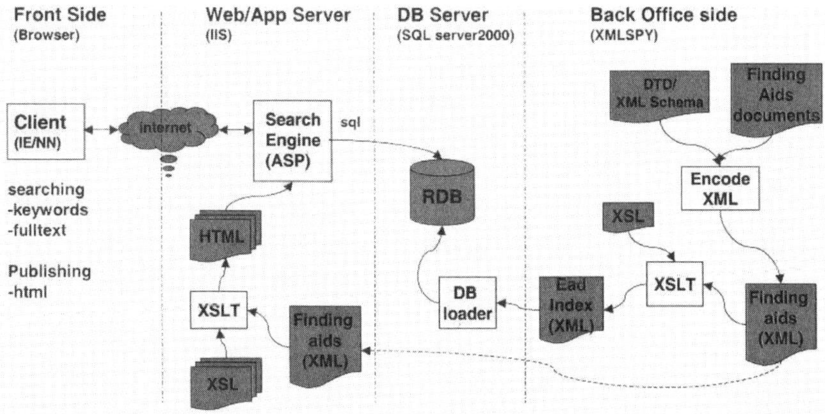

Figure 11.3. The Finding Aids system Architecture.

TRANSITION FROM PROTOTYPE TO CONTENT MANAGEMENT SYSTEM

CMS Foundation: Dublin Core Abstract Model

The Dublin Core (DC) Abstract Model was selected as the logical model for the CMS metadata storage. The DC Abstract Model is a schema for describing resources using (Element, Value) pairs that can be recursively resolved into elements from the Dublin Core Metadata Element Set. Because the Abstract Model defines an arbitrarily extensible cataloging schema, it is suitable as the foundation for a system intended to catalog arbitrary objects in the rapidly changing world of digital technology.

In the first phase of the transition from the Special Collections prototype to a design for the CMS, UML analyzed bibliographic, administrative, and structural metadata across databases. Based on the experience of developing the prototype and mapping the EAD-encoded metadata, UML examined the potential of mapping DC with qualifiers to a common element set for bibliographic metadata. UML was able to identify a common element set and adopt the schema as the foundation for the database structure.

Review of these collections yielded typical criteria and issues associated with digital library objects:

- Some objects were comprised of a single file, some were comprised of multiple files, and some had no files at all.
- Some objects have multiple representations. For example, a piece of sheet music might have image representations of the actual sheet music, text representations of the lyrics, audio representations of the music, and video representations of performers playing the music.
- Some objects are hierarchical in nature. For example, a single CD is an object, but so also are each of its tracks.
- Objects have a diverse range of access rights and authentication needs. Some objects are free for public access, some are available only to certain IP addresses, and some require barcode logins and are date-restricted.

The implications and decisions from this initial analysis were

1. The CMS would store structural and technical metadata: names and locations of files that comprise the digital object; information about how objects are displayed or presented; hierarchical structure; and associated descriptive metadata.
2. Every object would be stored with one and only one point of access (URL) in the CMS, even if multiple files or representations were stored.
3. The CMS would provide search and indexing only and would not be responsible for access authentication. If authentication was required, the point of access should point to the authenticator, not the object itself.

The last point imposes a requirement on any resource indexed by the CMS—that the application be capable of accepting an object identifier in a URL using a standard format, authenticating access if necessary, and then displaying the object appropriately.

COLLECTION-CENTRIC APPROACH

The CMS was designed to be flexible both in definitions of metadata elements and indexing for searching and browsing. The implication of flexibility is that rules have to be associated with digital objects at some level of granularity. At the lowest level, each digital object could have its own rules. At the highest level (the CMS itself), flexibility disappears because only a single set of rules exists. While per-object rule storage offers ultimate flexibility, it also imposes an unacceptable administrative burden in storage and management of rules. Clearly an intermediate level is needed.

UML decided to use the collection as a grouping level for storage of rules. Four types of rules or maps need to be stored for objects:

1. Metadata Harvest Maps (how the metadata elements of the object are mapped into the CMS)
2. Index Maps (which metadata elements are indexed)
3. Dublin Core Maps (how the internal storage is mapped to Dublin Core)
4. Display Maps (what elements are displayed and how they are labeled)

The initial population of the CMS resulted in over 35,000 objects harvested from 10 collections. UML stored only 10 sets of rules. The implication of the collection-based rule storage is that digital objects must belong to some collection. They cannot stand alone.

Collections are also a natural vehicle for viewing and browsing objects. Each collection normally has some primary entry point for end users. Collections are also hierarchical in nature; they can have subcollections. To accommodate subcollections, the collection subsystem was designed to allow a parent collection to be designated. This structure allows collections to be arbitrarily nested. Collections at lower levels do not need to have associated rules as the rules of the parent collection are used, and any object in a subcollection is also an object in the parent collection. The CMS also allows objects to be members of multiple collections. This approach not only makes it easy to browse objects at a subcollection level but it also makes it possible to include the same object in disparate multiple collections.

The collection structure also enables the CMS to function as a URI resolve if UML imposes a single constraint on any collection included in the CMS. Each collection has a single URL (the entry point for the collection). The constraint is simply that any collection must also have a URL that can accept a query string in the form "id=" followed by a unique identifier within the collection. This URL will perform authentication if needed and display the object if possible.

LOGICAL AND PHYSICAL DATABASE DESIGN

When considering any database design, it is important to distinguish the logical design from the physical design. The logical design shows how the database models the real-world objects that it describes. The physical design shows how the database is mapped into a set of tables or other structures in the specific DBMS in which the database is implemented. Differences between logical and physical design are particularly noticeable in relational database management systems, because the only structure available in a relational system is the two-dimensional table.

As previously noted, UML decided early in the design process that the CMS would be based on the Dublin Core (DC) standard. The Dublin Core standard by itself, however, is unsuitable as the basis for the physical database design for the following reasons. First, the DC core element set (DCMES) does not readily allow for administrative or structural metadata; it is primarily a bibliographic element set. Second, all DC metadata elements are inherently repeatable. Repeatable elements are a problem in only a few cases; title being the most prominent. Finally, "simple DC" using the DCMES is too broad for UML's purposes, e.g., UML would like to distinguish for display purposes authors, composers, and painters, all of which are tagged as "Creator" in simple DC.

The question of how to incorporate DC into the database design was resolved by treating DC as a communications channel or a view rather than a structure for database design. By "communications channel" UML means that the database is structured so that DC-tagged bibliographic metadata is acceptable as input and the database is capable of exporting DC-tagged metadata; in other words, the database can present a Dublin Core view of itself.

Because the CMS logical database structure closely parallels the Metadata Encoding and Transmission Standard (METS), it would be possible to add a METS map to the database and expose a METS view of the database as UMLll, or export the entire database or selected objects in METS XML format. The primary difference between the CMS physical design and METS is that the normalized relational design derived from Entity-Relationship modeling intermingles METS Administrative and Descriptive elements within single tables. METS does contain one structure that does not exist in the CMS design, the Behavior Mechanism Object (a description of and pointer to executable code), a model UML has discussed for the implementation of a central authenticator.

MAPPING METADATA TO AN RDBMS

The primary source of much of the metadata is in the form of MARC records from the online catalog. UML also mapped data elements from standalone systems that had arbitrary, collection-specific metadata elements that were often derived from MARC records. For example, Electronic Theses and Dissertations have a department that is cataloged as part of a 500 Note in MARC. The key to mapping cataloging metadata into a relational system is to identify single-valued and multivalued attributes. A multivalued attribute is a repeatable field in MARC terminology; for example, tag "650—Subject Added Entry—Topical Term." The reason that single-valued and multivalued attributes have to be identified is that they determine how data is stored in a relational structure.

Any metadata schema can be mapped to a relational database using a very simple schema that stores the name of the cataloging element with its value in a single metadata table. This is the approach apparently taken by the DSpace system. The schema (referred to below as the "Element, Value schema") in its simplest form has three columns:

ObjectID	identifier for the object
Element	cataloging element
Value	value of the cataloging element

The "Element" field stores the name of the cataloging element. A title derived from a Dublin Core system would have "title" in this field, and the title itself is stored in the "Value" field. A title derived from a MARC system would have (perhaps) "245$a" in the Element field and the title itself in the Value field. UML rejected this approach to a metadata storage structure for digital objects for several reasons:

1. The metadata table is very large, because each element occupies a single row, and the element name is stored together with its value. With metadata derived from a MARC system the cataloging data for a single object can easily occupy several thousand rows, because the basic unit of storage is the MARC subfield.
2. This table structure does not distinguish searchable from nonsearchable data. A search in this table has to explicitly name the elements to be searched in the WHERE clause of the SQL SELECT that performs the search. Search queries are difficult to construct and expensive to execute. SQL Server full-text search queries are even more difficult and expensive than the simple SELECT.
3. This structure does not distinguish single-valued and multivalued attributes. There is nothing inherent in the structure to prevent multiple

occurrences of Element 245$a. The distinction between single-valued and multivalued attributes determines where the attribute is stored. UML has only one entity of interest (the digital object). Single-valued (nonrepeatable) attributes of an entity are stored in a table with the relevant entity. Thus the title is stored in the Object table. Multivalued attributes (repeatable fields) are stored in separate tables.

4. Almost any RDBMS imposes an upper-size limit on character-data fields. In the case of SQL Server, this limit is 8,192. Cataloging data can sometimes exceed this size; for example, in a MARC 5xx Notes field. Where text to be stored exceeds this size, the RDBMS will provide a text or memo field type that allows unlimited text to be stored. But text or memo fields have limitations; for example, they cannot be used for sorting purposes.

Although this simple mapping was rejected for the object storage structure, UML does use it as part of the harvest process for MARC records described below.

DIGITAL OBJECT MANAGEMENT SYSTEM (CMS) 2004–2005

Basic CMS Bibliographic Structure

Bibliographic metadata is stored in a set of seven tables. The main table (Object) stores elements that UML treats as nonrepeatable. The other six tables store repeatable elements.

Object	Stores object identifier and nonrepeatable metadata elements such as title, publisher, and description.
Subject	Subject headings
ObjectDate	Any dates associated with the object
Contributor	Contributors of any type associated with an object
ObjectLanguage	Languages of the intellectual content of the object
ObjectRelations	Allows both internal object-to-object relations and object-to-external related object relations.
ObjectAttributes	A "catch-all" table that allows storage of arbitrary metadata elements not covered in other tables. This table implements the (Element, Value) schema, but only for a few, highly collection-specific elements.

The mapping between the relational structure outlined above and DC-tagged metadata is accomplished by the use of "type" fields in the tables that store repeatable elements. The "type" field is also used for display purposes. For example, the contributor table may contain:

Contributor Type	Qualified DC Element
Author	contributor.aut
Committee Chair	contributor.ths
Committee Member	contributor.ths
Vocalist	contributor.other

Here the DC contributor element has been qualified using MARC relator codes. The contributor type is used to provide an intelligible display of the record to the user. The structure allows UML to maintain distinctions (such as Committee Chair and Committee Member) that might be lost in translation to this particular qualified DC element. The elements that UML considers nonrepeatable are mapped to either simple or qualified DC elements.

The ObjectAttributes table corresponds to the simple (Element, Value) schema for mapping arbitrary metadata to relational databases that was described above. This table is one of the key reasons that the CMS is adaptable as a content management system to virtually any digital object type. It is a catchall table designed to allow storage of arbitrary attributes that are not otherwise captured in the relational structure. MARC has similar features for extensible cataloging; in particular, the 9xx fields are reserved for local implementation. The 5xx Notes fields are often used to store data that has no specific tag in MARC. Examples from ObjectAttributes table:

Department (Electronic Theses and Dissertations). Significant for display of theses; usually stored in a 5xx note field in MARC; no corresponding unqualified DC element.

Lyrics (Maine Music Box [sheet music scores]). Displays in full record display of sheet music; stored in a 5xx note field in MARC; no corresponding unqualified DC element.

The attribute name enables the CMS to provide an intelligible display of any object without presenting the user with technical cataloging terms. Because arbitrary attributes can be defined, the system is extensible as future collections are cataloged. The examples above demonstrate that UML can also store specific elements such as music lyrics that are not easily addressed in either MARC or DC.

OVERALL CMS ARCHITECTURE

The CMS database is divided into five separate areas, each with a different function.

1. Collections — Descriptive and administrative metadata describing the collections

2. Objects	Bibliographic, structural, and administrative metadata
3. Dublin Core	A set of tables that define a qualified DC schema and map the data in the Objects subsystem to the schema.
4. Metadata Harvester	A set of tables that describe how metadata in other systems are mapped into the Objects subsystem.
5. Index Harvester	A set of tables that define on a per-collection basis how elements from the Objects subsystem are mapped into the five full-text indexes.

Collections: The Collections subsystem consists of three tables. The primary table (Collection) provides a name, URL, and some descriptive metadata. Collections are linked by name to the metadata harvester where the input mappings are stored and to the index harvester where the index mappings are stored. This subsystem also has a table for re-mapping output labels from any source in the database. A third table defines element names used by the collection in the extensible ObjectAttributes table. For administrative purposes, the Collection table has an "Owner" attribute. This is used to assign rights to edit the collection.

The Collection subsystem is related to the Object subsystem through a table called "Contains." This table has only two columns: Collection and ObjectID. This very simple structure allows objects to belong to more than one collection.

Objects: The basic bibliographic metadata structure for the Objects subsystem was described above. Administrative and structural metadata are also stored in this subsystem. Some administrative metadata is embedded within the Object table, such as a suppress flag, create and update dates, and so on. Other administrative metadata such as object restrictions are stored in separate tables. Structural metadata is stored in a set of tables containing information about the actual files comprising an object. This information is related via file type to a MIME-type table that contains HTML templates that can be used to display an object.

Object Identifiers: Crucial to any object management system is the ability to uniquely identify any particular object with a single string of characters. Ideally, UML could use the Digital Object Identifier System (DOI) to provide the digital objects with unique identifiers that would be valid both within the system and outside the system. Budget constraints, however, precluded this solution because there is a cost associated with registering each digital object. For this reason, UML adopted an internal arbitrary unique identifier for each object (an 8-bit random number). This allows the CMS to be used as a local URI resolution system if needed. Given an object identifier, the CMS can produce its access point. Here the flexibility of the Dublin Core structure is an advantage. Identifiers are not normally repeatable elements in any system. Here UML has three identifiers: (1) Internal identifier, (2) Local collection identifier, and (3) Object URL. Each identifier can be presented in qualified DC (identifier.local, etc.), which resolves to elements in simple DC.

Dublin Core: This subsystem actually has two functions: It performs the mapping from the internal database structure to a Dublin Core view, and it also implicitly contains the "display rules" for tagging metadata in an end-user display. At the heart of the Dublin Core subsystem is a DC Element table. This table stores both qualified DC and simple DC element names. The structure of the table is designed to allow resolution of qualified names to simple DC ("dumbing-down") in either input or output of metadata. An example of mapping end-user display to DC qualified elements was discussed above.

Metadata Harvester: The Metadata Harvester consists of a set of tables in the CMS database, with a set of table-driven programs that interpret the content of the tables and execute queries to populate or update the database. The harvester currently has two input channels: (1) other databases that can be queried directly in SQL, and (2) MARC records from sources such as the online catalog.

Two different approaches to metadata harvest are possible:

1. The "push" approach—metadata sources publish metadata to be harvested.
2. The "pull" approach—the harvester visits sources and retrieves metadata.

OAI harvests use the push approach. Metadata sources publish metadata to an OAI-compliant repository that can be harvested by any OAI archive. UML initially considered using an OAI harvest process to populate the database but found that the system could not easily accommodate administrative and structural metadata. In addition, UML would have to construct both a collection-specific OAI provider and OAI harvester for each collection—not a trivial undertaking. Because multiple layers of maps are involved, the process is not easy to manage:

Collection (SQL Server) ->DC ->OAI provider ->OAI harvester ->DC ->DOM CMS

Compared with

Collection (SQL Server) ->SQL ->DOM CMS

The simplicity and low cost of the latter approach was appealing. UML decided to develop a custom harvester that uses the pull approach, as the metadata sources are stored in other, specialized relational databases as well as the proprietary online catalog in the form of MARC records.

Queries to other relational databases: When the harvest source is another relational database, metadata harvest is easy. The harvester opens a connection to the source database and executes a set of SQL queries. One table in the harvester subsystem specifies the set of SQL queries. The first query obtains a list of unique identifiers. The remaining queries are executed once for each identifier to obtain metadata. A second table in the harvester subsystem identifies each field returned by each query from the first table and specifies the destination field in CMS.

This structure is flexible, allowing a harvest from virtually any relational database, by mapping fields from one database into CMS fields. It is also slow and computationally expensive. Metadata sources in other relational databases, however, keep track of the last update to an object, so repeated harvests can return only new or changed objects.

Library of Congress Marc 21 XML Schema: LC's Marc 21 XML Schema is key to the MARC record harvest process. This is a simple and elegant schema for representing MARC records in XML. This schema can be used as a mechanism by which MARC records can be mapped to virtually any other cataloging system. The XML structure also is easily mapped directly to a relational database schema derived from MARC21Slim.xsd.

Ultimately all bibliographic data resides in either a <controlfield> element or a <subfield> element and can be obtained by either XPath queries to an XML file or SQL queries to the tables representing these elements. The simplicity of the structures used to represent MARC records in XML or a relational database, however, implies that the structures are not an efficient representation. One record in a MARC system can easily expand to several hundred <subfield> elements. This structure is in fact a variation of the simple (Element, Value) database representation of a cataloging system.

While not efficient for cataloging or application-building purposes, this structure is acceptable for the metadata harvester. The inefficiencies can be tolerated because of the infrequency of updates to individual objects. Because the structure has a relational representation, the same harvest process can be used for MARC records as well as metadata stored in a relational database.

UML has defined two input channels for the MARC harvest: online catalog review files that collect MARC records based on specific criteria and Z39.50 queries. The MARC—XML—SQL Server transformation process uses ZOOM—the Z39.50 Object-orientation Model to accomplish the transformation. In particular, UML uses Thomas Habing's Visual Basic Binding. For Z39.50 queries, the MARC loader can return MARC records in XML. For records collected in online catalog review files, the MARC loader first transforms the review file into an XML file that is then processed by the Microsoft SQLXML bulk database loader. Once the database has been loaded, the harvest process can run.

Index Harvester: The CMS contains material from a wide variety of digital collections. Each collection populates only a subset of available metadata elements, and some collections contain significant amounts of data stored as arbitrary elements or attributes, such as music lyrics. Some collections may contain data that is desirable for display but not for indexing.

In order to accommodate the indexing requirements of different collections, a table-driven index harvester (similar to the metadata harvester) was designed. A table-driven program reads the structures in the database. On a per-collection basis, the structures describe fields in specific tables that are indexed and the destination indexes. The index harvester copies data from the object metadata tables into the full-text table. For each collection, the tables to be indexed by the harvester are listed in a table. Then, for each listed table, the source columns (metadata elements) are listed in another table, along with one or more destination index columns. This process allows elements to be mapped into the indexes on a collection-specific basis.

EFFICIENT SEARCHES IN RELATIONAL STRUCTURED METADATA

One of the primary reasons for the design of the database was a more efficient structure for searching than the simple (Element, Value) schema. There are some efficiency problems associated with direct searches in the seven-table structure described above. In particular, because the data resides in separate tables, the database query engine has to "join" tables in order to perform a search involving several tables, such as a date-limited search for

Table 11.1. Technical Specifications for the CMS

RDBMS: Microsoft SQL Server 2000

Programming languages: Visual Basic.NET, VBScript, SQL Server T-SQL, JavaScript

Operating system: Microsoft Windows Server 2003 running IIS 6 Web Server

Web server scripting: ASP and ASP.NET

Metadata support: Dublin Core, MARC, design allows mapping to any other schema

Web presentation: OAI-PMH v. 2.0 compliant as a data provider; Z39.50 client

a particular subject. A simple keyword search would require the Object, Subject, Contributor, and ObjectAttributes tables to be joined—a very expensive operation. Database engines are designed to optimize joins, but the operation is still much more expensive than a simple index search.

Another problem arises in conducting full-text searches. This problem arises due to specific requirements of the DBMS (SQL Server), but any full-text search engine will impose similar requirements. Each table requires a separate full-text index, and each row in an indexed table must have a single-column primary key or identifier. The repeating element tables do not satisfy the second requirement, although UML could artificially impose a single-column identifier if UML wished. A more serious problem is that with separate full-text indexes for each table, the question of how to combine the separate relevancy rankings from each index is both problematic and computationally expensive.

The solution to the efficiency issue is to construct what UML calls a "full-text" table that contains text from all searchable fields. The object identifier identifies each row or record in the full-text table. Tables such as this, which contain redundant data, are normally very undesirable in a relational database because the redundancy imposes a dependency constraint. The full-text index table must be updated whenever any record is updated. Given the essentially static nature of the data, the dependency constraint is easily satisfied at low cost because updates are quite rare.

Going a step further, the full-text index was defined with five full-text fields, where the latter four are subsets of the first:

FT	All text associated with the object
TitleFT	Text from titles and alternate titles only
ContributorFT	Names of contributors and creators
DescriptionFT	Text from titles and descriptions
SubjectFT	Text from subject headings

This structure allows efficient searches to be conducted in any of five different areas, either by the full-text search engine or by direct query in SQL.

REVERSIBLE METADATA MAPPING

Mapping metadata from disparate systems into a single metadata schema populates the CMS. The current metadata maps are often "one-way" maps, primarily due to either concatenation of multiple source fields into a single destination field or to extraction or reformatting of data contained within a source field. It has become apparent that reversible metadata mapping would be a useful administrative tool to address application and display requirements that change over time, to track the source of data errors, and to correct erroneous data.

If display or search requirements change, the solution is normally a complete re-harvest, an expensive operation that can take 1 to 2 days for a large collection. With reversible metadata mapping, some re-harvest operations could be avoided by simply reformatting data internally.

The CMS provides end-user display of search results; some errors may be seen in the CMS before they are seen elsewhere. Without a reversible map, UML may not be able to pinpoint the source of the error in the original source. With a reversible metadata map, UML can find not only the exact source of the error but also could actually use the CMS to propagate a correction back to the source.

CENTRALIZED RIGHTS ADMINISTRATION

The CMS was designed to provide centralized rights administration and user authentication in the long run. To date, UML has not yet implemented this subsystem. Some of the issues that must be addressed include:

1. A flexible system for representing and storing rules for user authentication.
2. Whether the authentication programs should be implemented internally in the CMS or externally with the CMS pointing to the programs.
3. How to integrate disparate authentication lists into CMS (IP lists, patron/barcode lists, campus lists).

Currently the CMS operates under the rule that each collection is responsible for implementing its own rights administration. The CMS stores a URL that points to a collection-specific page for displaying an object. If authentication is required, the collection authenticates at this point of access. The problems of maintaining many different authentication systems with disparate data sources, however, are not much different from the problems of maintaining many different application-specific databases. If UML can build a single, central authenticator for all systems, it can reduce administrative costs considerably.

FUTURE DIRECTIONS: OBJECT-ORIENTED DATABASES

While relational databases are the current industry standard, another class of database management system began emerging in the early 1990s. Many of this new class of object-oriented database management systems (OODBMS) are still experimental in nature; some have been specially adapted to particular domains such as geographic information systems, and a few have emerged as robust, mainstream, general-purpose databases. Curiously, most of these "post-relational" systems actually have their roots in a pre-relational structure called a hierarchical database.

CONCEPT OF INHERITANCE

Object-oriented computer systems, whether programming languages, operating systems, or database management systems, share a common set of concepts and principles. All are based on the concept of an "object" as a computer model of a real-world entity. Objects have properties or attributes, which correspond to fields in a database or a metadata schema. Objects also have "methods," which are operations that act on an object or the data that comprises an object. Objects are typically defined by class definitions that specify the properties of the object and implement the methods of the object. Classes, however, can be defined as inheriting the properties and methods of another class. This concept of inheritance is what distinguishes object-oriented systems from conventional procedural systems.

Object types (or classes) created by inheritance have all of the attributes of the parent class but can add additional attributes necessary for the new class. Because the class (a database object itself) stores the definitions and methods (programs for accessing the data) the database remains manageable and easy to work with. New classes automatically inherit the methods of the parent class (unless overridden) ensuring that any code that works with the parent class will automatically work with new class.

CLASSES OF DIGITAL OBJECTS

When UML considered the domain of digital objects, it found a wide variety of object types with a wide variety of attributes. Attributes of one object type may be meaningless in terms of another object type. For example, duration is a property of digital audio and video objects that makes no sense for text objects, while the page count of a text object is irrelevant for audio and video.

In an object-oriented database, UML can define a hierarchy of digital objects:

Digital Object (Title, URL, Description)
- Text (Pages)
  - Image (Height, Width)
    - Moving Image (Duration)

Still Image (Color Depth)
Dataset (. . .)
. . .

Because hierarchies can be arbitrarily designed, UML can also design a collection-oriented hierarchy:

Digital Object (Title, URL, Description)
Maine Music Box Object (Rights)
Sheet Music (Pages, Height, Width)
Lyrics (Lyrics Text)
Audio (MIMEType, Duration)
Cooperative Forestry Research Unit Document (Pages, Rights)

Each subclass of digital object can be further subdivided, if there are distinguishing attributes to store for a particular subclass. In the first hierarchy example, all objects have Title, URL, and Description. But text objects also have Pages. Images also have Height and Width, while Moving Images also have Duration.

Object hierarchies also implement method inheritance. This means that a parent class can define a method that works for any object in the parent class and also for all child classes. The child class, however, can also implement the method and therefore override the parent class implementation.

Consider, in the simple hierarchy above, a method called DisplayBibData(). This method returns an HTML string that displays the bibliographic metadata associated with the object. For any object this will display the Title, URL, and Description. The Still Image class, however, could implement this method and also display Height, Width, and Color Depth. When an object reference is returned from a query, UML does not need to know or care what type it is. All UML needs to do is obtain the HTML string from DisplayBibData().

UML could also implement an Authenticate() method. At the Digital Object level this method might simply return the value True, corresponding to the assumption that all objects are accessible. Each object class can also implement the Authenticate() method, referring to internal object properties that determine the appropriate authentication technique.

WINDOWS ON MAINE, AN EXPERIMENT USING AN OODBMS

Work implementing an OODBMS to manage digital objects began a year ago with Windows on Maine, a pilot project to develop an online service offering streaming video programs and clips, and other primary and secondary digital resources, via broadband and wireless connections. It features a searchable database of complete programs and video clips from Maine Public Broadcasting Network and also includes a large number of related non-video, multimedia digital resources from cultural institutions in Maine.

UML selected Caché, the OODBMS from InterSystems Corporation, for two principal reasons: Caché is widely used in the health care and financial industries and has been shown to be a robust and stable system; and Caché projects both relational and object-oriented views of a database, thereby allowing easy integration with already existing application code and providing an easy transition from the relational world.

Using the relational database CMS structure UML had designed as a "universal" metadata structure, UML adapted this structure as the foundation design for the Windows on Maine database, a quick and easy process. This experience provided insight into how UML might merge the two systems in a full object-oriented database. The two different example object hierarchies referenced above exemplify the change in our approach. UML went into the Windows project with the file-centric approach illustrated by the first object hierarchy. UML quickly realized that this approach gained little over the relational solution of storing all possible attributes for all file types.

This is when the collection-centric approach again suggested itself. Certainly a moving image differs from a still image. But these differences are minor and are easily handled by a table-driven program that plugs values into parameterized HTML <object> templates. A far more significant distinction is that the image of a piece of sheet music is significantly different from the image of a piece of art, and both in turn differ from an image of a meeting taken from the William S. Cohen collection. They differ in that they are normally displayed in context (specifically, the collection context); and they are associated with different metadata elements.

The file-centric hierarchy can obviate the need for a small section of object handling code. The collection-centric hierarchy has the potential to eliminate the need for separate collection-specific applications by migrating the collection-specific code into the object hierarchy in the database. While the CMS in its current state has eliminated the need to build new, separate databases for new digital collections, each collection still has its own application. A transition to an OOD would allow the CMS to act as the repository for application code as well as metadata and could significantly speed the development of new collection interfaces.

LOOKING FORWARD . . .

In the approach to developing a digital content management system, UML adopted a plan that would meet the increasing needs of the library to capture, organize, publish, and disseminate digital collections in an integrated technology environment. Broad goals guided the system development: to provide for flexible, standards-based metadata management, to facilitate end-user access to multimedia digital collections, to build powerful indexing and retrieval tools to encompass the width and depth of collections, and to support access through standard protocols. The key to the system design is metadata: mapping, transforming, and managing the processing of MARC-based metadata into non-MARC schemes to build digital collections. UML anticipates that the design of the CMS positions UML to leverage the investment for integrating and adapting to future technology developments. Meanwhile, the work is incomplete, and the vision of migrating from the relational database structure to an object-oriented database management system has yet to be realized.

WEBSITES OF INTEREST

Digital Object Identifier System
www.doi.org/
Dublin Core Element Set
dublincore.org/documents/dces/
Dublin Core Abstract Model
dublincore.org/documents/abstract-model/
www.ukoln.ac.uk/metadata/dcmi/abstract-model/2003-08-11/
Encoded Archives Description (EAD)
www.loc.gov/ead/
Content Management System (CMS) (University of Maine)
libraries.maine.edu/gateway/
InterSystems Caché
www.intersystems.com
Library of Congress MARC 21 XML Schema
www.loc.gov/standards/marcxml/
Library of Congress METS Schema
www.loc.gov/standards/mets.xsd
MARC21Slim.xsd
www.loc.gov/standards/marcxml/xml/spy/spy.html
Open Archives Initiative Protocol for Metadata Harvesting (OAI-PMH)
www.openarchives.org/OAI/openarchivesprotocol.html
Thomas Habing's Visual Basic Binding
zoom.z3950.org/bind/vb/
vb-zoom.sourceforge.net/API.html
Windows on Maine
windowsonmaine.library.umaine.edu
ZOOM: The Z39.50 Object-Orientation Model
zoom.z3950.org/index.html

REFERENCES

DSpace. 2002. *DSpace version 1.1, MIT and Hewlett-Packard.* Available at libraries .mit.edu/dspace-mit/technology/system-docs/index.html

Fedora. 2002. *Fedora technical specification version 21.0.* University of Virginia Library and Cornell University. Available at www.fedora.info/; www.fedora.info/documentation/

Hurley, B. J., J. Price-Wilkins, M. Proffitt, and H. Besser. 1999. *The making of America II testbed project: A digital library service model.* Council on Library and Information Resources: Washington, DC. Available at www.clir.org/pubs/reports/pub87/contents .html and particularly, *part II: The MoA II digital library service model,* available at www.clir.org/pubs/reports/pub87/part2.html

Jeffrey, K. G. 1998. *What's wrong with the Dublin Core?* Available at www.ub.uib.no/ avdeling/fdok/cris/taskgroups/WhatsWrongWithDC.htm.

The Dublin Core working group in the development of the DC Abstract Model has addressed many of the issues discussed.

Kurth, M., D. Ruddy, and N. Rupp. Repurposing MARC metadata: Using digital project experience to develop a metadata management design. *Library Hi Tech* Volume 22, Number 2: 2004. Available at www.emeraldinsight.com/0737-8831.htm

Library of Congress. 2003. *METS: An overview and tutorial.* Available at www.loc.gov/ standards/mets/METSOverview.v2.html

Witten, I. H., and S. Boddie. 2003. Greenstone digital library version 2.6. New Zealand Digital Library Project at the University of Waikato, Hamilton. Available at www.greenstone.org/cgi-bin/library?e=p-en-home-utfZz-8&a=p&p=docs

12

Winning the Peace: An Approach to Consensus Building When Implementing a Content Management System

Edward Iglesias

Trying to implement a technological change in an academic environment requires dealing with viscosity. While there may be little apparent resistance to new projects, it may be impossible to get traction. Most of the articles and books published on the subject of using a Content Management System (CMS) in libraries focus on the technical details of setting up such a system as well as how to populate and customize the system. This article is not about such technical minutiae, but rather the often overlooked aspect of getting library staff to contribute and feel a part of the implementation of the CMS. Because a CMS is incredibly customizable with features that can be turned on or off, there is an imperative that as much information as possible be collected by the aspiring CMS administrator if such a system is to take hold. While it is a relatively simple matter to set up such a system, shaping and customizing it for the optimal use of staff is another matter.

PLANNING

An often overlooked aspect of introducing new technologies into the library environment is the need for formal technology planning. In his book on the subject, Joseph R. Matthews points out that "fewer than 30 percent of America's schools possess a written technology plan."[1] This will obviously vary greatly by the institution; however, there must be at least general backing and understanding by the staff who will be implementing the plan as well as support from administration. The good news is that technology planning does not have to be long and difficult. The key is to set ground rules early on and have a plan that involves:

- Evaluation
- Stakeholder involvement
- Needs assessment
- Infrastructure assessment
- Implementation
- Assessment and reevaluation

EVALUATION

The first step must be to evaluate what web technologies are currently being used. Evaluation of a website can be internal or external but is usually a combination of both. Pixey Anne Mosley in her 2003 article refers to this as "Realizing the Need."[2] In Mosley's case, LibQUAL provided some insight into the nature of the library's website. Daily interactions often provide more immediate evidence of issues with website design. This may manifest as student complaints or troubling web server statistics. Other obvious signs include content that is out of date or appears dated. Any of these are indicators of the need for library website reevaluation.

In "Web Site Redesign: Knowing When It's time,"[3] Kim Guenther addresses the critical issue of timing and what the signs are that an "overhaul" is necessary. Ms. Guenther observes that:

> While redesigns aren't usually driven solely by content management issues, growth in new content and the need to rearrange or retire existing content can be a primary driver.
>
> Paradoxically, the use of a Web content management system (CMS) can actually exacerbate the problems of "cube farm" design since a CMS makes developing a web site easier.[4]

Here we see one of the dilemmas of CMS implementation. It may make things worse. Years ago at a LITA conference the author had the opportunity to hear a speaker on open source tools. The speaker referred to them as kitchen-sink items that would be used as needed once staff know they were there.[5] This could cause some real problems if there is no agreement on style of content, templates, and some sort of editorial review. All of these issues can be dealt with through a good CMS and effective templates, assuming there is consistent staff buy-in.

Obtaining this kind of staff involvement and cooperation is far from an easy process. Many times there are conflicting visions of what the website should be. One librarian may find it very important that the site be fast loading and usable while another may want a flash tutorial. Some may find the language used to be a huge issue. One way to defuse or at least mitigate some of these conflicts is to use tools to help objectify the problem and build consensus.[6] Another factor to keep in mind is that other departments are likely to want a say in the look and feel of the final website. One example in the author's personal experience involved the university publications department wanting an exact shade of maroon in the header. The fact that this color did not exist in HTML did not seem to matter.

STAKEHOLDER INVOLVEMENT

There are many good resources on consensus building,[7] but the main point is to include the stakeholders early on. This does not mean everyone has to be on the committee/team/working group. It does mean that everyone in the library who will be affected should feel they have some representation. A meeting where everyone in the library is invited to brainstorm some of the difficulties and benefits of the current website is a good way to discover and quantify underlying issues and interests of different constituencies. There should be an understanding that these are just some of the library's constituents. Others include users, administration officials, public relations (PR), and information technology (IT). Getting these stakeholders involved at the beginning can save a lot of time down the road.

Once there is a group, a moderator should be appointed to keep the peace. This needs to be someone with "mediation skills" and whose job is "to get agreement at the outset on how the group wanted to proceed."[8] It is important to remember, "consensus does not mean unanimity" but that "everyone agrees they can live with the final proposal."[9] Obviously, this method will only work if the participants feel they have a voice in choosing the product early on. If one person is firmly set on using Drupal because it can be installed quickly on the server and at minimal expense, while another member feels that a formal RFP must be put forth, there must be exploration as to why these positions are held. Perhaps that institution requires a formal bidding process. Perhaps the IT department has just purchased a portal product that will not interact with your proposed solution. Library technology planning and deployment must be placed within the larger institutional context.

NEEDS ASSESSMENT

Many of the issues listed above can be dealt with by doing a thorough needs assessment. This helps everyone start on the same page. This should be a familiar process by now to most librarians and can include such tools as surveys, usability studies, and gap analysis.[10] One often overlooked area is workflow management. Suppose there is a dedicated web designer who converts content from MS Word files to HTML. Thought must be given as to where this person will fit in the new workflow. There may be new skills involved in maintaining a CMS that the web designer does not possess. Issues of job description and retraining may arise. While a designer usually thinks in terms of overall website design and usability, the toolkit for implementing his or her vision will have changed. Instead of designing pages from scratch, most of the work will involve modifying templates. Additionally, the web designer may fall into a teaching role for the new staff who will have to be trained to use the CMS. Other aspects of CMS likely to change a job description are the administration tasks. Someone on staff will have to focus on backups, updates, and permission structures. It is important to work out a service level agreement with IT so that there is a clear understanding of where these duties fall. Martin White makes the observation on workflow management that:

> Often organizations think they have such procedures, but they tend to be flexible, with the organization almost self-adjusting to the resignation of a member of staff or a departmental restructuring. That is very difficult to engineer in workflow software terms, especially when two or more workflows meet in the middle, such as the preparation of an annual report . . .[11]

Whatever instrument is used, it must take into account not only the needs of the users who visit the system from outside but also the needs of those who will have to publish content on the system.

INFRASTRUCTURE ASSESSMENT

After evaluating user needs it is critical to look at infrastructure. If the preferred library solutions run on a type of platform that is not supported by IT, some adjustment may be necessary. Decisions must be made early on regarding organizational priorities and mission. If accessibility is a primary concern this will tend to trump many design decisions. Bandwidth can become a major consideration depending on the type of content that will be hosted. One way to look at these issues is to impose a hierarchy such as:

- Accessibility is more important than usability.
- Usability is more important than design.
- Content is more important than all of the above.

IMPLEMENTATION

Once evaluation has taken place and decisions have been made, it is time to implement. There will need to be installation of a test environment to get the bugs out, staff training, and eventually a "go live date." Taking these in sequence, the test environment is very important. Initially someone will have to take on the role of systems administrator and set up templates, create user accounts, and set parameters. This will include policy decisions that will assign staff roles such as who is a "content creator" and who can "publish." Other tasks will include deciding what format data must be in before uploading into the CMS and arranging for regular backups as well as all the other tasks that come with a system of this type.

Staff training should have been part of the plan from the beginning, but now it will be time to implement this as well. Staff should have a "sandbox" on which to experiment. Some of the staff used to working with HTML will probably have to learn different markup schemes and may experience frustration at not being able to do tasks that used to be routine. Uploading large files with many individual pages, for example, might not be possible in some systems and should not be circumvented due to data integrity issues. On a side note, staff retraining should be part of any CMS deployment plan. Staff will want to learn basic features at first but will undoubtedly have new projects that will require different skills. A departmental secretary may start out only wanting to be able to edit a contact list but may soon need the skill to create new pages using a variety of templates. Reference librarians often need to create specialized pages with pathfinders or webliographies that are subject-specific. This should be encouraged as long as everyone understands the ground rules and abides by them.[12]

ASSESSMENT

Assessment is an integral part of any technology plan and a helpful way to set goals and assess progress in a regular manner. If the move to a CMS came out of an assessment instrument such as LibQUAL, then there is an objective way to evaluate growth already in place. Even in this case, however, implementation of a more customized survey instrument may be necessary for a variety of reasons, ranging from the need for more specific data to an instrument that focuses on process more than outcome. Whatever the case, there should be a focus on how the CMS is serving the core mission of the institution. If one of the goals in the mission statement is to empower users, a method of quantifying this outcome must be established. An outcome such as "empowered five librarians to publish subject-specific bibliographies" tends to convey more than "allows users to create web pages." Specificity is crucial. If one of the library's goals is cost cutting then there must be a way to measure it. Time and subject expertise must be factored into cost analysis. If a webmaster position is eliminated but a Unix Systems Administrator is added, the library may have incurred more costs. Similarly, if everyone in the library is expected to change workflows there must be compelling, measurable reasons for doing so. Thinking users will like it more without any evidence is unlikely to be sufficient. Wayne Powell and Chris Gill put together a list of lessons learned that has as their first item "Get buy-in from the top."[13] The only way to do this on a consistent basis in today's academic environment is to focus on assessment and measurable outcomes. The plan may not work perfectly, but there does have to be a reasonable expectation of mission fulfillment and user satisfaction.

CONCLUSION

The process of implementing a CMS is long but worthwhile. If there is sufficient buy-in from the various constituencies, with good planning and assessment there will almost certainly be success. This success can be measured by the participation of staff who had never contributed to the library website, the improved architecture of the website in general, and the ability of users to find what they need in a more efficient manner. Additionally, as content is created in a more uniform manner with appropriate metadata, this opens up possibilities for future technologies that may be leveraged in future redesigns. CSS and HTML are only the beginning. As CMSs become more sophisticated in storing their data in XML, the way is cleared for a variety of interfaces improving user experience and driving users to library content. Perhaps future plans will involve experimental search interfaces such as XML Topic Maps as front ends or customizable environments where users are able to log in to the areas that interest them.[14] More importantly, it will be relatively trivial to set up environments that allow users of adaptive technologies to find their way to the libraries' rich content. Further developments with AJAX[15] (Asynchronous JavaScript And XML) technologies suggest that the idea of a static and passive web is giving way to a Web 2.0[16] type of environment where users help determine content. None of this is possible unless the idea of static web pages, based on HTML and magically placed on the web by the select few with FTP accounts to the server, is abandoned. In its place we need to look to our websites as social constructs potentially co-developed by any user with an interest and ability. At the same time, CMSs provide a way to ensure that content standards are maintained while making the publishing of that content a role that is not only available to all staff but also encouraged. Finally, CMSs are a sign that the technology of the web is maturing. Just as every staff member needs to be comfortable enough with a computer to use some form of office application, so must we expect new staff to feel comfortable with the web as just another medium. CMSs simplify this process by removing unnecessary barriers caused by outdated technological models left over from a bygone era. Some librarians will always be more comfortable creating web pages from scratch, fearing a loss of control. The library as a whole must decide if the core responsibility of librarians is to create content or create websites. If the primary role of the librarian is still to provide access to information through the use of finding aids, bibliographies, and search tools, then the CMS is an ideal environment in which to pursue these tasks. The true value of libraries and librarians lies in their uniqueness. Anyone can create a website. Only librarians can create authoritative metadata or subject bibliographies trusted by the public. The key to letting librarians do what they do best is to implement technologies that lower the barriers to effective content creation. Fast, easy creation of content as well as better search capabilities and display options make CMSs a natural choice in a library environment.

NOTES

1. Joseph R. Matthews, *Technology Planning: Preparing and Updating a Library Technology Plan* (Westport, CT: Libraries Unlimited, 2004), 2.
2. Pixey Anne Mosley, "Re-creating a Web of Service at TAMU with a Content Management System," *Texas Library Journal* 79.1 (2003): 18–19.
3. Kim Guenther, "Web Site Redesign: Knowing When It's Time," *Online* 29 (2005): 58.
4. Guenther, "Web Site Redesign."
5. May Chang, LITA (2004).
6. The National Parks Service has an excellent site of tools available online at www.nps.gov/phso/rtcatoolbox/index_comtoolbox.htm
7. See "A Short Guide to Consensus Building" available at web.mit.edu/public/disputes/practice/cbh_ch1.html
8. "A Short Guide to Consensus Building," 2.
9. "A Short Guide to Consensus Building,"3.
10. For a really good start see Guenther, "Key Steps to Guide Your Planning Process," 60.
11. White, "Managing Content Management System Selection," *EContent* 25 (2002): 42–43.
12. See the note on "cube farms" above.
13. Powell and Gill, "Web Content Management Systems in Higher Education," *Educause Quarterly* 2 (2003): 43–50.
14. See SIRSI's "Rooms" concept.
15. See en.wikipedia.org/wiki/AJAX.
16. See en.wikipedia.org/wiki/Web_2.0.

REFERENCES

Guenther, K. 2005. Web site redesign: Knowing when it's time. *Online* 29: 58.

Matthews, J. R. 2004. *Technology planning, preparing and updating a library technology plan*. Westport, CT: Libraries Unlimited, 2.

Mosley, P. A. 2003. Re-creating a web of service at TAMU with a content management system. *Texas Library Journal* 79.1: 18–19.

Powell, W., and C. Gill. 2003. Web content management systems in higher education. *Educause Quarterly* 2: 43–50.

White, M. S. 2002. Managing content management system selection. *EContent* 25: 42–43.

13

Enterprise Content Management System (CMS) for a University Photographic Museum: A Case Study of Selecting a CMS for Integrated Collections

Yu Su

University libraries, like other large enterprises, have seen dramatic changes in the last decade. New technologies have presented libraries with extraordinary new opportunities, and along with those developments have come fundamental changes in the function of their information technology (IT) management. As businesses are increasingly relying on a global IT workforce and commercially available off-the-shelf software to address IT needs, colleges and universities have also seen the shift away from self-built systems and have invested more efforts in evaluating and acquiring commercial products. In a complex organization like a modern university and its libraries, the IT department is no longer developing and implementing information systems in the traditional way but focusing on the positioning of IT to support business strategies. Specifically, integrating new and continually evolving IT applications with the rest of business operations is viewed as critical (Tanniru 2005).

Having always been stewards of knowledge and information in society, university libraries, museums, and archives face the challenge of how to manage it effectively in the digital age. Because these organizations are usually complex and perform a wide range of functions, it is often a demanding task to even comprehend all the needs and issues as a whole. Consequently, "content management system (CMS)" has been loosely used to refer to any software system that performs some aspects of management of any information content, ranging from data repository and records manipulation to file directory and website management. Further, content is no longer specific to a certain type or format, nor is it specific to a certain location of the information, such as a book catalog, an archival finding aid, or a museum catalog. This changing concept of content contributes to the evolving complexity of content management.

While many current publications on CMS focus on web content management systems, the definition of content management goes beyond an organization's website. This chapter will take a close look at content management in the context of the enterprise of university libraries and discuss how one software system has been selected to meet different needs in managing and integrating museum, archive, and library collections. The particular case of selecting and implementing a CMS at the Center for Creative Photography at the University of Arizona will exemplify the accomplishments and lessons constituted by and for the new IT project management in the age of software acquisition.

THE NEED FOR AN ENTERPRISE CMS

The Center for Creative Photography (CCP), a division of the University of Arizona (UA) Libraries, is a world-renowned photographic museum and research center. Founded in 1975 by Ansel Adams and then UA president John P. Schaefer, the CCP is based on a novel idea of not only being a repository of historical materials but also an active research center and exhibition space to facilitate a wide range of audiences from advanced scholars to an expanding public interested in photography. This foundational idea is reflected in the three components of the CCP's holdings: a photographic collection of around 80,000 fine prints, a research library, and an archive of 3.8 million items including artists' journals, correspondence, and personal memorabilia. Besides his archive of more than 2,500 fine prints, Ansel Adams also entrusted the CCP with his decades of papers and correspondence, negatives, cameras, work prints, and even personal items such as his trademark hat. Today the CCP is the home of the life-long work of over 50 photographers. Its curatorial philosophy is not to seek perfect-but-isolated masterpieces but to collect an artist's body of work and the surrounding documents (Rule and Solomon 2002). This approach allowed the CCP to create interrelated subject matters so that the individual works of the artist are interconnected with his/her journals, correspondence, diaries, and other documents. For example, in the web environment, when a user clicks on a photograph, they would have the opportunity to explore digitally these related materials through web links. This positions the CCP to pursue high interconnectivity in interpreting its holdings and presenting photography as a process of art creation.

Despite the richness of its content, the CCP had few ways to present its treasure to the world. Its photographic collection was indexed in half a dozen binders for onsite use only. While the fine prints were cataloged and stored in a nonrelational database known as InMagic, acquisition decisions and registration information were handled through a combination of email messages, InMagic records, and registrars' own filing systems. Only a small portion of the CCP's 3.8 million archival items were described in 200 some finding aids, and only 8 of these finding aids were arranged with the Encoded Archival Descriptor (EAD) and were actually searchable online. This archive, the largest collection of North American photographers' archives in the world, was housed in boxes and folders and only benefited those who could make a trip to Tucson, Arizona, for a personal visit. Bibliographic holdings at the research library, although searchable through the Online Public Access Catalog of the UA Libraries, were completely separate from the photographic collections and the archive. In the 2002 introduction book of the CCP, *Original Sources*, it was stated that ". . . an international audience experiences the Center, not through these physical spaces, but through publications such as the scholarly journal, catalogs, the newsletter, and through traveling exhibitions originating at the Center." Like most art museums prior to the digital revolution, the CCP's website was nothing much more than a bulletin board offering "information about current exhibitions and programs, new publications, rights and reproductions, traveling exhibition schedules, and how to make appointments to use the Research Center and PrintViewing facilities" (Rule and Solomon 2002).

Looking for an institution-wide CMS was triggered by a digital initiative and a massive digitization plan of the CCP to make a complete online presentation of its content. This five-year initiative, started in 2004 and led by the fourth director of the CCP, Dr. Douglas R. Nickel, aims at activating the archive, bringing the life work of the world's most important photographers to the web, and making them accessible to those of all ages and educational background. In order to support these public web presences, a solid data foundation including unified collections and fully developed metadata will be the first step toward the goal. Over the years, however, different departments of the CCP have developed their own protocols, and information about the collections as well as individual records were dispersed as well. These situations created an obstacle to integrating the holdings of the CCP and revealed the need to centralize the data into an institution-wide system.

THE SELECTION METHODOLOGY AND THE REQUEST FOR PROPOSAL PROCESS

Starting in 2004, the CCP staff has developed a series of scenarios to envision the future functions of the web collections. These scenarios, created by two archivists, two curators, and one museum cataloger, encompass a wide range of innovative ways that the future CCP customers could explore its web collections. One scenario created by archivist Amy Rule provides the following details:

> A researcher is writing an article about the role of photojournalist scripting or directing the action in documentary photographs. He/she is familiar with W. Eugene Smith's photo essay for *Life* magazine titled "Spanish Village," and wonders how much Smith had to do with setting up the scenes and how much control he had over the final product in the published essay. Through a simple search by the photographer's name, the researcher learns that we have an array of research materials. We have:
>
> - Portraits of Smith
> - Books in our library about Smith
> - Photographs by Smith cataloged in our fine print collection
> - Archival materials about Smith and his career

By choosing to pursue the link to archival materials, he/she is given these options:

- Look at the Finding Aid
- Look at scans of selected archival materials related to most important projects
- Do a keyword search of Smith archival materials

The researcher knows that he/she wants to see "Spanish Village" materials, so any of the three choices would be useful. If he/she looks at the Finding Aid, it is possible to search the terms "Spanish Village" to see the descriptive inventory. They would also have the choice to look at scans selected by staff of important components of "Spanish Village." This would include scans of the published essay in *Life* magazine. These could be compared with scans of all the contact sheets, front and back, with Smith's annotations. By examining these, the researcher could use the contact sheets to learn how Smith approached his subject matter, how he directed his subjects, and which views were excluded from the final product. The researcher could also look at scans of the pocket diaries Smith kept on this assignment, reading for relevant commentary on his work in the field.

Once the researcher has examined these materials online, it is important for him/her to know what additional materials exist that have not been scanned and are not online. We could make this point obvious in the Finding Aid, allowing the researcher to plan to come to Tucson to conduct in-person research of numerous other archival materials such as captions and story scripts as well as letters between Smith and his editors at *Life* magazine.

The researcher will also find intuitive, easy links to information about:

- Making research appointments (with confirmation return email)
- Policies about copying archival materials
- Guidelines for citing our website in publications and copyright guidelines

Functional scenarios like this one later became major criteria in the selection process of the CMS. Vendors were asked to respond in detail how their product would accommodate these types of encounters and provide the best possible foundation to deliver interrelated data as described in these scenarios. This process-oriented method effectively examined the flexibility and overall capability of each candidate system and helped overcome the weakness of a specification-oriented requirement list.

In August 2004, a project group was formed to create a Request for Proposal (RFP). This group had a combined expertise in archiving, cataloging, registration, curation, information technology, and digital projects. The museum CMS project was positioned to meet requirements from the photographic museum collection, the archive and the research library of the CCP. It was also a shared expectation that this CMS must fit into the rest of the infrastructure of the UA Libraries for future growth and expansion. The target goals for this system are as follows:

1. Standards-based connectivity and extensibility: Records from the photographic collection should be integrated with the archival finding aids and bibliographic records from the research library. There needed to be a framework to allow additional data fields and linkages to be established in order to accommodate future growth of the collections. The CMS should be able to accommodate potential connection with content from other major museums and art collections in future. There had to be a platform for web development to utilize new web technologies and deliver electronic content.
2. Good search capability and easy-to-use interface: There had to be good search capability within the system, and it should also support external searching functionalities of both the photographic collections and the archive via the web. The system should have the ability to function under a single interface and manage information of a variety of types including objects, images, texts, and sound recordings. An easy-to-navigate interface design was a must to keep any interference or confusion at a minimum level for staff working with the system on a daily basis.
3. Integrated information management framework and tools: The system should provide a framework for tracking a variety of collections-related activities, including task management for acquisition, cataloging, exhibition, photo reproduction licensing, and various accesses

to collections. A flexible tool set for customized functions such as report writing and data import/export was required to provide staff with the ability to use data for a broad range of purposes; for example, education, research support, and various administrative responsibilities.

Based on these goals, the RFP detailed requirements in three areas: Vision and Discovery, System Specifications, and Technical Requirements. Weight was assigned to each of these areas as well as other sections, i.e., pricing and after-sales support. This way, the final evaluation matrix could be kept within the predefined parameters, because sections with more questions were not necessarily more important than those with less.

The first area, Vision and Discovery, was weighted 35 percent in the evaluation matrix. It was a collection of six user experience scenarios describing what the CCP collections would support at the completion of this project. (One of the scenario's content was explicated in the synopsis from Amy Rule, which was inserted above.) Derived from the scenarios that the CCP staff developed, these six "stories" covered user perspectives from curator, researcher, faculty, student, enlightened collector, and virtual customer respectively. The vendors' systems were pitted against the various ways the CCP collections could be organized and pulled together to serve a wide range of audiences.

The second area, System Specifications, weighted 35 percent in the matrix, was broken down into ten areas: System Administration, Data Management, User Interface, Query, Reports, Collections Acquisition and Deaccession, Collections Documentation, Collections Care, Collections Control, and Collection Use. In each area, individual requirements were marked as "mandatory," "extremely desirable," and "highly desirable." It was proved later that these rankings provided good guidance in the evaluation process, but they were not non-negotiable. For example, a CMS product was not excluded automatically even if there was a "no" answer to a "mandatory" requirement.

System Administration covered issues that were related to the system administrator's ability to configure, control, monitor, and report on system-level activities. These activities involve security, access, backups, restores, and crash recovery. Many of these procedures are standard in the industry and are commonly shared by different vendors. Some newer capabilities or customized requirements, however, still remain in question. For example, utilizing Lightweight Directory Access Protocol (LDAP) for login and password access was not available in every CMS yet. Also, although most software has logging and audit trails built in where log files were available at the system level to the database administrator, there are cases when some CMSs, oddly, create log files of errors on the client PC.

Data Management is a core capability of CMS. It is also one of the most diverse and customizable aspects, which demands a closer look by any potential buyer. This section of the RFP focused on the database management framework. It specifically looked for an expandable toolset, the extensibility of the system, and the amount of flexibility that the users would have in controlling the data at both the entry and retrieval level. The number of records and tables can influence the functionality of the system, and a CMS which normally handles 1 million records could run into functionality degradation when 8 million records are required. A field length limit of 4,000 characters may sound more than sufficient, but would not the limit of 2 trillion be more satisfying? Although most CMSs have a large number of fields designed for expected potential usage, many do not allow new fields and new tables to be added without major work on the system. Allowing the expansion of new data fields is usually a good indication that a CMS is based on a more robust design, which is likely to have flexibilities in other areas, too.

While other sections of specifications covered database configurations and general data manipulation capabilities, Collections Documentation touched on a more vital issue; namely, the different ways that different types of materials were processed and managed. Museums and archives have almost completely opposite approaches toward collection documentation. Whereas museums register and catalog individual objects when they come in and build a collection with objects, archives on the other hand describe entire collections first and then go down to the item level as necessary. Because of these distinctive ways of processing different collections, the need to seamlessly integrate all collections at the CCP would require a system that was able to handle both item and collection level descriptions and effectively maintain connection among related entities.

The third area of the RFP requirements, Technical Requirements, stood for 10 percent in the evaluation matrix and was dedicated to the CMS's ability to complement the existing infrastructure of the UA Libraries system. Because the photographic collection and the archive at the CCP serve the same campus as the rest of the libraries do, it is critical for the CMS at the CCP to be able to interface with the main library system. Federated searching, which allows users to search both the UA Libraries' catalog and the holdings of the CCP, is essential in the university environment. This feature requires either Z39.50 connection or Open Archives Initiative (OAI) capability. Therefore, while most individual museums are less concerned about issues like federated searching, a CMS's ability to access any Z39.50 compliant server and accept XML documents that are compliant with the OAI standard would be mandatory in this case.

This RFP attracted three formal responses from Gallery Systems, Willoughby, and MINISIS. The selection team gave scores on a 1 to 10 scale to each RFP section, and the total numbers were rebalanced with the weight assigned to each requirement section. While all three companies could provide adequate management capabilities to the CCP collections, after lengthy discussions taking into consideration both the needs from within the CCP departments and those from the CCP as part of the university library system, the MINISIS Integrator (MINT) was selected for this particular case.

MINT can provide comprehensive workflow management for most museum, archive, and library functions that the CCP will perform, including registration, cataloging, loan tracking, auditing, accounting, and rights and reproduction, etc. A standard application toolkit is available for the local database administrator to build and change databases, add and delete fields, add and change screens, build and change reports, etc. These customizations can then be managed locally. MINT approaches the integration of museum, archive, and library collections through a centralized registration mechanism. This essential idea will be discussed further in the following sections.

REFLECTIONS AND FURTHER DISCUSSIONS

Mission-based Selection Process

The selection of a CMS should always begin and end with looking into the characteristics of the original collections and the primary functions they serve. In this case, the mission for this technology solution was the seamless connection among different types of materials from different locations, i.e., the integration among museum, archive, and library collections. As 25-year veteran archivist Amy Rule pointed out:

> The most powerful theme that emerges throughout the [CCP] collections and archives is that of synergy. The relationships among collections multiply as each small addition brings its own interconnections and overlapping relevancies. The complex web of friendships among photographers suggests synergistic flow in many directions. We find Keith Smith's letters in Robert Heinecken's archive, just down the aisle from the archive of Judith Golden, a student of Smith and a colleague of Heinecken. . . . Who knew that such dissimilar artists as Heinecken and Bullock would be connected through the evidence of a fanciful hand-made greeting card?

To automatically make these kinds of linkages among content like an archivist with 25 years experience does in her head, a CMS needs a well-established infrastructure with a design that is backed up by good understanding of various types of information collections. From this will come a substantial amount of metadata development that ultimately supports a great variety of resource discoveries. The selected product, MINT, is an integrated solution designed to manage curatorial, archival, and bibliographic information under one umbrella. Through a central registration database, MINT pushes data down to its museum, archive, and library components respectively. Information about an item or collection is entered once and kept throughout the entire system. For example, name authorities and metadata created in the registration and cataloging processes are centrally stored. Once some information is entered for one item, these fields will be automatically populated whenever this item is brought up. Newly added information is stored and managed in the same fashion.

MINT relies on the field "Descriptive Focus" to determine how to proceed with an entry. The descriptive focus is a field in the database that has a predefined validation list that asks if the accession is curatorial, archival, bibliographic, a curatorial grouped item, an archival group, a bibliographic group of items, or finally a mixed group of curatorial, archival, and bibliographic items. While the values of this field can be changed according to the local situation (for example, add "archaeological item" and "archaeological group," etc.), the field still performs the first "cut" to any material that comes to an institution. While records of all types of materials go into the museum module, the archival and bibliographic records are also sent to the archive module and library module for further description. This way, all the metadata is collected and presented in a unified way, regardless of the different functions that one item may perform in different situations.

Setting Correct Objectives through Requirements

When a group of stakeholders get together to create an RFP, it is not hard to get lost in the details. Knowing the future system will directly affect everybody's day-to-day life, RFP creators can have a tendency to try to exhaust every minute aspect they can ever think of. While a comprehensive list of system specifications provides rigorous evaluation aid, pinpoints some important demands and to some extent provides political satisfaction among different parties, a "checklist"-only RFP can put both the vendor and the organization in a passive position. A "checklist" not only leaves most of the burden on the RFP creators, requiring them to understand all the different technical options and decide the best way to achieve their goals, but also restricts the vendor from demonstrating certain problem-solving capabilities if they are not specifically asked to in the RFP. In short, a specification-heavy RFP may have addressed all the functionalities well but happened to miss the function that an organization has set out to perform.

In the case of the CCP RFP, the employment of user experience scenarios helps balance the "yes/no" questions. By inviting each vendor to read six functional "stories" and provide a technical solution through their products, the organization keeps itself as well as the vendors focusing on the correct objectives that the system is expected to achieve. Like CMS consultant Martin White pointed out, "Current CMS applications have more than enough power to handle the most complex of content management processes, but how many organizations have worked through the workflow behind document preparation, and (of even greater importance) identified where there could be benefits in re-engineering the workflow to gain the maximum benefit from the CMS application?" (White 2002). An RFP needs to be written in terms of deliverables or performance objectives containing most rigors that keep the evaluation process on target. Some vendors responded to these functional scenarios with standard answers, while others provided more thoughtful and creative solutions, tackling one question from different perspectives and providing options. By comparing and evaluating these responses, one can get a better handle on how well a system is aligned to the organization's business goals.

Changed IT Project Management

While libraries and other institutions today constantly make case-by-case choices between building from scratch and acquiring commercial products to meet their IT needs, the shift away from the traditional "waterfall" model to design and develop applications in-house from the ground up (plan, analyze, design, implement, and maintain) is inevitable. Efforts invested in internally structured and developed applications have been gradually replaced by an evolutionary or spiral approach, as application development begins to focus more on less-structured business problems. Research in the late 1990s showed that more emphasis was being paid to the analysis and requirements gathering phase due to process redesign or re-alignment in view of software acquisition such as Enterprise Resource Planning (ERP) (Sharma and Tanniru 2000). A hybrid of both development approaches is being used to manage applications today, being referred to as "strategic IT life cycle." The strategic IT life cycle explores new technologies or commercially available software tools for strategic advantage, and it seeks opportunities to leverage advanced IT within an organization. Once a technology is considered viable, it is adopted through process realignment, acquisition, integration, and implementation processes, following the normal commercial off-the-shelf application development, so that the acquired software can be institutionalized.

The implementation of an enterprise CMS at the CCP is an example of acquiring commercial off-the-shelf software in a large and complex organization. The new IT management presents the feature of interorganizational activities guiding application development in support of building business relationships. As newer technologies are introduced, the organization is looking to explore their potential for viability in the early stages of investigation. Once a decision is made, it is introduced to the organization. Although design and construction take less effort due to external acquisition of software, tailoring and gluing code to reflect any customization and integration is needed.

Further investing time up front is worthwhile. Even with commercial products, making superficial changes on the system without good homework to discover real requirements can cause costly rebuilding of the system down the road. One lesson learned from the case of the CCP CMS project was that the implementation of the selected product could have moved forward faster if the workflow review had been completed prior to the RFP process. Because of the delay of the workflow analysis, the team had to set aside time during the implementation phase to complete this task. Although the local workflow benefited from the new system despite the setback on the time line, an organization could definitely be more proactive in determining what the desired processes were in the earlier stage of selecting a new technological solution.

FINAL THOUGHTS: IT AS A SOLUTION TO SUPPORT BUSINESS STRATEGIES

The selection and implementation of a CMS can be one of the most complex IT projects a library or museum has to manage. With the changing technological environment and transforming organizational functions, this task requires the reevaluation of the business objectives and the adoption of new project management methods. When it comes to IT solutions, organizations constantly have to make choices among self-built systems, open-source software, and commercial off-the-shelf products. The decision needs to be based on the function of the work, the analysis of the costs, the size of the applications, and most of the time the business strategy of the organization, i.e., where an organization wants to place its budget and FTEs.

Regardless of what type of system an organization chooses to implement, workflow is essential in content management. A successful CMS implementation is based on a good understanding of the business functions and workflow of an organization. Even if it is recognized that the integration involves different types of collections such as museum collections and archive and bibliographic collections, it is easy to follow the big strokes that museums are museums, archives are archives, and libraries are libraries. In reality, once one looks closer at what an organization does, each has a bit of variation. Many organizations make general rules but allow exceptions. The moment at which a CMS is implemented often reveals how unclear the workers are about the processes of their own day-to-day workflow. A thorough workflow analysis can not only speed up the customization of the system after a CMS has been selected but it also usually reveals existing problems and thus initiates changes.

In summary, implementing a new CMS is not just an issue of mapping the old system to the new. It is a time to customize the product to fit the organization's needs as well as to reassess an organization's processes and potentially establish new traditions. An organization needs to be open to exploring possibilities and developing new systems empowered by new technologies and adopting new ways to improve the existing business processes. It is important for everybody involved to understand the different functions of the organization as a whole and think at an institutional level what processes can help improve the organization.

Further, the view towards customization remains: If there is not a good business role for a new customized feature, it should not be done. After all, new technology is not replacing the core business value of an organization and its functions. For example, a new system may release the archive department from typing up finding aids and creating EAD records manually, but it will take the very same skill of an archivist to analyze a pile of paper and pull out the key elements to describe it. Finally, any system is only as good as one makes it, and the opportunity to implement an enterprise CMS may be a prime time for an organization to reflect on its own business roles and strategies and take a giant leap forward.

ACKNOWLEDGMENTS

This chapter is based on the work of the staff members at the Center for Creative Photography and the Digital Library and Information Systems Team of the University of Arizona Libraries. The author would like to thank all the project team members, including, but not limited to, Barbara Allen, Travis Bowen, Leslie Calmes, Adele Edwards, Cass Fey, Denise Gose, Yan Han, Dr. Krisellen Maloney, Betsi Meissner, Tim Mosman, Dr. Douglas Nickel, Dianne Nilsen, Trinity Parker, Lisa Richmond, Amy Rule, Britt Salveson, Elizabeth Saxes, Marcia Tiede, Amy Verheide and Andrew Wallace, for their vision and dedication that made this CMS project a success. The author would also like to thank Sara Heitshu and Judy Kamin for their advice, without which this chapter would not have been completed.

REFERENCES

Bramscher, P. F., and J. T. Butler. 2006. LibData to LibCMS—one library's evolutionary pathway to a content management system. *Library Hi Tech* Vol. 24, No. 1: 14–28.

Doyle, B. 2005. Where the wild CMSs are! *EContent* December 2005 issue. Available at www.econtentmag.com/?ArticleID=14534.

Goodwin, S., N. Burford, and M. Bedard. 2006. CMS/CMS: Content management system/change management strategies. *Library Hi Tech* Vol. 24, No. 1: 54–60.

Han, Y. 2004. Digital content management: The search for a content management system. *Library Hi Tech* Vol. 22, No. 4: 355–365.

MINISIS Inc. 2006. *MINT.* Available at www.minisisinc.com/index.php?page=mint.

Rule, A., and N. Solomon, ed. 2002. Original sources—art and archives at the Center for Creative Photography. University of Arizona, Tucson, AZ.

Sharma, S., and M. Tanniru. 2000. *Managing projects in a software acquisition environment—issues and challenges.* AIS Conference 2000, Long Beach, CA.

Tanniru, M. 2005. *A program template for the graduate MS program in MIS.* Available at mis.eller.arizona.edu/mtanniru/MISProgramOverviewBE1.pdf.

White, M. 2002. Managing content management system selection. *EContent* July. Posted 1 July 2002. Available at www.econtentmag.com/?ArticleID=826.

Yang, Y., J. Bhuta, B. Boehm, and D. Port. 2005. Value-based processes for COTS-based applications. *IEEE Software* Vol. 22, No. 4: 54–62.

14

Using the Library Intranet to Manage Web Content

Sarah Robbins, Debra Engel, and James Bierman

CMS AT THE UNIVERSITY OF OKLAHOMA LIBRARIES

Intranets have differing roles within organizations. Some organizations use intranets to share reports and minutes, post policies, procedures, and announcements, and link to databases or other electronic resources. Intranet applications, however, are not limited to static files and documents. As Fichter (1999) notes, "Some libraries have also added interactive discussion forums, collaborative workspaces for teams, election wizards for academic communities, and special news areas" (108). A significant aspect of the intranet at the University of Oklahoma Libraries (UL) is to provide a communication tool where employees can find information about the organization and their unit in one place—work schedules, organizational forms, information for specific employee groups, and employee rosters. While fostering communication is one aspect of UL's intranet, providing access to content management tools serves as a primary function of the intranet.

Content management, generally defined, is a system of collecting, managing, and publishing data (Boiko 2002). Browning and Lowndes (2001) expand upon this definition and write:

> A CMS is not really a product or a technology. It is a catchall term that covers a wide set of processes that will underpin the "Next Generation" large-scale web site. The pervasive nature of the Web means that it has become the preferred vehicle for content delivery. "CMS" should therefore be read as "Web Content Management System." Institutions have no shortage of "content"—be it data, information or knowledge. When the creation and publication of content is well managed then the organization functions more cost-effectively; it is also likely to lead to better decision-making.

University Libraries' content management tools were designed to permit library personnel to manage content related to their areas of responsibilities, while systems staff retained control of the technological and design aspects of the library website (Robbins and Engel 2005). The process of locally developing content management tools at UL began in 2002 with the initial launch of a database-driven website and has continued to evolve since the initial launch.

UL's intranet currently contains 19 systems for managing content, both on the public website and on the staff intranet. Library personnel use these systems to manage and generate statistical reports and to organize resources as well as to create and display content. Thirty-four library employees (13 percent of UL's total personnel) are tasked with using these systems in some capacity to manage content. Many of these employees use several of these systems to update content. Some systems are used by only one or two employees to manage a specific area of the website. Systems employees, while responsible for the creation and maintenance of CMS, do not utilize CMS to manage content, and thus were not included in the 34 employees responsible for managing content.

At UL, the Web Steering Committee (WSC) oversees the development of content management tools and web content in general. Formed in 2002, the WSC provides stewardship and oversight to the continuing development of the libraries' website, web services, and web-based tools. This includes setting priorities for web development, providing a governance structure, and coordinating the planning, implementation, and evaluation of the UL website. The WSC also provides training to employees on how to use content management tools as they are developed and promotes the use of CMS for creating web content.

Encouraging library employees to use content management tools, while maintaining centralized control of the site design and navigation, can be a precarious balancing act. Intranets often serve a wide and diverse audience and thus will likely have numerous content providers, each with his or her own unique view of what the intranet should offer in terms of content and how that content should be presented (DiMattia 2002). Having a specifically designated person or group with final control and authority over both intranet content and design can assist in maintaining forward momentum in developing tools, even when all parties do not agree. The WSC serves in this capacity at UL.

Without a group like WSC overseeing content development and without employees assuming ownership, intranets risk falling into what Zauha (2003) refers to as a "No-Man's Land," wherein "no one is ultimately responsible for day-to-day maintenance and few in the organization have the power to add content or make changes" (10). Low contribution and a lack of ownership can lead to dated and inaccurate information, turning the intranet into a stagnant repository that lacks usefulness and value. An unfavorable perception of the intranet and its content exacerbates the problem. Vidgen, Goodwin, and Barnes (2001) explain, "In many respects, there is a vicious circle; the intranet is not perceived as useful as there is little useful content, but because it is not perceived as useful, there is little incentive to add more content" (476).

Planning and implementing locally developed content management tools has inherent advantages and disadvantages. Before deciding whether or not to create management tools locally or to outsource this task, the WSC and the Library Systems office carefully examined the issues. Developing a custom solution is not simply a one-time expense. Locally developed content management tools demand ongoing technical expertise and budgetary commitments. One advantage of a locally developed CMS is that it can be custom-tailored to fit the needs of the content managers and of the organization as a whole. A commercial or open-source CMS solution usually does not allow the same degree of individualized customization. The advantage to outsourcing the intranet application, however, is that the library staff does not need the same level of technical expertise.

When UL started building the database-driven website, commercial software that could handle the type of web portal needed to meet systems' requirements was prohibitively expensive. In addition, the commercial software did not have the ability to handle the type of authentication that UL has to do to broker access to IP-restricted resources for distance education students and researchers working from off campus. There were no open source packages available that met the needs of UL's website and intranet development at that time. Because of these limitations in commercial and open source products, UL proceeded with the development of content management tools. This study attempts to examine usage of content management tools on UL's intranet and provide a framework for future intranet development.

METHODOLOGY

While the WSC is keenly aware of why UL is migrating to a database-driven website and is also familiar with the rationale behind the development of each of the content management systems available to library personnel on the intranet, the committee is uncertain of how these systems are actually used by the personnel and the extent to which personnel find these systems meeting their needs. To obtain information about staff usage of the content management systems available on the library's intranet, the authors sent a nine-item survey (Appendix A) to all faculty, professional staff, classified staff, and student assistants employed by UL in June 2005. A total of 264 surveys were sent, with 168 surveys distributed to student assistants, 56 surveys distributed to classified staff, 14 surveys distributed to professional staff members, and 26 surveys distributed to faculty.

In the survey, participants were asked to identify their personnel classification (student, classified, professional, or faculty) and the area of the library in which they worked (public services, technical services, systems, special collections, or administration). They were also asked to identify how frequently they logged into the intranet, and then how frequently they used various content management systems available as well as how often they used the intranet to find organizational information. In addition to these questions, participants were asked three open-ended questions on the strengths and weaknesses of the library intranet and features that participants would like to see added to the intranet to increase usability.

SURVEY FINDINGS

Response Rate

Of the 264 surveys that were sent, 84 surveys were returned. This yields a 32 percent response rate. The response rate by personnel classification is as follows: 20 percent of the student assistants responded, 38 percent of the classified staff responded, 57 percent of the professional staff responded, and 81 percent of the faculty responded. At UL, personnel classifications are defined as:

- Faculty: librarians who hold an academic rank of Professor, Associate Professor, or Assistant Professor and are eligible for tenure in accordance with the University of Oklahoma faculty rules
- Professional staff: librarians in public services and technical services that do not hold an academic rank, information systems professionals, and accounting professionals
- Classified staff: full- and part-time employees who provide support to all library departments and branches
- Student assistants: temporary employees currently enrolled as students at the University of Oklahoma

By area of the library, the response rate is 45 percent of the public-services staff, 16 percent of the special collections staff, 27 percent of the technical services staff, 67 percent of the Systems staff, and 40 percent of the administration. Faculty and professional staff make up the majority of those who would be using the intranet to post or manage content on either the public website or on the staff intranet itself. Classified staff and student assistants primarily use the intranet to obtain organizational information, though some do have permission to manage content.

Reported Usage

To determine overall intranet usage, participants were asked how frequently they logged into the staff intranet—daily, 2–3 times per week, once a week, 2–3 times per month, once a month, once or twice a year, and never. For the purposes of this analysis, those who logged in at least once per week are considered regular users. Of the respondents, 42 percent claim to be regular users while 26 percent claim to use the intranet from once per month up to three times per month, and 31 percent reported using it seldom or never.

When looking at the responses of faculty and professional staff, 48 percent claim to be regular users, 38 percent use it at least monthly, and only 7 percent report never using the intranet (Figure 14.1). By looking at the data by area of the library in which respondents work, 51 percent of the public services staff, 33 percent of technical services staff, 50 percent of Systems staff, 29 percent of special collections staff, and 25 percent of administrative staff identify themselves as regular users of the intranet.

Usage of Content Management Systems

On the survey, participants were asked about the frequency of their usage of three specific systems and then of content management in

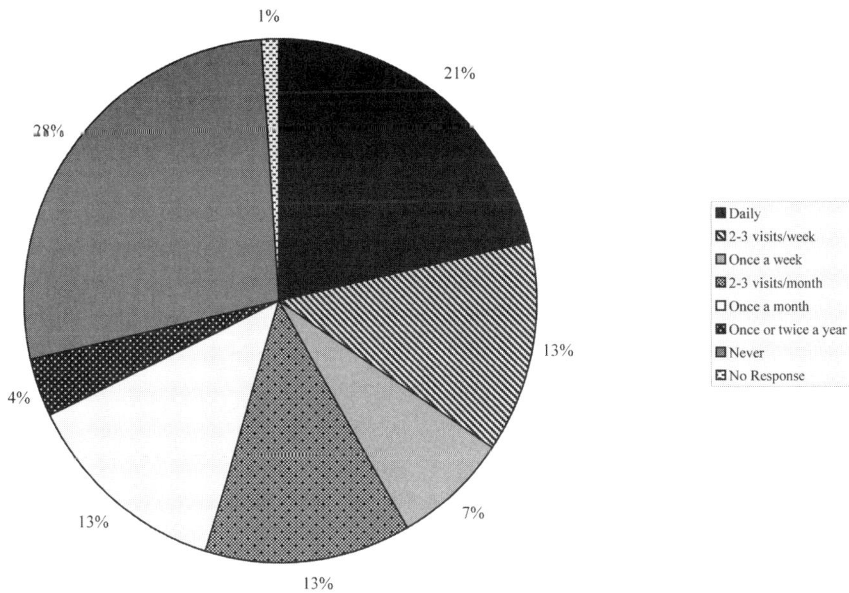

Figure 14.1. Frequency of general intranet usage.

general to encompass the other 16 systems. At UL, these systems are defined as:

- LORA CMS: allows employees to organize UL's electronic resources by subject and alphabetical listing
- Unit Page (Public) CMS: allows employees to organize their public unit pages by adding links, uploading documents, and providing location directions and contact information
- Unit Page (Intranet) CMS: allows employees to organize their unit intranet pages by uploading documents such as rosters and schedules and managing access permissions
- Other Content Areas: allows employees to add announcements, post unit hours, change front-page web content, manage electronic reserves, associate metadata to digital images, and create usage reports

Within the survey results, those who reported using a content management system at least monthly to update content are defined as regular users. Since most student assistants do not even have permission to edit content management areas on the website, their responses were removed from the data analyzed for this section.

As depicted in Figure 14.2, the majority of the respondents reported never using content management systems located on UL's intranet. This was not an unexpected response, however, since all UL employees were surveyed even

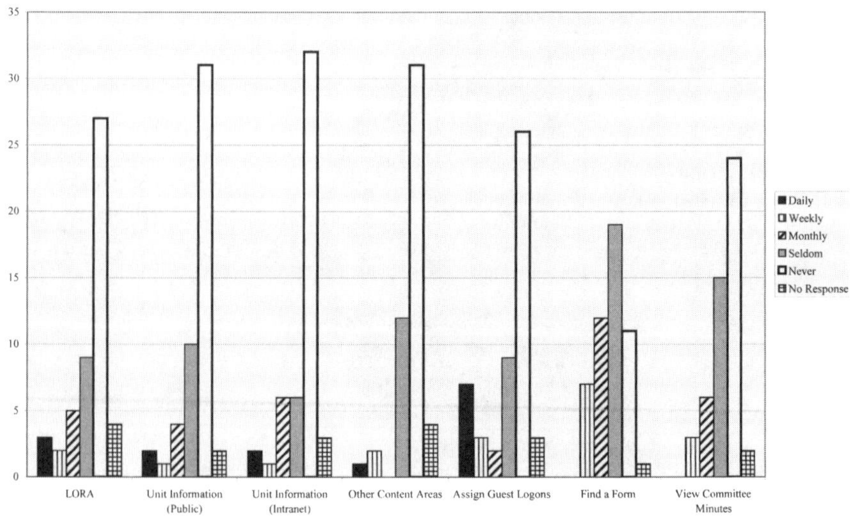

Figure 14.2. Faculty, professional staff, and classified staff frequency of use by intranet content area.

though a mere 34 employees have access to content management systems. Fifteen faculty and four classified staff are responsible for managing LORA. When considering that only 19 people could respond to updating LORA at all, the responses suggest that at least 53 percent of those with access are regularly updating their areas within LORA. Unit information, both public and intranet, can be updated by a total of 22 individuals (faculty, professional staff, and classified staff). When considering the data gathered in respect to the 22 employees who have permission to edit unit information, 32 percent regularly update their publicly accessible unit pages, and 41 percent regularly update their unit information available on the intranet.

Figure 14.3 shows the distribution of regular users of content management tools by area of the library in which they are employed. Though the number of regular users per system is relatively low regardless of area of the library, the graph confirms that public services employees use the CMS more heavily than any other area of employees. Also, it shows that special collections employees are not regularly using any of the content management systems and that administration employees are only regularly using one system.

Open-Ended Responses

Respondents were asked to provide answers to three open-ended questions. The questions asked respondents to list strengths and weaknesses of the libraries' intranet as well as provide suggestions for improving the intranet. Sixty

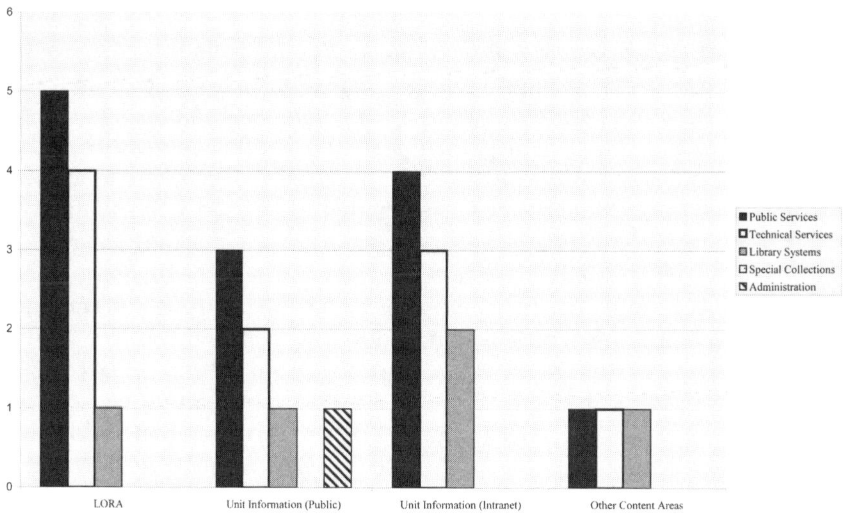

Figure 14.3. Regular users (faculty, professional staff, and classified staff) of content management tools by area of the library.

percent of those responding to the survey completed at least one of the open-ended questions. While not everyone responded to these questions, from those responses that were received, several common themes emerged.

Strengths of the intranet. Many of the respondents noted the abundance of content available and the accessibility of this content to all areas of the library as strengths of the intranet. Respondents also commented on the effectiveness of the intranet as a central site for communicating and referencing library policies and announcements. Regarding content management specifically, technical services faculty members noted the "ease of updating unit pages" and "CMS tools" in general as positive aspects of the intranet.

Weaknesses of the intranet. Many respondents were unaware that the library had an intranet. While most of these comments came from student workers, one technical services faculty member wrote, "I have no idea what is on it, and nobody ever told me that there were useful things on it even though I supervise employees. I figured it was only useful for the reference librarians and administration."

From those who knew the library has an intranet, reported weaknesses included a lack of obvious organizational structure to content on the intranet and not knowing when to turn to the intranet versus some other means of finding information regarding library policy and procedure. Intranet usability was another concern. One public services faculty member noted that, "Sometimes features are added that don't work." Another faculty member cited "having to go through Systems to update a document or to post a new one" as a problem of the existing intranet. A couple of respondents indicated that they only turned to the intranet when they needed to update something.

Suggestions for improvement of the intranet. Respondents provided a wide variety of suggestions for improving the intranet and making it more useful to them. One public services faculty member requested tutorials for the CMS and LORA content management systems. Another thought the addition of staff blogs accessible only to employees in a specific unit as a possible improvement. Several employees suggested improving access to the content on the intranet through implementing a site search or an RSS feed to alert users as new content is added. One technical services faculty member wrote, "While intranet use may be higher by faculty or professional librarians or in departments with constantly developing content, in my experience, staff have little use for it. In order for the intranet to be a key component of staff daily routine, content found there cannot simply be duplication of what they otherwise access on the I: [shared, network] drive. It might help if things like timesheets, schedules, and such were available only on the intranet. It might also help if use of the intranet was actively promoted by all department heads, not just those in public service areas." A professional staff member in the library Systems office noted a need for more administrative pages and features that would eliminate direct edits to the Oracle database.

ANALYSIS OF WEBTRENDS DATA

In June 2005, the same month the authors disseminated the paper survey to UL personnel, the libraries' Systems office used WebTrends software to analyze usage of the staff intranet. Systems gathered data regarding the number of visits per month, the number of visits per user, the location of users when they visit the intranet, and intranet access by library unit. In addition, Systems analyzed usage by intranet content area.

General intranet usage. Since its launch in June 2003, OU Libraries' intranet has had a steady increase in the amount of content and tools available. As a result, intranet usage has steadily risen as well. Intranet usage peaked in February 2005 with approximately 1,400 visits.

Systems gathered the data by unit in which each employee belongs. These logins per units were then grouped into the broader categories of public services, technical services, Systems, special collections, administration, and the WSC. With the exception of the addition of the Web Steering Committee as a distinct group, these categories mirror the categories used to analyze the data collected from the survey responses. Systems removed the WSC from their units because they felt the WSC members' extremely high usage of the content management tools would skew the data. The data presented in Figure 14.4 confirms this supposition, as the four-member WSC constitute 14 percent of the total intranet usage, while public services personnel account for 55 percent, technical services for 12 percent, Systems for 16 percent, administration for 2 percent, and special collections for less than 1 percent of the total intranet usage.

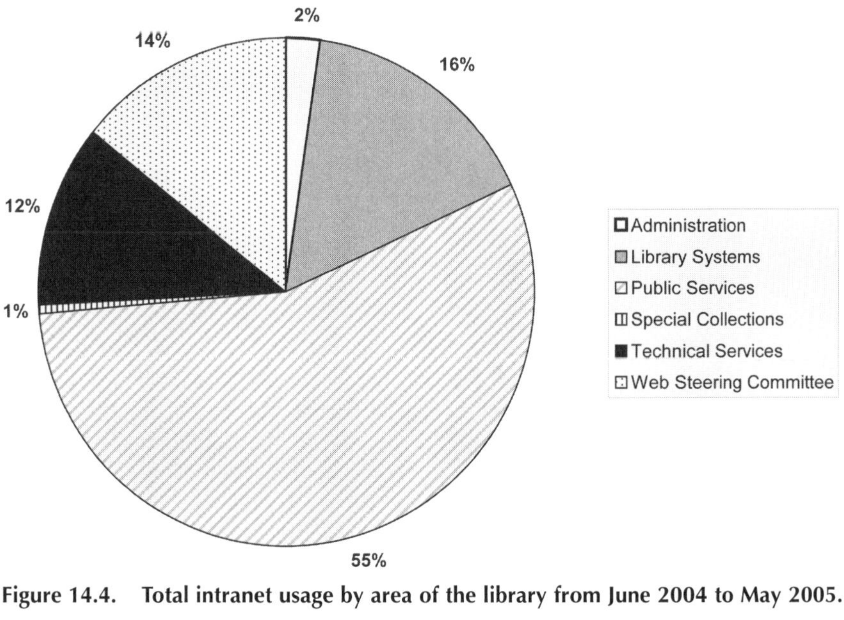

Figure 14.4. Total intranet usage by area of the library from June 2004 to May 2005.

Usage of content management systems. Figure 14.5 depicts total intranet usage by system. The various content management systems comprise 21 percent of the total intranet usage. Most heavily used is the system designed to assign guest logons to those patrons who wish to use library computers but are not affiliated with the university. Employees working in public services areas assign guest logons; this helps to explain why there is more usage of the intranet by public services personnel than personnel in other areas of the library.

Recommendations for improvement. Systems ended their report on intranet usage with several suggestions for improvement. These suggestions included adding a search capability to the intranet, creating an internal knowledge base, creating an internal content management system, expanding the electronic resource management system to include administrative and licensing information, and creating RSS support for intranet-based news and announcements.

DISCUSSION

The self-reported survey data and the WebTrends data complement one another and may be used together to create a complete picture of intranet usage at UL. The data, however, cannot be easily compared because each set of data is distinct. The findings from the self-reported data indicate how frequently individuals log in to the intranet and how frequently they perceive using various areas of the intranet. The WebTrends data show average and

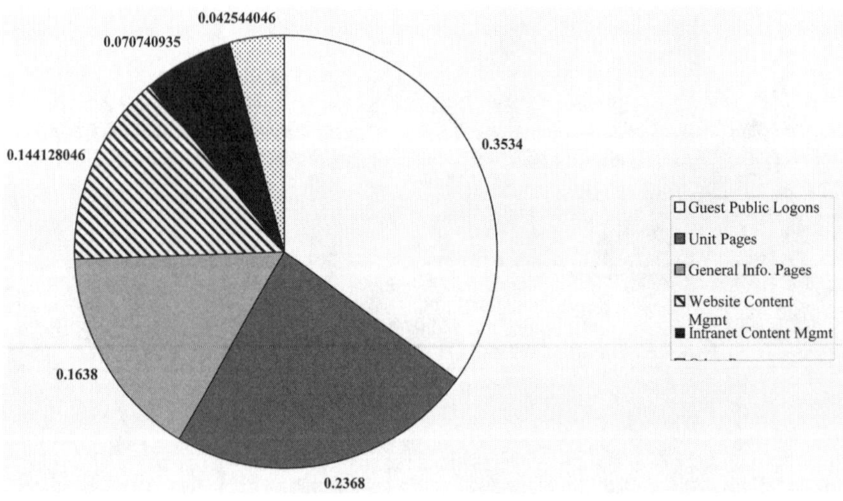

Figure 14.5. Total usage by intranet area visited from June 2004 to May 2005.

cumulative usage over a period of time. When looking at the WebTrends data, the content management systems accounted for 21 percent of total intranet usage. By comparison, more than double that percentage (44 percent) of the total internet usage is for viewing content on the intranet. Survey data presented in Figure 14.2 support this information gathered from WebTrends and indicate that while content management tools are part of the usage of the intranet, they are not the sole reason employees use this organizational tool. In both the self-reported survey data and the WebTrends data, the most heavily used system is the system for assigning guest logons. The WebTrends data illustrate that the primary users of the intranet were the public services personnel. The public services personnel include the librarians and branch managers who are responsible for managing content in LORA as well as for assigning guest logons.

As the anecdotal evidence and the open-ended responses suggest, the intranet is perceived as a tool for the public services employees and for faculty and professional staff. While the intranet was not designed specifically for public services employees, they are the primary users of many of the content management tools and typically invest significant time updating their unit pages. In contrast, technical services employees do not perceive that the intranet is a tool for their areas and thus do not invest time in developing their unit pages, perpetuating the belief that the intranet has little to offer them. Survey responses also indicated that the intranet is more heavily used by library faculty and professional staff, while classified staff and student workers either do not know what the intranet is or believe it is not for their use. Reducing the redundancy of content available on the intranet and on shared network drives may decrease the confusion some employees expressed regarding when to go to the intranet for information and when to consult other sources.

Intranet applications are not new, so why is the UL intranet not utilized more fully? One of the challenges in intranet development is to build compelling applications that provide useful tools for content managers. Ideally, when the UL intranet fully matures, every employee will log in to the intranet daily to view announcements and updates. Building an intranet that is vital to the employees within an organization requires organizational commitment to developing tools that are easy to use and vital for the development of the website. Adding value to the content management tools and delivering those tools on schedule will help increase user confidence in the value of the intranet. At UL the intranet development, and specifically the development of the CMS, took much longer than projected by the Systems staff. As a result, content managers experienced frustration as their control of the content on their pages was delayed. In addition, when the CMS was ready for implementation, there was some doubt on the part of the content managers that the CMS could deliver promised results. This has caused a skeptical attitude towards most content on the intranet and has slowed the adoption and integration of new tools as they became available. As White (2004) writes, "How to increase usage merits focus because, whatever the measure used, there is almost always reason for an organization to make more effective use of its intranet" (41).

Based on the feedback provided from the survey, UL should develop an intranet site search that will assist in the discovery of intranet-based information. Additionally, a system such as RSS feeds needs to be implemented to alert users of new content. A concerted marketing effort needs to be made at all levels to inform new and existing employees of content available on the intranet and how to integrate the intranet into daily workflows within the organization. The UL administration needs to encourage supervisors and unit managers to develop their unit pages on the intranet to give employees a reason to use the intranet.

CONCLUSION

University Libraries continues to endorse website and intranet development and the use of CMS as a high strategic priority. UL's intranet is developing a regular base of users among the library faculty and staff. As the faculty and staff who use the CMS become more comfortable with the interface and trust the stability of new tools, the WSC expects intranet usage to increase. As the roles and responsibilities of content managers, Systems staff, and WSC become better defined, content management tools will be fine-tuned to produce information products that consistently meet employee needs and expectations.

Developing an internal knowledge base of best practices for CMS and intranet development will help the continued development of the intranet. Users of the intranet want the organizational assurance that planned structure and process with built-in quality assurance are part of the implementation plans for CMS. Building measurable success criteria for CMS and the intranet will increase the employees' confidence in the system. Developing clear and simple objectives with realistic schedules and avoiding long project cycles will also increase the viability of the intranet. The UL intranet has evolved from a rudimentary to a more sophisticated tool, and therefore the trust in the content management tools has increased as employees perceive these tools as organized, managed, and sustainable.

In the next year, UL will begin a new web and intranet development planning process. A committee will ask the library faculty and staff what they want to accomplish through the website, what new features they want to offer, and what new services should be developed for library customers. In addition, web usability tests will be conducted on the website and intranet. The WSC will evaluate the existing, locally developed content management tools and will once again compare these tools with commercial and open source intranet applications that are now available.

Developing the library website and library intranet is a continuing challenge. While libraries have had an intranet for many years, many libraries do not have an overall intranet strategy or clearly articulated strategic plan for CMS and intranet development. Using the information from this study, continuing to monitor WebTrends data, and examining how other libraries are developing their intranets will assist University Libraries in planning a practical strategic vision for content management and intranet development.

REFERENCES

Boiko, B. 2002. *Content management bible*. New York: Hungry Minds.

Browning, P., and M. Lowndes. 2001. Content management systems: Who needs them? *Ariadne* No. 30, available at www.ariadne.ac.uk/issue30/techwatch/ (accessed 9 August 2005).

DiMattia, S. 2002. Creative intranets. *Library Journal* Vol. 127, No. 12: 40–2.

Fichter, D. 1999. Intranets: Librarians dive in! *Online* Vol. 23, No. 3: 107–8.

Robbins, S., and D. Engel. 2005. Developing committees to create a web content management system. *Content and workflow management for library websites: Case studies*. Holly Yu (ed.). Hershey, PA: Information Science Publishing.

Vidgen, R., S. Goodwin, and S. Barnes. 2001. Web content management. *Proceedings of the 14th Bled electronic commerce conference*. O'Keefe, R., C. Loebbecke, J. Gricar, A. Pucihar, and G. Lenart (eds.). Bled, Slovenia: June. 465–480.

White, M. 2004. Does your intranet have a win-win strategy? *EContent* Vol. 27, No. 3: 41.

Zauha, J. 2003. Library intranets as knowledge management tools: Box of tricks or box of junk? *PNLA Quarterly* Vol. 68, No. 1: 9–10, 23.

APPENDIX A: LIBRARY INTRANET USAGE SURVEY

1. What is your position classification?
   - ☐ Student Worker
   - ☐ Classified Staff
   - ☐ Professional Staff
   - ☐ Faculty
2. In what area of the library do you work?
   - ☐ Public Services
   - ☐ Technical Services
   - ☐ Library Systems
   - ☐ Special Collections
   - ☐ Administration

3. Did you know the library had a staff intranet? Yes No
4. How frequently do you login to the library intranet?
   - ☐ Daily
   - ☐ 2–3 times per week
   - ☐ Once a week
   - ☐ 2–3 times per month
   - ☐ Once a month
   - ☐ Once or twice a year
   - ☐ Never
5. With what frequency do you perform the following tasks on the intranet?

	Daily	**Weekly**	**Monthly**	**Seldom**	**Never**
Assign Guest Logins	☐	☐	☐	☐	☐
Update LORA Content Areas	☐	☐	☐	☐	☐
Update Unit Pages—Public	☐	☐	☐	☐	☐
Update Unit Pages—Intranet	☐	☐	☐	☐	☐
View Announcements	☐	☐	☐	☐	☐
View Department Page	☐	☐	☐	☐	☐
Search for Employee Information	☐	☐	☐	☐	☐
Log a Long-Distance Phone Call	☐	☐	☐	☐	☐
Find a Policy	☐	☐	☐	☐	☐
Find information about a service	☐	☐	☐	☐	☐
Find a form	☐	☐	☐	☐	☐
View committee minutes	☐	☐	☐	☐	☐
Update other content areas (reserves, *Sooner* Magazine, etc.)	☐	☐	☐	☐	☐

6. Do you access the intranet from home? Yes No
7. In your opinion, what are the strengths of University Libraries' intranet?
8. In your opinion, what are the weaknesses of University Libraries' intranet?
9. What content or features would you like to see added to the intranet to make it more useful to you?

Index

About the Editor and Contributors

Bradford Lee Eden is associate university librarian for Technical Services and Scholarly Communication at the University of California, Santa Barbara. Previous positions include head of the Web and Digitization Services for the University of Nevada, Las Vegas Libraries; head of the Bibliographic and Metadata Services for the UNLV Libraries; and Coordinator of Technical Services for the North Harris Montgomery Community College District. He is editor of *OCLC Systems & Services: Digital Library Perspectives International* and *The Bottom Line: Managing Library Finances*, associate editor of *Library Hi Tech* and *The Journal of Film Music*, and series editor of the *Routledge Music Bibliographies*. He has a master's and a PhD degree in musicology, as well as an MS in library science. He publishes in the areas of metadata, librarianship, medieval music and liturgy, and J. R. R. Tolkien. He recently edited *Innovative Redesign and Reorganization of Library Technical Services: Paths for the Future and Case Studies* (2004), and is the author of *Metadata and Its Applications* (2002), *3D Visualization Techniques* (2005), *Innovative Digital Projects in the Humanities* (2005), *Metadata and Its Applications: New Directions and Updates* (2005), and *FRBR: Functional Requirements for Bibliographic Records* (2006).

Ray Bailey is the instructional technology librarian at Morehead State University (MSU). He holds a BA in psychology and philosophy from MSU, an MA in clinical psychology from MSU, and an MLS from the University of South Florida.

Regina Beach is the head of Technical Services and Collection Development at the Jernigan Library at Texas A&M University, Kingsville. She holds the rank of assistant professor, and her research interests include management of library technology and strategic uses of technology.

Jeff W. Beaird is the computer operations supervisor at Buswell Memorial Library, Wheaton College, Wheaton, Illinois.

Martha Bedard is associate dean and director of the Medical Sciences Library, Texas A&M University and holds the Lila B. King Endowed Professorship in the University Libraries. She has served as the chair of the Web Implementation Team since its inception in 2001.

Matt Benzing is information technology librarian at Rensselaer Research Libraries.

James Bierman is a recent graduate of the University of Oklahoma's School of Library and Information Studies.

Paul F. Bramscher is a web applications developer at the Digital Library Development Lab, University of Minnesota, Twin Cities, Minnesota.

Nancy Burford is an assistant professor and resources management librarian at the Medical Sciences Library, Texas A&M University. She was the primary web page designer for the Medical Sciences Library in the pre-CMS era and has served on three Web Implementation Team subcommittees.

John T. Butler is the director of the Digital Library Development Lab at the University of Minnesota, Twin Cities, Minnesota.

Esther Carrigan is deputy director of the Medical Sciences Library, Texas A&M University. She has served on the Web Implementation Team for three years. Her research and professional interests include the management of information resources and organizational development.

Miqueas Diál is an assistant professor of CIS at Texas A&M University, Kingsville, where he teaches database and programming courses. His research interests include neural networks and the semantic web.

Christos Douligeris works in the Department of Informatics at the University of Piraeus in Piraeus, Greece.

Debra Engel is the director of public services at the University of Oklahoma Libraries.

Ronald W. Fordham is the computer support coordinator at Buswell Memorial Library, Wheaton College, Wheaton, Illinois.

Doug Goans has been the web development librarian at the Georgia State University Library since 2000.

Susan Goodwin is an assistant professor and coordinator of Instructional Services for Texas A&M University Libraries. She has served as the Secretary of the Web Implementation Team since its inception in 2001. Her research interests include the effective utilization of various technologies in the provision and delivery of library instruction and information literacy.

Yan Han is systems librarian at the University of Arizona Libraries.

Gale C. Hannigan is director of Informatics for Medical Education at Texas A&M Medical Sciences Library and holds joint faculty appointments at the College of Medicine and School of Rural Public Health where she teaches informatics. She is a member of the Web Implementation Team's Usability Committee.

Terry L. Huttenlock is the head of Systems and Technological Services and assistant professor of Library Science at Buswell Memorial Library, Wheaton College, Wheaton, Illinois.

Edward Iglesias is systems librarian at Central Connecticut State University.

Tom Klingler is assistant dean for Technical Services, Libraries & Media Services, Kent State University.

Tom Kmetz is the coordinator of Reference and Online Services in the library at Morehead State University. He earned an MSLIS from the University of Illinois at Urbana-Champaign in 1997, and he is one of the two principal designers of *The Kentucky Encyclopedia Web Edition*.

Guy Leach joined Georgia State University Library as the humanities liaison for music and modern/classical languages in 2000.

Marilyn Lutz is the director of library information technology planning at the University of Maine Library, Orono, Maine.

Curtis Meadow is the director of IS development at Trefoil Corporation (Orono, ME) and instructor in computer science, University of Maine.

Ioannis Papadakis works in the Department of Archives and Library Science at Ionian University in Corfu, Greece.

Jeph Remley is multimedia/web developer, Libraries & Media Services, Kent State University.

Sarah Robbins is the web & digital initiatives coordinator at the University of Oklahoma Libraries.

Yu Su is Information Systems librarian at the University of Arizona.

Teri M. Vogel was the science liaison for biology and chemistry at Georgia State University Library from 2001–2004 and is now the chemistry librarian at the University of California, San Diego, Science and Engineering Library.

Rick Wiggins is web programmer, Libraries & Media Services, Kent State University.